SAINSBURY'S
THE RECORD YEARS

SAINSBURY'S

THE RECORD YEARS
1950–1992

GILES EMERSON

Haggerston Press
London 2006

Frontispiece: John Sainsbury receives the Food Marketing Institute of America's global award for 'Outstanding Supermarket Chain' in 1984

First published in 2006 by Haggerston Press,
38 Kensington Place, London w8 7PR

Printed in Great Britain by
Cambridge University Press, Cambridge

CONTENTS

ILLUSTRATIONS

FOREWORD

by Lord Sainsbury of Preston Candover KG – 'Mr JD'

Between 1950 and 1992, Sainsbury's grew from being a relatively small, family-owned company with a chain of traditional shops, selling provisions and groceries, to become the country's most successful and profitable food retailer, a public company with 395 supermarkets in the UK and the US, and a DIY chain of 64 stores.

How that happened is of most interest to those who worked in the company and contributed to its success during those 42 years. It is for them that I commissioned this book to be written and it is to them that it is dedicated. One of our greatest strengths was the loyalty of those who worked for JS during this time, their belief in what we did and in the values we espoused. There was great pride throughout the company in what we achieved, and a high proportion of those in the company chose to be shareholders – it was their company in more ways than one.

What happened to 'our company' after 1992 naturally caused the greatest distress to those who were responsible for the success we had enjoyed, whether they were on the shop floor or in the boardroom. Personally, it was a very painful period, all the more so as I know I must bear responsibility for the structure that I left in place in 1992. However, I felt that there should be a record of what we achieved in the 40 years from 1950. Hence this book covers the period for which I could supply the author with papers relevant to the company's development, including my very full annual presentations to senior management.

It was a period of unprecedented change in food retailing. We went from post-war rationing, shortages and controls, through a revolutionary transformation in the method of selling food. This time also saw a great increase in the purchasing power of our customers, their mobility, their sophistication and their desire for variety and greater choice. We sought to lead the way, to anticipate our customers' changing needs and to be constantly innovative in what we did and how we did it. To do that we had the great advantage of having a very strong executive board, including some of the most able professionals in the retail industry. Those who were on the JS board between 1950 and 1992 are all listed in Appendix 2 (pp. 227–8). They all deserve great credit for the company's achievements during these years. In particular, I should like to pay tribute to the contributions made by my brothers, Simon and Tim, and to Roy Griffiths, Joe Barnes, Gurth Hoyer Millar and Tom Vyner.

A fundamental influence on us was our inheritance; that was the tradition, established so successfully by the founders of our business and so ably upheld by each generation that preceded us, that the quality of the goods we sold and the service and value we gave our customers should be unrivalled. We knew that our greatest asset was the reputation that our predecessors had established for the company.

I hope this book will interest not only those who were in the business during this period, but also those who work in the company now, or will in the future. I am a strong believer in the value of history for a better understanding of the present and wiser judgement for the future. I hope, too, that our long-term suppliers, who were crucial to our success, and some of our many loyal and lifelong customers will find this account of how we worked interesting.

I should like to express my appreciation to Simon Learmount, of the Judge Institute, Cambridge, for the extensive and detailed research he undertook into Sainsbury's post-war history, which has been invaluable for this book. I should also like to thank the many JS people who so generously gave their time to assist Simon. Those whom he and the author interviewed are listed on page 11. I wish to express my appreciation and special thanks to Joe Barnes and Ivor Hunt for their great assistance, and also to thank Araminta Whitley and Adrian House for their invaluable help and advice. Finally, my congratulations and thanks to Giles Emerson, our author, for devoting such care and skill to understanding and assessing the Sainsbury's story, and for turning a long and complex series of events into a book that tells so well 'what we did and how we did it'.

AUTHOR'S NOTE

I would like to add my thanks to those expressed by Lord Sainsbury in his Foreword for the work of Simon Learmount. This book would not have been possible but for the considerable time he spent preparing a statistical record of the progress of Sainsbury's since the early post-war period. He also interviewed many former Sainsbury's employees and associates in order to provide as wide-ranging and objective a view as possible of the company in its buoyant post-war years. I am very grateful to all those interviewed, many of whom are quoted in the book, but all of whom have contributed to a resource of first-hand information which has underpinned my assessment of the Sainsbury's story. I should, of course, thank Simon and Timothy Sainsbury for their help.

Former employees and directors interviewed were: Dino Adriano, Joe Barnes, Angus Clark, Ian Coull, Sir Peter Davis, Bert Ellis, Derek Henson, Colin Harvey, Gurth Hoyer Millar, Ivor Hunt, Bob Ingham, Dennis Males, Ross McLaren, Len Payne, David Smith, Tom Vyner, Robin Whitbread, Jim Woods and Ron Yeates. Others interviewed who were associated with the company include: John Beaumont, former president of the Institute of Grocery Distribution (IGD), Mike O'Conner, former head of the Supermarket Institute of America (SMI), Lord Prior of Brampton and Sir James Spooner, non-executive directors at Sainsbury's 1985–92.

Among those listed I would single out Joe Barnes and Ivor Hunt, who, with Lord Sainsbury of Preston Candover – better known to so many as 'Mr JD' or 'JD' – spent long hours discussing work in progress to help me establish the facts and get the right balance of material. While I have been influenced by the opinions and experience of so many people, and significantly by JD, Joe and Ivor, I hope it will be clear to readers that the 'voice' in the book is my own and not theirs. My intention has never been to propound a particular version of events, but rather to make a credible, objective assessment of what Sainsbury's was like, both for customers and for the people who worked for the company, and to describe how it changed with the times and what drove its success.

The research and writing of this book has also been made

possible through open access to numerous papers covering the period. These include all the speeches and presentations that JD made to senior managers and shareholders, and other memos and papers drawn from the Sainsbury's archive. I am particularly grateful to Clare Bunkham, Sainsbury's archivist, and her staff for responding so efficiently to many requests for photographs at a time when the entire archive was being packed up and moved to its present home in the Museum of London in Docklands.

Former Sainsbury's archivist Bridget Williams's excellent history of Sainsbury's, *The Best Butter in the World,* has also been an invaluable source of information for which I am very grateful. Other books that have helped to throw light on the period include Ian Mac-Laurin's *Tiger by the Tail,* Carol Kennedy's *The Merchant Princes* and Andrew Seth and Geoffrey Randall's *The Grocers.*

I am particularly grateful for the substantial editorial support from Adrian House, who showed great wisdom in helping me adjust and strengthen the narrative structure. My thanks also go to Roger Hudson and to Joe Whitlock Blundell of the Haggerston Press for the former's editorial assistance and eye for detail and the latter's strong design work. Finally, I would like to thank Araminta Whitley, my agent, who has been involved in the project from its early days and has been a fount of energy and good advice.

Giles Emerson, December 2005

SAINSBURY'S
The Record Years

Part One

THREE GENERATIONS
1869–1967

Chapter 1

THE INHERITANCE
1869–1939

'QUALITY PERFECT, PRICES LOWER' read the bold slogan on the fascia of one of the earliest Sainsbury's shops, in Chapel Street, Islington, in the 1870s. The promise of good quality at low prices was one of a number of selling points that started to set the new chain apart from its many nineteenth-century competitors serving mostly working-class populations in London. In those days each high street would have a number of food shops trading in the same area and often selling a similar range of staples – cheese, ham, bacon, pickled pork, rabbit, poultry, tea – with 'egg boys' working the market from stalls at the front.

The busiest periods on the street were Saturday nights, after the family breadwinners had been paid for their long working weeks, with trade often continuing well into the early hours of Sunday morning. Among the duties of the Sainsbury's sales assistants in the early hours of Sunday would be to collect beer tankards left behind by customers and return them to the pubs where they belonged.

John James Sainsbury and his wife, Mary Ann, opened the first J. Sainsbury dairy shop in Drury Lane in 1869. Serving a population in the capital that almost doubled during the second half of the nineteenth century, the family built a highly respected chain of food shops in and around London, mostly selling dairy products. When he passed control of the firm to the eldest of his six sons, Mr John, more than 40 years later, there were 114 shops, and the business had a turnover of almost £3 million.

Mr John took over in 1915, just after the beginning of the First World War, and built the business steadily, extending the number of shops across Greater London, the south-east and gradually further afield. When he handed over to his two sons, Alan and Robert, in 1938, on the eve of the Second World War, there were 248 shops in the chain, now a 'high-class provisioner' with a turnover of £12 million and some 8,000 employees.

As joint general managers, Alan and Robert Sainsbury were almost immediately faced with the problems of running a food business in wartime, but as soon as it was over they set about a programme of modernisation. They led the way among British food retailers in the development of self-service and the first wave of supermarket outlets. Alan Sainsbury retired as the company's chairman in 1967, and his brother, who took over for a short time, retired during the company's centenary year in 1969. By then Sainsbury's was a fashionable and popular food retailer with 244 outlets, half of which were supermarkets and half a combination of small self-service, part-self-service and older-style counter-service branches. The company had a turnover of £166 million and more than 23,000 employees.

In 1969, John Sainsbury, Alan's eldest son, took over leadership of the company, with his brothers Simon and Timothy, and his cousin David Sainsbury, son of Robert, among the main directors. Over the next 23 years something extraordinary happened. In 1992, when John Sainsbury retired as chairman and chief executive of the company after a career in the family business lasting 42 years, J. Sainsbury plc recorded a turnover of some £9.2 billion, and profits before tax of nearly £630 million. The main supermarket company employed 72,000 full-time-equivalent staff, a considerable percentage of whom were Sainsbury's shareholders; some of the longer-serving of these would still have been holding shares apportioned to them when the company went public in 1973 – shares that had become 50 times more valuable. Many of the eight million loyal customers who visited Sainsbury's 313 stores during an average week in 1992 were also shareholders. It was surely a good thing to be, for not only was this the leading food retailer in the UK – in terms of sales, profit and market share – but in 1992, Sainsbury's was also the most profitable of *any* type of retail company in the UK.

How was this achieved, and how did each of the four generations contribute to this success?

Over time, John James, the founder, evolved a particular style of buying and selling which had a deep influence on the development of the company. Buying involved long-term relationships that were assiduously fostered, sometimes over many years. At the heart of Sainsbury's buying approach was a tendency to reach deeply into the supplier's own business, following the trail of supply to the point of origin in order to understand production processes and also to be able to improve the product's quality or suggest new products. A prime example of this was the relationship that John James and his sons established with Lloyd Maunders. Once just a farm in Devon that had caught John James's eye in the early days, today it is a major meat processor and still a supplier to Sainsbury's. The relationship with Lloyd Maunders was also innovative – and innovation is fundamental to Sainsbury's success – for it allowed John James to source good-quality fresh meat outside the traditional London wholesale markets and to transport it to the London-based chain of shops using the modern railway system.

The more Sainsbury's grew, the greater the firm's purchasing power and the more it was able to achieve a high level of control in its buying policies – it might almost be called 'ownership' of products, even if they were made by Sainsbury's itself. Both Sainsbury's and its key suppliers gained enormously from this process. Buisman's is another example of this kind of buyer–supplier relationship. In 1880, John James had found a Dutch merchant called Mr R. Buisman to source Dutch butter from the most reliable dairies in Friesland. Initially working as an agent for Sainsbury's, Buisman eventually established a major business, and the company was still a supplier of butter to Sainsbury's in the 1970s. Another such was George Payne, a supplier of tea for Sainsbury's from the early days of the firm's foundation to the 1980s.

'Ownership' is an important theme in Sainsbury's development and in its distinctive approach. Over time – including John James's and Mr John's period as well as those of subsequent generations – the company preferred to own its branch premises, headquarters buildings, factories, farms, land and other property freehold, or on long leases as a second option. The competitor food multiples that had established themselves in the second half of the nineteenth century generally took a different approach. Some started by renting cheap property and moving on quickly if the outlet was not successful. Lipton's developed its once very considerable turn-of-the-century retail business by setting up in rented properties and selling only a handful of products; in its early days there were only eight or ten grocery staples in a shop, with tea predominating.

In 1882, John James invested heavily in establishing a completely new style of shop to serve the wealthier burghers of Croydon. This had grown from a sleepy place of 6,000 souls in 1801 to become

London's largest neighbouring 'suburban' town, with a population of 80,000 in 1881 – and many of these people were commuters. Croydon was served by 11 railway stations operated by four different companies, and each day 400 trains travelled between it and London. Sainsbury's new shop was established opposite one of the busiest of these stations, on the London Road. This was a lavish branch by any standards, more a reminder of Fortnum & Mason in Piccadilly than Drury Lane. The front windows bore spandrels of stained glass portraying pheasants, hares and other game; the central window proclaimed 'J. Sainsbury High Class Provisions'. A contemporary advertisement described the premises as 'well lighted and elegantly fitted with mahogany, the walls being lined with tessellated tiles, whilst marble slabs and counters give to the whole an inviting air of coolness and cleanliness at the hottest season.' This – No. 9–11 London Road, Croydon – became the model Sainsbury's shop.

Other traders and critics thought John James would get his fingers burnt and would never be able to recoup such outlays. John Benjamin – known to all as 'Mr John' – later recalled, 'The critics missed the point . . . and that was to produce a shop to ensure perfect cleanliness and freedom from the menace of all the food shops in those days – mice and rats. For all time my father must stand as the founder of the modern provision trade.' The shop was successful, and the relatively wealthy inhabitants of Croydon were happy to buy there a greater range of products than could be found in other shops. John James may have kept the rats and mice at bay at 9–11 London Road, but he also raised the status of his business, establishing Sainsbury's as a provisioner for the middle as well as working classes.

John James's next great contribution was the setting up of the firm's new headquarters. In 1890 he took a 78-year lease on 11 Stamford Street, Blackfriars, and on the adjoining building at 10–13 Bennett Street, on the south side of the Thames. Unlike that of the firm's former headquarters in Kentish Town, this location could not have been more appropriate for the business of retailing. It was close to Tooley Street, where butter, bacon and other continental produce arrived at the wharves, and a short distance from the main wholesale markets of Smithfield and Leadenhall; Blackfriars Station was near by, and Liverpool Street, London Bridge and Waterloo were also readily accessible. It was, indeed, right next to the South

Bank's 'London Larder', where most of the principal firms dealing with imported provisions were based.

The headquarters was the focus of activities in other ways. In the 1890s, Sainsbury's first ventured into food manufacturing on its own behalf by building bacon-smoking stoves at Gravel Lane in Blackfriars. Sides of bacon were hung for two or three days at a time on metal grids above foot-deep smouldering sawdust, economically spread with token chunks of peat, allowing the firm rather optimistically to advertise its 'peat-smoked bacon'. The sale of good bacon remained a theme in the company's subsequent development.

The excellent position of Blackfriars meant that all goods passed through the depot before they were distributed to the branches. In comparison with other retailers developing in this period, this was an early and perhaps inspired form of centralisation which made it possible to establish rigorous quality controls. Bulk goods could be broken down, repackaged and distributed to the shops in optimal condition. Most branches traded within a 15-mile radius of headquarters that was comfortably served by the two-horse delivery vans. This centralisation gave a substantial boost to the company, so that in the ten years between 1890 and 1910, the number of shops in the chain more than doubled in the County of London.

In 1915, Mr John took over as head of trading, and worked hard to keep customers supplied during the First World War. To cope with the need to attract women into the firm, he started the first training centre at Blackfriars in the same year. Only when a quarter of the merchant ships sailing to Britain were sunk by German U-boats in April 1917 did the government realise that rationing was inevitable. Sainsbury's ability to keep up supplies became greatly inhibited. Turnover went up from £2.7 million to £3.7 million during the war, but severe wartime inflation actually disguised a downturn in volumes sold and in the firm's fortunes. Profit margins were badly affected, and no new branches were opened between November 1916 and July 1919.

After the war it took another two full years before sales and profits returned to former levels. However, the centralised administration and distribution system at Blackfriars strengthened Mr John's hand as he extended the chain and attracted a considerable following of loyal customers. Some filled their baskets at Sainsbury's with as much of their weekly food shopping as they could buy and carry, while others took advantage of Sainsbury's home-delivery service. This enabled Sainsbury's buyers to increase the range of food on offer, in particular by adding further grocery items, over and above tea, coffee, sugar and other staples.

In 1922, Sainsbury's became a limited company – a change of status that Mr John and his father had partly been persuaded to adopt by Mr John's eldest son, Alan, who joined the firm in 1921. During his 23 years as head of trade and then as chairman, after John James's death in 1928, Mr John demonstrated a fantastic grasp of the business. In this period, the number of Sainsbury's shops more than doubled, from 122 to 248; turnover rose fourfold in real terms to a figure of about £12 million, and the company's reputation for range, quality and value was extended from Greater London into the Midlands, East Anglia and the south of England. The number of products on sale in the average shop increased from about 200 in 1915 to more than 550 in 1938.

Mr John's style as head of the company was hands-on, thorough and often uncompromising; he was a perfectionist who demanded only the best, and made it his business to achieve this – traits that echo down the family line. While approving of and admiring the way Mr John grew the business, the editor of the *Grocer's Gazette* referred to him as an 'unapologetic dictator' whose desire was to control everything, whether the sites of the shops or the way products should be arranged on the counters. At the same time, his capacity to inspire and his ability to create a purposeful and committed team were acknowledged.

Above all, Mr John was an intuitive retailer who was clever at spotting and exploiting new trends. In particular, he buttressed the company's reputation for 'home-manufactured' cooked meats, sausages and pies. These were prepared initially at the company's 'kitchens' at Blackfriars, and later at the imposing cooked-meat factory built in 1936 across the road from the headquarters and depot. This had the latest facilities, and was the first pre-stressed concrete factory built in the capital. A seemingly impregnable construction, the building still stands today and has been listed, perhaps less for its beauty or architectural importance than because of the difficulty of dismantling it. Mr John was also a pioneer in the early development of 'own-label' products: 'J. Sainsbury's Pure Teas' were popular, as was 'J. Sainsbury's Crelos Margarine'. These were heavily promoted through billboards and displays in the shop windows: 'Buy Crelos Margarine and reduce your butter bill' read the large display banner. Crelos was a bargain at 9d per pound, and a popular alternative to other margarines.

Customers flocked to buy Sainsbury's cooked-meat products and fresh viands and its increasing range of poultry and game; French, Danish and Dutch as well as English butters; imported and English cheeses; York, Cumberland and Irish hams; beef from Scotland and Argentina; lamb from Australia and New Zealand. The firm established a reputation for introducing good-quality foodstuffs from all over the world.

As London grew and the former villages on its outskirts were linked by ribbon development, there was plenty of scope for expansion into the new suburbs. Usually when Mr John decided to locate a new shop in a particular area, other well-established retailers would soon book their places near by. A Sainsbury's shop's location was always regarded as critically important to its success, and this would hold true for the rest of the century. Location decisions were also determined, in the early days at least, by the distance that could be travelled by horse and van in one day from the company headquarters at Blackfriars. Mr John presided over a major and ineluctable change in this respect, with the new motor era arriving in the pre-war period. Nevertheless, the Sainsbury's chairman was reluctant to lose his delivery teams entirely, and the Blackfriars stables were not finally swept out until 1937, when Sainsbury's new motor vehicles were already extending deliveries upwards of 100 miles from headquarters.

And as the number of branches grew, it became increasingly important to maintain a disciplined approach in all aspects of the expanding business. Long-retired staff have reported on a kind of a 'Sainsburyness' about Sainsbury's, which in large part resulted from the imprint of rigorously applied standards and disciplines. Indeed, the whole organisation of the company in the inter-war period, and for a long time after the Second World War, could be said to have been both military and paternalistic in style. We see this in the control exercised from the centre, in the hierarchical structure, methodical training, stringent quality control and scrupulous attention to health, safety and hygiene; also in the emphasis on punctuality, neat appearance and the uniforms worn by sales staff. By having a combination of written and unwritten rules concerning all aspects of work, the Sainsbury's name and identity was created as an early form of retail 'brand'.

The displays in the shop windows promoting a particular product were usually changed weekly, and there would be exactly the same promotion in every Sainsbury's shop in the chain. The prices of all provisions would also be the same whether you were visiting Sainsbury's in Oxford, Leytonstone or Bournemouth. Equally, there would be consistency in the layout of the departments, manner of displaying biscuits, 'knocking up' Sainsbury's butter, trussing the poultry, serving the popular Sainsbury's Pure Tea and the growing range of grocery items. Customers were always served by well-groomed and courteous staff. Each shop manager – invariably a thoroughly experienced tradesman – had a company rule book as his bible and a stock book which he kept up to date at the end of each day; he received regular bulletins instructing him about the preparation and display of new products and any other decisions that derived from headquarters. Control was fastidiously and constantly applied, and it was respected without question.

It was the manager's job to maintain a presence on the shop floor and to lead by example. Usually his post would reflect his seniority and expertise as a tradesman rather than his abilities as a manager in anything like the sense in which these are understood today. The hours were long, the work was hard and the dedication to minutiae was exacting. The manager was also a kind of paterfamilias – a family leader concerned with the welfare and skills of his own team, a man who was always accountable to those at the centre of the company. He would generally stay a long time in the company, perhaps having started in the very junior position of 'egg boy', and would finally leave as a retiring manager after a career that might have lasted 45 years or more.

Sainsbury's standards were reinforced through formal training, a process that was virtually unheard of among competing retailers. Within the trade as a whole, Sainsbury's training was widely perceived to be the best in the business. 'Sainsbury's trade-training preferred' was a phrase commonly seen in advertisements for staff in this sector well into the 1950s. The training took place in short but intensive courses held at Blackfriars. Eager young staff were, for example, shown how to cut up and prepare an 80-pound round of cheese leaving only two ounces of waste. Recruits would continue their training in a particular branch department under the supervision of senior tradesmen. Many would stay their entire working life. For years before the Second World War and right up to the end of the 1960s, these young salesmen and, later, women would not only work at the Sainsbury's branches but lived, under the watchful eye of housekeepers, in the hostels that were owned and run by the company and situated directly above or close to their branch. Their career, and inevitably much of their social calendar, was thus regulated with almost military precision.

But outside the well-ordered shop and the discipline, what was Sainsbury's position in the general struggle for market share that occurred among food retailers of this period? After the First World War, and with the return of some confidence in the late 1920s, food retailing had changed rapidly. The three largest groups of multiples in the 1930s were Home and Colonial, International Tea and Moores Stores. Home and Colonial was mostly owned by the prominent food, soap and detergent manufacturer, Unilever – which was attempting to extend its power by adding retail to production. These groups bought up their smaller competitors at a frenetic pace. By 1931, Home and Colonial operated more than 3,000 stores nationwide. Maypole, Lipton and the Meadow Dairy Company all traded under their own names but were absorbed under the Home and Colonial umbrella. These would still be well-known high-street names in the sluggish aftermath of the Second World War.

Among the new chains was Tesco Limited, founded by T. E. Stockwell and Jack Cohen in 1932 – 'Tesco' is an elision of the founders' initials and names. Tesco worked energetically to establish a presence in the high street by buying small shops and supplying them through the principal wholesalers, or by means of Cohen's opportunistic dealings. But while Cohen became famous in the trade for his buccaneering style, his company only started to become truly noteworthy during the 1950s.

In the face of this competition, Mr John's tactic of opening relatively large shops (although tiny compared even to a 'local' modern supermarket) in increasingly upmarket locations proved highly effective. By 1938, Sainsbury's had achieved remarkable progress in the way food was prepared and sold and in the way buyers maintained quality and sought to develop the range. Buyers were always the heroes among Sainsbury's staff and, as illustrated later, the family heads of trade continually drove them to do better and take on increasing responsibilities.

Uniquely among the food-retailer multiples of the period, Sainsbury's also established 'the Laboratories' at Blackfriars, where all food products were sampled and tested and where the buyers worked with suppliers and scientific staff in the development of new product lines. Laboratory staff – early 'mystery shoppers' – regularly visited the shops and bought products which were then brought back to Blackfriars for rigorous checks to ensure that quality at the point of sale had been maintained.

When one generation of Sainsburys decided the time for succession was ripe, the next generation was inevitably well prepared for the job in hand. So it was in 1938, when Mr John passed full executive control to his sons. Since joining in 1921, Alan had already demonstrated great ability on the trading side of the business. In 1930, Robert Sainsbury had joined the company as a professionally qualified accountant. The division of responsibilities between the brothers was clear from the outset: Alan, always 'Mr Alan' in his generation, would handle the trading side of the company – the buying and the management of the shops; Robert, known as 'Mr RJ' because there was already a Mr Roberts in the firm – the chief accountant – would control the finances, administration and personnel. Their cousin James Sainsbury, also on the executive board, was responsible for manufacturing operations. Once he had passed on control, Mr John held the title of chairman, and continued to maintain a close interest in the company's progress until his death in 1956.

By the time of reporting in March 1939, Sainsbury's turnover from its 248 branches was £12.6 million, while Home and Colonial's chain of nearly 800 own-title shops produced £9.9 million, Lipton's 450 stores produced less than £7 million and Maypole Dairy's almost 1,000 shops produced only £9.1 million. This is an early record of another thoroughly important and prevailing theme in the firm's subsequent development: Sainsbury's could sell more per square foot of selling space in its branches than any other food-retailing company. The third generation seemed set for a good innings.

Chapter 2

WAR AND RECOVERY
1939–1954

I N THAT LAST SUMMER OF PEACE, one glance in a high street or parade in Greater London would tell you which shop was Sainsbury's.

Outside, an imposing façade, generally taller than neighbouring premises, is surmounted by a large 'J. Sainsbury' in gilded lettering. Below this the high windows, either side of a substantial central doorway, are set into a frontage usually combining red Norwegian and grey Swedish granite. The frontage is relatively narrow compared with the long inner space, on both sides of which are counters and shelves of white Sicilian marble. They are immaculately clean and easily seen to be so in the brightly lit interior. The floors are decorated with colourful mosaics and the walls are covered with highly glazed ceramic tiles that were specially produced by Minton Hollins of Stoke-on-Trent. The patterns are complex and stylised, including upper borders depicting dolphins and fleur-de-lis. The tiles on the front of the counters are a deep colour know by Minton as 'Sainsbury's teapot brown'. An ornate wooden screen, like a reredos in a Wren church, is built against the back wall of the shop; this separates the office area.

The shop is busy. Customers are being served at one of the six principal departments dividing the length of the marble counters. There is Dairy, Bacon and Hams, Poultry and Game, Cooked Meats, Fresh Meat, and Grocery. Everything is carefully arrayed. A busy hubbub greets us from the back of the shop as well as within it, and we sense the presence of food-preparation rooms and supply areas out of sight. Like all the others in the Sainsbury's chain, this branch is a mini-industrial unit as well as a shop.

Outside, passers-by may notice a gleaming Sainsbury's delivery van easing its way from the kerb into the mid-morning traffic.

Far more than an echo of that early slogan, 'Quality Perfect, Prices Lower' remained. The company had achieved an excellent

reputation; to shop in a Sainsbury's branch conferred a kind of dignity in itself. The chain was still well represented in many areas that
would have been considered largely working-class, but these shops
offered a range and a service that combined the everyday with the
aspirational. In the more well-to-do locations, Sainsbury's branches
were not dissimilar from the best independent food retailers in the
smartest streets of London. But unlike the royally appointed food
provisioners of Piccadilly, the Sainsbury's 'offer' uniquely combined
good quality in presentation and product with affordability. The
style and operations of this typical Sainsbury's branch had not
notably altered since the early twentieth century – at least not compared to the remarkable changes that were to come.

The Second World War made trading extremely difficult, and seriously set back Sainsbury's progress. Many shops were damaged
during the blitz. There were about 600 bombing incidents, some
devastating, others requiring hurried repairs after the dust had
settled before reopening for business. Even the head office was
bombed, with direct hits on the garage workshops, the kitchens and
the Union Street bacon stoves which were then being used by the
Ministry of Food to store frozen meat. One person who watched
that particular blaze was Fred Salisbury, a close personal assistant
to Mr John who became the first non-family member of the board in
1941. He presciently observed: 'This will set us back fifteen years!'
    The war affected Sainsbury's more than its rival companies. It
had developed a reputation for a variety of high-quality fresh foods,
cooked meats, sausages, bacons, pies and dairy products. But with
rationing and price controls the food that was available was generally the same standard and price in all shops. Families were
required to register at a particular shop, and, with the standardisation of food quality and increasing travel difficulties, many
cus-tomers otherwise loyal to Sainsbury's had little option but to
register at their nearest available food-retailing outlet. The result
was a drastic reduction in turnover.
    The joint general managers resorted to occasional compromise
and constant ingenuity in order to continue to trade. To make up for
the shortfall in staff caused by conscription they recruited women
vigorously, but it remained hard to find adequate numbers because
many families were evacuated from London. By March 1942 sales
sunk to their lowest possible level, only 65 per cent of their value in

1939 – and profits were almost non-existent. Mr R J later admitted
that if sales had gone any lower, 'we couldn't have survived'.

The general managers believed fundamentally in fairness and
integrity in all customer dealings, and this certainly helped to maintain customer loyalty in a difficult period. They introduced a 'Fair
Shares' scheme using 'points' which enabled the fair distribution of
those goods that were generally in short supply, such as sausages,
bacon hocks, meat pies, cake, blancmanges and custard powder.
And customers came to expect that the least good quality cut of
bacon, for example, would always be placed on top of the display, so
that they knew the unseen product below was likely to be no worse
and possibly better. Sainsbury's also had a clear policy against the
giving of favours to customers, or having a little something 'under
the counter', which often happened in other establishments.
Branch staff had to sign a declaration stating that if they broke the
rationing regulations they would be dismissed immediately. The
title of this declaration was 'Food is a Munition of War'. There was a
real sense that anyone breaking the rule was a low form of traitor. So
Sainsbury's survived the war not only with its reputation for quality
and value intact but with immense good will from its customers.

After the war Mr Alan's and Mr R J's main concern was to rebuild
Sainsbury's damaged trade and begin the necessary process of
modernising the business. As head of trading, Mr Alan, like his
father, had a good eye for new trends, and he was convinced that
the economic climate would improve, bringing gradual increases in
food production and availability, as well as a demand for more variety and range in the shops. Both brothers were keenly aware of the
social upheavals caused by the war and how this affected the business. For example, the Education Act of 1944 stipulated that the new
school-leaving age should be 15 from 1947; later it was raised to 16.
This had an impact on traditional patterns of youth work and
apprenticeships, and Mr R J responded by reforming Sainsbury's
training programmes. Mr Alan's abiding interest in politics – as a
member of the Labour Party since 1945 – assured his sensitivity to
more general changes in society. The fact that the middle classes
had few if any domestic staff affected food retailing and demanded
new thinking.

But new thinking was one thing, putting new plans into motion
was quite another. Modernisation within Sainsbury's and among

competitors in the food-retailing market was hampered by a number of obstacles that lay outside their control. First and foremost, the ration book was still very much in operation. Within just three weeks of VE Day in 1945, when the dust from the celebrations had scarcely settled, rations of bacon, cooking fat and fresh meat were further reduced. Food supplies at that point were even more limited than before May 1945 because the needs of the newly liberated countries of Europe had to be accommodated. Bread had not been rationed during the war but its sale also became controlled from 1946; even potatoes were subject to post-war controls.

Many other staples in the nation's diet remained rationed for years after the war, including meat, eggs, cheese, sugar, butter and margarine. The rationing of petrol also continued. Daily deliveries from Blackfriars had to stop, and the vans set out from Stamford Street just three times a week, instead of six. Drivers and shop staff worked long hours to make deliveries and unload the vans. The depot at Blackfriars had partly been able to respond to these pressures by replacing the three-ton vans with new five-ton 'cars', as they were called. Thankfully, in 1950 petrol rationing ceased and six-day delivery could resume. Sainsbury's transport department could then also introduce highly effective night-loading and driving schedules. This meant that the output from the factory could reach the shops early in the morning along with other perishable goods.

There was also a chronic post-war shortage of skilled staff, and manpower generally. All sectors of the economy needed labour, and returning servicemen and women were often lured to better-paid jobs elsewhere. Again, this factor contributed to the reform of recruitment and training policies at Sainsbury's. Mr R J was keenly aware of the balance required between maintaining the quality of trade and service skills required in the shops, and training men and women who had no former retailing skills whatsoever.

There was another fundamental barrier to any programme of modernisation. The Board of Trade controlled the issue of licences for construction work of any kind. Building supplies and indeed building labour were severely limited because of the massive task of reconstruction required across the country, and the need to set priorities. Although about half of the post-war portfolio of Sainsbury's shops had not been substantially upgraded since before 1914, the fact that the company had built their shops so well made it harder to plead for licences to refurbish old stores or build new ones.

Such 'external' problems faced by Sainsbury's were also faced by all the other retail multiples and independents that had survived the war, and by the brave new multiples that tried to establish themselves in a difficult environment that would last until halfway through the 1950s. According to Board of Trade figures, the multiple grocery retailers operated 15,247 shops across the UK in 1950, though probably less than 20 per cent of this number were located within Sainsbury's south-eastern area.

Mr Alan's approach to his competition was rigorous. He personally maintained a deep and up-to-date knowledge of the market in which he operated, and his pricing policy reflected this. Each Thursday morning, he had a meeting with the senior buyers in Stamford House to decide on the prices of goods that needed to be changed the following week. He would carefully brief himself on the prices that competitors were charging before approving each price change. He did not, however, set the meat prices, for this was Fred Salisbury's domain. Once all price changes were decided, they were typed up in the form of a bulletin which was again checked by Mr Alan, copied and then sent to every branch over the weekend. While this was time-consuming, it was a necessary means of offering customers the best possible value. It was the firm's unwavering policy both to keep prices keen and to charge the same amount throughout the chain.

While keen pricing was important, Sainsbury's competitive hand was strengthened by other factors in the company's inheritance. The maintenance of high standards in food retailing, carried forward by Mr Alan and Mr R J, tended to be the exception rather than the norm as the number of multiple-owned grocery shops started to grow after the war. Lacking the kind of discipline and the centralised control that characterised Sainsbury's, many of the war-shocked older multiples and the opportunistic new ones had little more than price to fall back on to maintain their own competitive edge. The Co-op movement had by far and away the largest share of the total food market – 25 per cent in 1950 – and was particularly strong in the Midlands and the north of the country. The ideal behind the foundation of the Co-op was fair trading and honesty, if not remarkable value or spectacular quality. But the various different groups comprising the democratically run Co-operative Societies had not moved with the times; their mode of operation was dated in many respects, and they generally lacked capital and the obvious means to raise it. This would make their share of the market relatively easy prey.

Despite the ructions and changes that had occurred as a result of the war, Sainsbury's style of leadership remained consistent. Attention to detail, for example, was a factor of paramount importance in the incessant pursuit of quality. James Sainsbury, cousin of Alan and Robert, was famously particular about the quality of the sausages and cooked-meat products produced in the factory that it had become his responsibility to run since its construction in 1936. He visited the factory every day for long sampling sessions, and it has been suggested that he developed so beady an eye that he even knew which worker had prepared a particular sausage mix by its colour and texture. He would usually mutter complaint if the best mixer was absent for any reason, however legitimate. Perfection alone was good enough.

Mr James may have been singular in his focus on sausage meat, but this level of attention to detail had a far wider target range in the person of Mr Alan. As head of trading he was, after all, the man whose wishes had to be respected most, and his abiding concern was to maintain high quality – the freshness, shape, colour, texture, presentation, temperature – of all the food that went into his shops. Quality control at Blackfriars was attended to religiously. Every batch of butter arriving from the English countryside or continental Europe was tasted at Blackfriars to ensure that it was good enough for Sainsbury's customers. The same scrutiny was applied to the cheeses; each individual round of the many that were delivered weekly into the storerooms had to be checked and approved.

Being so close to his buying and trading team at Blackfriars also allowed Mr Alan to spot-check the work of subordinates. He regularly turned up at the weekly meetings of, for example, the grocery department. Buyers would be busy checking through lists of stock, records of previous weekly sales and other data. Mr Alan would pick up and thumb through the data sheets, taking note of any discrepancy and making pre-emptive comments if he found, for example, slow sales of particular products relative to stock.

In such an atmosphere of vigilance, it is not surprising that Sainsbury's developed an ethos in which its buyers were renowned throughout the trade both for their expertise and their stringency. An article in the company newsletter, *JS Journal*, in May 1950 offers an insight into the daily activities of the company's main poultry buyer visiting London's wholesale market for poultry and game, at Leadenhall Street. The article describes how every individual bird bought for Sainsbury's actually passed through the buyer's hands and was discerningly checked, a great many being rejected:

> The technique changes from bird to bird and even, with some species, from season to season. When wild fowl such as wild duck, widgeon or teal are examined in the early part of the season, the main attention is paid to flesh in the centre of the back, whilst in winter our buyers would pay more attention to the flesh near the tail feathers.

Bob Ingham, who joined Sainsbury's in 1952 as one of the company's first graduate recruits, was initially astonished by the time and energy that Sainsbury's devoted to guaranteeing these standards: 'The scientific part of buying food is about product specification, but that only really works if you have a buyer who is absolutely committed to quality – and Sainsbury's made sure that you were absolutely committed.' Jim Woods, Mr Alan's personal assistant at the time, testifies to the fervour of Sainsbury's commitment to standards more generally: 'The trouble they went to . . . to make sure everything was right, everything was the best, would be unbelievable today.'

Such a comment applied particularly to Mr Alan's method of ensuring that all Sainsbury's branches were running to order. Visiting the shops unannounced was a distinctive part of his leadership, as it would be for his successor. Each Tuesday was set aside for the purpose of visiting five or six branches in a particular area, the purpose being to see how these were operating in normal trading conditions – as customers saw them. If anything was found to be wrong in a particular shop, the manager could expect fireworks, but he would receive praise if all was going well. One branch manager recalled a visit from Mr Alan in the early 1950s. It was just before closing when the boss unexpectedly entered the store and walked right round, finishing at the bread aisle where there was just one large loaf and one small loaf remaining on the shelves. Mr Alan called the manager over, who waited anxiously for a verdict. Mr Alan simply pointed to the remaining bread and said, 'Very well judged,' then left the store. On this occasion, the store manager was caught unawares by the visit, whereas in most cases there was an excellent company grapevine sounding the alert to local branches.

This anecdote points to a fundamentally important aspect of Sainsbury's approach. All Sainsbury's staff – in the branches, depot and head office – worked unusually hard to ensure that both rationed and non-rationed products were available in every shop on a daily basis. To fail in this respect risked losing valued customers. Ron Yeates, who joined the company in the late 1940s as a shop employee and later rose to senior management, recalls that it was considered a crime to be out of stock of a product when a customer asked for it. In his role as a store manager he recalls how he, in common with all Sainsbury's managers, meticulously recorded daily sales in his day-book, adding other pertinent information such as the weather conditions, the time goods were sold out if they did sell out – anything that would assist judgement about the optimal order level for his shop. The head-office supply system was even more paper-heavy, each clerk taking pains to interpret order volume and get the balance right between availability in the warehouse and factories and allocation in the branches.

In October 1950, John Davan Sainsbury, eldest son of Mr Alan, joined the family firm and started, from scratch, to learn an entirely new trade. He had by then taken a degree in history at Worcester College, Oxford, after doing his National Service in the Life Guards. Following such a stimulating time, when he had been able to foster his love of the arts and music, the 22 year-old had mixed feelings as he embarked on a career as a food retailer. There had not been any explicit pressure upon him to join the firm, but there was undoubtedly some expectation that he would follow in the footsteps of his father, grandfather and great-grandfather before him. John Sainsbury – known as 'JD' to distinguish him from his grandfather, Mr John – keenly remembers his feelings at the time: 'I thought it might not stretch my mind much, but I could always pursue other interests to get intellectual fulfilment. How naive I was!'

A core activity in the business – the job of getting appropriate supplies of goods into the central warehouses – was the responsibility of the departmental buyers, and theirs was a challenging task. Production and availability may have started to increase in the late 1940s and early 1950s, but the whole process of food supply in the

UK had become manacled by many years of government-imposed controls. Food suppliers and manufacturers were entrenched in a system of allocating food, rather than meeting market demand. Their agents were neither geared nor easily moved to respond to multiple food retailers such as Sainsbury's who were determined to grow their range and increase volumes of goods to satisfy customers' needs.

JD cut his teeth in the family business as an assistant grocery buyer under Arthur Trask – one of the company's foremost buyers at the time and later a director of the company. He quickly became aware of the kinds of problem that buyers were facing in the early post-war regime. By early 1952, JD was a biscuit buyer in the grocery department. Although biscuits were not rationed, suppliers tended to approach Sainsbury's with a predetermined allocation which was usually based on pre-war sales levels. As a number of Sainsbury's shops did not even sell groceries before the war, JD faced the challenge of trying to convince suppliers – some of whom he recalls were notoriously arrogant – of the need for more. His exasperation at seeing the company unable to meet demand was a significant early lesson, and one that fuelled his desire to make improvements.

Sainsbury's paternalistic culture differentiated the company from other food retailers, and continued to be an important part of its strength in the post-war years. All those who joined the company became part of the larger 'family' – a family to which they became committed and which took care of them in turn. Mr Alan and Mr RJ continued the tradition of providing exemplary working conditions and welfare for the staff, even at a time when resources were thoroughly stretched. Exceptionally, within the trade during this period, Sainsbury's had introduced a pension scheme, originally set up in the 1930s by N. C. Turner – and staff were entitled to paid holidays.

In 1922, Mr John had also established a 'Good Fellowship Trust' to provide discretionary payments to staff in times of sickness and adversity. This measure was most unusual before the war, and was partly the result of the persuasive voice of Mr Alan, a pre-war Liberal and post-war Labour supporter who always believed deeply that all those involved in the company should be well looked after and should share in the company's success. Both Mr Alan and

Mr R J publicly expressed their approval of the Beveridge Report, in effect a blueprint for the welfare state, in a letter published in *The Times*. In this document, published in 1942, William Beveridge had argued the merits of having a general insurance scheme to which every worker would contribute in return for the equivalent of unemployment benefit and comprehensive medical care. The joint general managers of Sainsbury's both believed in what was at the time a highly controversial political vision of offering protection for British citizens 'from the cradle to the grave'.

The benevolent approach to employees extended further than pay and conditions of work. There was the Griffin Sports Club, a sports ground at Dulwich Village with excellent facilities not only for football, netball and cricket but also for dances and social events. The *JS Journal*, which was started in 1946, emanates a sense of 'Sainsbury's people' at work and play, and is packed with information about individuals, groups, events in the firm and news items concerning activities in the branches. It also educates its readers about many aspects of the company's operation outside the actual shops. There are features on London's wholesale markets and detailed accounts of the food-manufacturing processes of key suppliers such as Unilever and McVitie's. Some articles offer a kind of social induction and welcome, perhaps intended primarily for young employees who have been trawled in the provinces and have come to London and its busy suburbs to start their working lives. There are descriptions of the theatre and verbal tours of particular London streets and their histories. Each successive monthly journal has a coy optimism, reflecting the emergence of new confidence, the rediscovery of the value of ordinary things as people found their feet after the traumas of war.

Ron Yeates recalls: 'The morale in those little shops was fantastic. Everyone helped everyone. There was a real family atmosphere, a strong sense of community in all the shops. And the strong discipline and regular visits from supervisors and the Sainsbury family directors just served to strengthen the common bond we all felt.'

It wasn't until 23 February 1950, the day of the general election that returned the Attlee government to power for the second time, that Sainsbury's opened its first new shop since 1939. This was a small branch by Sainsbury's pre-war standards, situated at Selsdon, to the south of Croydon. The building licence had been granted mainly because the shell of the shop had already been completed in the first year of the war. In an article in the *JS Journal* of March that year, Fred Salisbury, assistant general manager and a driving force behind the design and fitting-out of the new premises, talked up Selsdon as a 'turning point' in the company's history. Although small, this shop did indeed contain a number of innovations, some of which had been planned for several years and only needed an outlet for trial. Corrugated perspex made its first appearance, as did an early form of fluorescent lighting. The teak window frames were conspicuously absent from the front of the shop, all of which was now granite-fronted with armour-plated glass; the blinds were on the inside of the windows so the Sainsbury's name was emblazoned round the clock. There were both automatic and semi-automatic counter scales, curved counter screens and electrically heated water (a hygienic improvement on former gas-heating methods). The emphasis was on function and hygiene, with white or pale-coloured tiles extending across all shop walls and into the fluorescent-lit preparation and storage rooms. Not least, Sainsbury's abandoned the wooden till for the thoroughly modern cash register – an American import, this was a major innovation in retailing in 1950.

The previewing public clearly approved of the aura of wall-to-wall hygiene, efficiency and modernity. But Selsdon was tiny, and as Fred Salisbury writes in the newsletter, 'It is by no means a hundred-per-cent post-war shop, for the finishing work of 1950 has had to be applied to the 1940 structure'. Nevertheless, the directors were pleased to have at least one testing ground for their modernisations, particularly as they were working towards the launch of something far more spectacular. Following a visit to the United States in March 1949, Mr Alan and Fred Salisbury had become convinced that the future of food retailing lay in self-service shopping. The primary purpose during their two-week visit had been to study American methods of displaying and selling frozen foods, which were a completely unknown quantity in the UK. But what really caught the directors' imaginations was the wonderland of huge American supermarkets.

For two frenetic weeks the pair virtually lived in supermarkets during an exhausting tour of these outlets in New York, Boston, Buffalo, Chicago and Philadelphia. As Mr Alan recalled, they returned to England on the *Queen Elizabeth* 'to get some sleep'. The range of food, size of store, refrigeration methods, customer facilities, existence of adjoining car parking – all this was impressive; the Americans were clearly well advanced in food retailing compared to Britain and continental Europe. But then they had been helping themselves from the shelves in one form or another since 1916, when the Piggly Wiggly self-service grocery store was opened by Clarence Saunders in Memphis, Tennessee. The idea had developed rapidly during the Depression as a way of keeping down distribution and labour costs; customers mostly took goods straight from open cases in large warehouse premises. Then in the 1930s Michael J. Cullen had started to professionalise self-service and open a number of supermarkets, thus planting the roots of an international retail chain.

Seeing at first hand what was happening in post-war America was a kind of road to Damascus for the visitors from Blackfriars. Mr Alan seized his opportunity when John Strachey, the Minister of Food, who was also becoming interested in the potential of self-service, offered to grant licences to up to 100 shops for experiments in self-service techniques in the UK.

On 26 June 1950, the doors of the thoroughly refurbished branch at 9–11 London Road, Croydon, were thrown open to reveal the company's very first self-service store. It was appropriate that an entirely new style of shopping should be offered from the company's original Croydon 'model' premises; but this was pure coincidence. The reason for choosing 9–11 was its suitability for conversion: it was double-fronted and therefore of good size, offering an eventual sales-floor area of some 4,000 square feet; there was good access for delivery at the rear; the shop could be reconstructed to include a lower-ground-floor area for preparation and storage. Croydon was also close enough to Blackfriars to allow easy monitoring.

Mr Alan and Fred Salisbury had been utterly painstaking in the development of this store. The only component of its design and internal furnishings that was handled by an outside contractor was the tiling. Everything else was the work of a small army of in-house engineers, draughtsmen, craftsmen, joiners, plumbers and electricians. Led by Ralph Hall, the firm's chief engineer, the engineering department had carried out lengthy experiments to develop an effective 'blister-plate' refrigeration unit for use in the temperature-controlled, open-top cabinets. The very concept of an 'open' refrigerator was completely novel to customers in this period. The main shelf display units, known as 'gondolas', were the result of further detailed research and development that took careful account of factors such as the height and comfortable reach of the housewives who would browse them. Everything was robustly made and spotless. The gondolas were raised on foot-long stainless steel cylinder legs, so that the lowest shelf was accessible and the free space underneath could be swept and polished easily.

The store opened at 8.30 am on the first morning, admitting an eager queue of one person, Mrs Fowler, who happened to be the manager's wife. But the drum soon beat and more customers stepped in to explore the new venture. The self-service gondolas shone pristine in the fluorescent overhead lighting, with spotlights highlighting promotional items at each end. There was the usual relatively limited range of non-rationed grocery products arrayed in perfect displays: tinned meats, canned fruits, jams and preserves, tubs of Saxa salt, Kellogg's cornflakes and Campbell soups. Mr Fowler and the sales assistants hovered and offered guidance.

Two long service counters on either side of the store were a reminder that rationing was still in force; there could be no such thing as full self-service of rationed products such as butter, bacon, cheese and fresh meat. On the other hand, pork sausages, cream biscuits and canned fruit were still rarities at this time, and the presentation of limitless supplies of sausages ('come and help yourself') certainly helped to sell the new format to bedazzled customers. With very few exceptions, the Croydon residents took to the new approach immediately, recognising that something quite different had taken place on their high street and was being done well. They browsed among the biscuits and other pre-wrapped goods, all of which had been prepared below the sales floor and packaged for presentation. Customers took their rationed and self-selected goods to the brand-new checkout desks in wire baskets, where purchases were placed in a sliding wooden 'rake', checked though the brand new cash register and wrapped by a packer. For a number of years the 'packers' in question tended to be young management trainees.

Recalling his inspirational visit to the US, Mr Alan later reflected: 'We were convinced that this was the future for JS . . . we couldn't visualise a return to the old type of trading . . . no old-fashioned counter shop could offer the customers of the future the range of choice that would be expected with a higher standard of living.' This recollection combines the hindsight of later years with the optimism of the times, for the 'old type of trading' was to continue, alongside the slowly rolled-out new format, for many years to come. By contrast, Fred Salisbury's contemporary account of the US visit, in the September 1950 *JS Journal*, is prosaic and cautious: 'We came to the conclusion that up to the outbreak of the war, America had very little to show us in the sphere of retail food distribution but in the last decade they had certainly far-outstripped us in many directions, particularly in packaging, refrigeration, self-service and the establishment of the super-market [*sic*].' He concludes with the note that 'there is the more difficult task of applying our experience to existing branches, for much of what we have learned at Croydon can be of use elsewhere, self-service or no'.

This inference about how lessons learnt were to be applied is important. Not only was it difficult to change the old order of things because of barriers to trade beyond the control of Sainsbury's directors, but it was just not possible to convert a considerable number of shops to self-service. Most of the existing Sainsbury's premises were not big enough, and they were the wrong shape, offering depth instead of breadth. It would in fact be many years before Sainsbury's could close or replace all the counter-service stores upon which the firm's name and reputation had been built.

Nevertheless, the new format created a real buzz of excitement around the company, and aroused the attention of the entire retail food trade. Many commentators at this stage were sceptical about whether this style of shopping could be successfully transplanted from the US to Britain, arguing that the UK market and general environment were so different from those in the US that self-service would never be taken up by the British public. But proof of Croydon's success came when the company realised that the turnover of the new self-service store was significantly outstripping that of the traditional counter-service shops. Only five months after 9–11 London Road opened, a market researcher working for the Co-op wrote in *The Producer* that 9–11 London Road was 'certainly doing a weekly volume of trade greater than that of any grocery shop in the country'.

Of course, the overall reaction of long-term, loyal Sainsbury's customers had also to be carefully assessed in the early days of self-service. The majority took quickly to the new approach in Croydon, but a small minority found it an affront to their dignity to have to serve themselves. There is a famous story of Mr Alan, on opening day, offering the new-fangled wire basket – there were no trolleys at this stage – to a customer who handed it straight back; she was outraged that she should have to serve herself *and* carry her own purchases. Some customers continued to demand to be served appropriately and smartly at the counters.

The first half of the 1950s was a difficult time to open new self-service stores, and only three more were built by 1954. One was at Terminus Road in Eastbourne, where a licence had been granted to rebuild a severely bomb-damaged shop. This was Sainsbury's first purpose-built self-service store. Unlike Croydon, customers either loved or hated the new self-service format; fortunately the disgruntled of Eastbourne had access to another Sainsbury's counter-service shop near by.

The other two stores in the first wave were built at new post-war estates in Grange Hill and Debden, where Sainsbury's was invited by the London County Council (LCC) to introduce its 'experiment'. The LCC was keen to promote its own social experiment, and what better way than to have the highly reputable Sainsbury's name among the small row of shops in the parades of these marsh-bound Essex estates. Still partly rather than fully self-service, the tiny new branches, once again fronted in granite and armour-plated glass, were tiled literally floor to ceiling. All the goods were set out particularly low, as this was believed to assist the comfort of shoppers. The result was an impression of bareness and sterility as you entered the branch. Following his own inspection of the Debden premises, Mr John returned to Blackfriars and commented to his grandson, JD: 'It's a bit like a bathroom.'

During the same period, the very last counter-service shop was built – or rather rebuilt – at East Grinstead, on the severely bomb-damaged site of a former Sainsbury's shop. Out of the rubble emerged a familiarly deep and well-lit shop, spotless and – by the standards of the day – thoroughly modernised. Behind the scenes, the engineers and architects had incorporated the very latest and best in staff facilities, warehouse plant, preparation and store rooms and equipment. Even the staff cloakrooms were considered a marvel of ingenuity and convenience by the *East Grinstead Observer*: 'the most modern food store in the country', opined the eager reporter who joined swarms of residents and visitors previewing the premises in the week before its opening.

In March 1954, Sainsbury's appeared to have finally shaken off the cobwebs of the war when turnover crept above the company's pre-war high point. It had taken 15 hard years to achieve this.

Chapter 3

A CHANGED WORLD
1954–1962

I N THE SECOND HALF of the 1950s and the early 1960s, a sense
of stability gradually returned to the whole country, and with it
more optimism and a growing affluence. It was as if people were
waking up, rediscovering all the advances that had been delayed or
blown away by the war, and developing an appetite for new ideas.
This was the environment in which Sainsbury's could develop the
self-service format further and continue to lead progress in selling
food. Whatever the claims might be for a thoroughly 'modern'
counter-service shop like the one at East Grinstead, it was now clear
to the general managers that the self-service format would be the
key to the company's growth – also that constant innovation was
needed to harness the potential of this exciting new method of
retailing.

An important early showpiece was the 5,000 square-foot self-
service store in Southampton which Sainsbury's opened in September 1954. This was only two months after the end of rationing of
meat and bacon – the last rationed items; the little ration books of
coupons that had to be snipped out with a pair of scissors became
mementoes or were eagerly binned. Southampton was therefore
the company's first truly all-self-service store, including refrigerated
cabinets for pre-wrapped fresh meat. The shop floor was serviced
from the basement preparation rooms by means of a 'magic eye'
control, a goods lift and four compressed-air 'push-ups' – these
were specially designed hydraulic lifts that delivered food to the
sales floor from the lower preparation areas. Not only the most
modern of the self-service shops in this respect, it was also a venture into southernmost territory, and there was some apprehension
about how local customers would take both to self-service and to a
name that was relatively unknown to them. But directors need not
have worried; the gleaming modern premises and thoughtfully
presented products attracted plenty of custom and acclaim.

The directors were often surprised and impressed by the increasing quantities of food that could be sold through the various departments in the new stores. Dennis Males, who became highly influential in the operations of the company's supermarkets 20 years later, was a young and eager recruit into Sainsbury's self-service stores at this time. He recalls, 'Everybody underestimated the sheer volume that would go through these stores. It was such a learning curve with our day-books, just trying to keep track of sales.' Males was one of many who saw Sainsbury's move into self-service as a real chance to get involved in something exciting and innovative. He comments: 'Self-service gave you opportunities; things that were not possible beforehand. It was right for the time.' More broadly, this sense of optimism was felt throughout British society, which was becoming less formal, more meritocratic and affluent as the clear water became visible after the war.

Although retailing and the service sector generally was not high on the government's list of priorities, there had been some initial political interest in self-service in that it was believed that the new format would create labour efficiencies, thus releasing vital manpower to be used for rebuilding other sectors of the economy. But labour efficiencies did not immediately come about, particularly in Sainsbury's where the processes supporting the product in the shop were remarkably labour-intensive. Throughout most of the 1950s, Sainsbury's self-service stores still required substantial effort in preparing, wrapping and packaging goods. Fewer staff may have been visible in the early self-service branches, but they had in effect moved from the front of the shop, or from Blackfriars, to preparation and storage areas in lower ground floors, or at the back of the store. Here there was a hive of activity taking in and sorting deliveries, slicing or trussing joints, knocking up butter in a specially screened area and wrapping it in one-pound and half-pound packs, wiring cheese and packing tomatoes and biscuits. Through activities such as these, food retailers led the way in the packaging and presentation of food to suit the self-service format. Suppliers caught on later, and became responsible for much of this side of developments, but largely because of the practical demands for more efficiency, ingenuity and hygiene coming from the multiple retailers.

Some aspects of the work, at least in the early years, actually increased the labour requirement. Sainsbury's self-service format required on-site electricians and technical engineers to maintain the hydraulic push-up lifts; they also looked after the stock conveyors, air pumps and condensers supporting the open-topped refrigeration cabinets. This largely unseen element of labour doubtless contributed to the sense of magic felt by customers browsing the well-stocked gondolas. During this decade, the trade in Sainsbury's largest self-service stores increased significantly but the greater staff numbers were gradually offset by developments in pre-packing and by many refinements to working practices.

In September 1955, Sainsbury's opened in Lewisham what was then believed to be the largest self-service store in Europe, with a sales area of almost 8,000 square feet. This is about one-fifth or less of the size of a typical modern out-of-town supermarket. The branch was the centrepiece in a brand-new shopping development in Lewisham High Street which, unusually, had its own multi-storey car park. As a foretaste of future difficulties, both Sainsbury's and other retailers involved in the scheme had suffered planning battles and delays in their combined effort to establish the shopping centre on a bombed-out former site. Nevertheless, for Sainsbury's the result was impressive. The thoroughly modern look of the new branch literally astonished some visitors, with its massive glass 'front' entrances on both sides of the three-storey building and its elongated upper-storey windows and large metal-framed windowpanes. For several weeks leading up to the official opening, crowds gathered on the streets and gaped at the final stages of work in progress.

Inside, the branch incorporated the latest developments in refrigeration, further modernisations in plant, refined and improved gondolas and new product-packaging materials. The store presented customers with the largest range that Sainsbury's had ever offered, in the region of 950 lines, including the company's first dedicated 'produce' department (produce being the term borrowed from the US to describe fresh fruit and vegetables). In total this carried potatoes, tomatoes, cucumbers, apples, bananas, grapes and citrus fruits – a modest offer, but everything was fresh. Before Lewisham, only tomatoes and cucumbers were usually available in Sainsbury's shops as a traditional accompaniment to the dairy and cooked meats.

Although Lewisham had plenty of problems and was not particularly profitable, the shop nevertheless presaged a new era for the company, the era of the 'large' self-service store. One day, but not for about ten years by Sainsbury's itself, these would be called 'supermarkets' in the American style.

From the mid-1950s other multiples were also realising the benefits of self-service, and this stimulated the creation of numerous new multiple food retailers. The more vigorous of these companies, including Tesco, were hungry for expansion. It was Jack Cohen's intention to build his chain of shops rapidly, acquiring premises as fast as he could and seeking to imitate the largest chains, particularly Allied Suppliers and International Stores. But Tesco's business style was very different from Sainsbury's. The philosophy of customer service started and ended with 'Pile it high, sell it cheap', and the best business advice that the brilliant but piratical Jack Cohen could offer his managers and colleagues was 'Always keep your hand over the money and be ready to run'.

The total number of shops owned by multiple chains grew during the decade, even as some of them, like Sainsbury's, were set on a course to find larger self-service premises, rather than more standard outlets. Only after 1961 would the total number of almost 16,300 multiple outlets start to fall, as the trend for larger shops caught on more widely. JD particularly recalls being approached by Sir Lancelot Royle, head of Allied Suppliers, at an industry function when he first joined the business: 'He took me aside to give me some friendly advice. He said, "Never forget that it's the small shops that make the money." And I believe he really meant it.' The self-service revolution was soon to prove Sir Lancelot wrong.

By December 1955, Sainsbury's had 11 self-service branches, four of them conversions of existing stores and three on LCC estates. Gradually, the pace of developments picked up, and in the second half of the decade another 15 self-service stores were added. Four of these were built in the new towns of Hemel Hempstead, Crawley, Harlow and Stevenage, where such developments brought ready approval from politicians, matching the reformist zeal of the times. Prime Minister Harold Macmillan visited the Harlow store, while Herbert Morrison, former deputy leader of the Labour Party, visited Crawley: 'A very clean and most ingenious way of serving the public and doing business,' said Macmillan afterwards. 'Damned good!' was Morrison's response. But almost any food store would have been 'damned good' in the circumstances; from one new estate to the next, the planners grossly underestimated the shopping needs of inhabitants, with the result that the new Sainsbury's stores over-traded hugely from the moment they opened.

Driven by the success of self-service, Sainsbury's also used the second half of the decade to build on the quality and range of its products, to implement new packaging and design, to modernise some of the older stores where modernisation would bring benefit, and to close down the shops that could not be appropriately refurbished or converted to self-service. By 1959, 29 such shops were closed, although these were mostly replaced with new-format stores near by. Poignantly, 173 Drury Lane, the firm's founding shop, was closed in 1958 on the same day that a self-service branch opened on the other side of the street.

In 1956, JD's brothers Simon and Timothy joined the firm to swell the ranks of the family involved in this modernising effort. Simon had qualified as a chartered accountant and worked on his uncle Robert's side of the business. During the following years he took increasing responsibility for the company's financial management, and also became involved in negotiations with the unions and in reshaping personnel policy. Although Timothy joined in the same year, he then spent 18 months outside the company gaining knowledge of land and property development. He worked with estate agents, architects, quantity surveyors and builders before returning in mid-summer 1958 to become involved in the management of Sainsbury's building and engineering division and the estates department. He reported to Fred Salisbury, whose overall remit as a director included the development programme.

As part of the drive to ensure the quality of products as the range gradually increased, Sainsbury's laboratories took on broader responsibilities. Set up initially to check the quality of Sainsbury's own cooked meats and sausages produced in the factory, staff in the laboratories were now equally scrupulous in the examination of the gradually developing range of 'own-label' brands. Technicians carried out thorough bacteriological and chemical tests, and Sainsbury's food scientists, nutritionists and engineers in the laboratories became a source of advice and feedback to suppliers about how a product might be improved to meet the standards that Sainsbury's expected for its customers.

Reflecting this growing role, the laboratories moved to new

premises in Blackfriars Road in November 1956. The building contained laboratories for routine bacteriological and chemical tests, research laboratories for biochemistry and physical chemistry, preparation rooms, a media room and darkroom, an office and library facilities. There were also pilot plant rooms on the ground floor and basement, where the company's engineers could develop and test new equipment such as refrigeration units or ventilation systems essential for hygiene and increasing technical efficiency. These facilities were unique in their day. The laboratory research and technical staff worked at the vanguard of developments in new packaging and were exhaustive in their examination of cellophane, 'rayophane' and other new materials. They contributed enormously to the steady transformation in presenting and preserving self-service food in this decade and the next.

Developments in particular products illustrate how the self-service format had started to drive some pioneering changes in food production and retailing. Bacon production is one such example. After derationing in 1954, JD moved from the grocery department to become bacon buyer. As he had earlier found with the supply of biscuits, he was exasperated to find that bacon suppliers were stuck in the old methods of allocating food rather than producing to meet demand. Few suppliers were interested in negotiating prices or attending to quality issues – or even considering any form of pre-packaging. JD persuaded his father to let him travel to Canada on what was to become an eye-opening visit to the bacon-production facilities of Canada Packers. Mr Alan and Mr R J had been initially reluctant to fund the visit in full, and JD paid half the costs himself on the basis that the trip would be part-holiday, part-business. In Canada, he learnt about new production techniques and processes that resulted in more attractive, leaner, less salty bacon. And, of great importance, this bacon could be pre-packed to suit the self-service trade.

On his return, JD convinced his father of the benefits of emulating these modern techniques in order to provide a unique product for the UK market. The company was in a good position to do this, having its own pig-buying set-up and an abattoir in Suffolk, under the direction of Mr James, and its own bacon-smoking stoves at Union Street, close to headquarters. Mr James suggested forming a joint company with Canada Packers to build a pilot plant to produce Sainsbury's own 'Tendersweet' bacon next to the Blunt's Hall abattoir near Haverhill in Suffolk.

In 1958, the new company, Haverhill Meat Products (HMP) – 50 per cent owned by Canada Meat Packers and 50 per cent by Sainsbury's – began production. With hindsight, HMP was the perfect example of a highly successful joint-venture company in which Canada Meat Packers provided the process know-how, and Sainsbury's, under JD's direction, did the marketing. Soon the company was supplying all Sainsbury's shops with the highly successful 'Tendersweet' bacon. As the name suggests, this was leaner, sweeter and more tender than any bacon sold in the UK in the 1950s. It was also of a consistently higher quality than other bacons, and it was all pre-packed by HMP and ready for sale.

Today's consumers, so used to a seemingly endless variety of supermarket products, might wonder at the excitement that a new style of pre-packaged bacon caused in the late 1950s. JD comments: 'There was terrific competition to sell the bacon in the shops, and it was great to be unique in the country, at least before others started doing the same thing some years later.' The project clearly demonstrated the value of investing in innovation to differentiate Sainsbury's from its competition and to provide real benefits for customers. The year 1958 was a good one for JD, who joined the board of directors in October. Simon Sainsbury joined the board a year later.

At around the same time JD sought to develop a modern version of Sainsbury's age-old method of smoking Wiltshire bacon at the Union Street stoves. Considerable time and money was devoted to experiments with different filters, fans and temperature-control systems before a process was developed, based on the method used for fish-smoking in Scotland.

Another example of product innovation stimulated by self-service was the introduction of 'ready-to-cook' frozen chickens. Inspired yet again by North American methods, Max Justice, then head of the poultry department, worked closely with leading chicken breeders and producers – including Lloyd Maunders, Buxted Chicken and the Western Chicken Growers Association – in the mass production of frozen chickens. Great strides in production were made by transferring the drawing and dressing of the birds from retailer to producer, who also became responsible for freezing and packing. Thanks largely to Max Justice, with Mr Alan's close support, Sainsbury's were once again pioneers, this time in a trade which over time led to chicken becoming the most affordable and popular meat in British households.

In its turn, this project led to innovation of another type when Sainsbury's launched its first-ever television advertising campaign to promote its new offer of frozen chicken. Sainsbury's branch in Putney was used for the film. Jim Woods, then head of advertising and marketing, recalls that the actress who played the customer had to remove her shoes because they squeaked on the mosaic floor in this older-style shop. Later television adverts were produced in studios using Sainsbury's purpose-made fitments as background; these were usually borrowed from the company's newly modernised and much enlarged training suite which opened at Blackfriars in 1957. Television advertising was a distinctly new form of marketing within the retail trade, and for Sainsbury's it became a component in a mix of marketing activities associated with the development of Sainsbury's own-label products.

Sainsbury's commitment to own-label in the late 1950s gradually extended to the whole range of products it sold, from 'own-manufacture' with the Blackfriars Factory and the Tendersweet plant – which between them provided bacon, cooked meats and bakery goods – through products developed closely with suppliers such as frozen chicken, to the own-label goods produced entirely by other manufacturers but to Sainsbury's exacting specifications. In the development of these goods the company had a maxim that would remain inviolate for the next 30 years. All own-label products had to be either as good as or better than the leading brand, and lower-priced. Every month saw Sainsbury's name appear on yet more products; the *JS Journal* sported photographs of the latest selection so that all staff kept pace with product developments. Over time, Sainsbury's own-label marketing became one of the greatest trading strengths of the company. There were very considerable savings in the costs of products bearing own labels compared to proprietary-label products: own-label did not carry the advertising, marketing and selling costs of branded goods; distribution costs were also much lower. There were often savings in packaging material and benefits gained from the close working relationship between the buyer and manufacturer.

One of the keys to the success of own-label was the design and presentation of these products and the way the Sainsbury's brand identity was developed across all aspects of the company's public face. Back in 1950, Mr Alan had employed a graphic designer called Leonard Beaumont as the company's design consultant. At a time when other food shops were littered with handbills and fussed with manufacturer-associated symbols and advertisements, Beaumont used just two typefaces, Albertus and Trajan, to reaffirm Sainsbury's brand identity. Trajan was adopted for the bold name on the fascias above the shop; Albertus was used for virtually all Sainsbury's printed material and packaging.

Beaumont's brief from Mr Alan was to simplify and make lucid. He thus used colour sparingly in his package designs and sought function and clarity in the presentation of everything from Sainsbury's Ground Mixed Spice, complete with new resealable-style metal lid (the 'flavo-tainer' as Jim Woods dubbed it), to Sainsbury's Walnuts, packaged so that the contents could be immediately clear to customers, from whichever angle they might approach the shelves. Mr Alan told *Design* magazine, 'I wanted to get discipline into the look of things, and an avoidance of fussiness . . . it may be my reaction to Victorianism . . . Simplify, Simplify!' He even required that point-of-sale advertising put forward by some manufacturers be redesigned to conform to Sainsbury's house style.

Joe Barnes, who joined as an accountant in 1956 and became retail director in 1976, comments: 'The focus had to be on the food – what was on offer to our customers and how it was presented; everything else in the environment was a low-key backdrop.' He adds: 'This remained the case right the way through to the 1990s. We did not have the dump displays and clutter, fliers, handbills and other distractions that you saw and still see in so many supermarkets.'

In the development of the range of all food products, both own-label and proprietary, Sainsbury's responded quickly to customer demands. Canned goods, for example, were extremely important to the grocery trade in the era before frozen food and ready meals. They had a much appreciated shelf-life, vital at the end of the 1950s when three-quarters of British households still lacked a refrigerator. Sainsbury's buyers went all over the world to ensure improved supplies of canned fruit, potatoes, tomatoes, carrots, beans, spam, corned beef and other popular products, always seeking to develop own-label versions once a local supplier's quality and reliability could be verified. Jack Russell, the buyer of canned fruits, remembered: 'It was impossible to buy enough of any given packer's brand . . . Soon I was on the plane to Australia, South Africa and Italy to persuade packers to pack our own-label to our specifications. I used to have to go out and pass every batch code before it was shipped.'

Back at Blackfriars, all products placed in front of customers continued to be tasted and checked by the buyers themselves with a fastidiousness beyond that of any other food-retailing company of the day. In the sampling rooms, the buyers would arrange the contents of Sainsbury's own-label tins and packages alongside the fullest possible range of other manufacturers' offerings and own-label brands put forward by competing retailers. Small regiments of goods were laid out in the tasting trays: how many per tin, what quality, taste and texture were the potatoes, carrots and beans? What variety and what resemblance to fresh fruit was there in the contents of the canned fruit cocktails? In general, the other retailers who ventured into own-label in this period did so to provide cheap goods with little attention paid to quality. In due course only products offered by Waitrose and Marks & Spencer resembled the standard that Sainsbury's was managing to sustain across its whole range – as a fixed principle of trade.

The method of serving Sainsbury's customers was changing fast, although the emphasis on customer service – where this concerned attention to customers' needs in the stores – remained an imperative. Some departmental services were rationalised as a direct result of the self-service movement. For example, until 1955 Sainsbury's had still provided a home-delivery service for a small proportion of customers. The general managers then decided that providing credit and delivering to customers at home no longer made economic good sense and were contrary to the principles of self-service, so home delivery was stopped. In 1959, Sainsbury's also closed down its catering and wholesale food department. This was a service for restaurants, hotels and institutions which Sainsbury's had set up during the war in an attempt to offset the great loss of trade in the shops at the time. But, like home delivery, it had become an unnecessary minority concern compared to the self-service stores.

In November 1959, following the opening of a new self-service store in George Street, Croydon, Sainsbury's still had 250 branches, although there were now considerable differences in the size and composition of the stores. The chain included 26 self-service stores, although only four of these could be called 'supermarkets' in what was starting to emerge as the food-distribution industry's definition of the term. To be eligible as a 'supermarket', according to the Institute of Grocery Distribution (IGD), a store had to have at least 4,000 square feet of sales area. In 1959, this was considered a handsome size, although by comparison with today's supermarkets it is tiny, probably no larger than a local convenience store serving an urban population. The total selling space in Sainsbury's 26 self-service stores amounted in that year to almost 100,000 square feet, and, in terms of volume and turnover, each square foot was doing more trade than its equivalent in any competitor food-retailing multiple. In real terms – that is, allowing for inflation – Sainsbury's turnover was up threefold in the ten years since 1950, and profits had more than doubled. This was a solid achievement. The decade of modernisation and improvements had set the course for the future growth of the company.

As a new decade began, Sainsbury's thus occupied a strengthening position in an exciting marketplace. The company was now a major player in its heartland in the wealthiest part of Britain, in Greater London and the south-east, and its territory was gradually extending. Alongside the modernisation programme and the emerging new style of the company, the family had assured that traditional trading principles were firmly in play: Sainsbury's was steadily introducing new, good-quality products and selling them at prices that offered good value to customers.

The company's high-street competitors had for some time now been busy developing their own self-service outlets, but these were generally smaller than the average selling area of a new Sainsbury's self-service branch. In 1960, this amounted to some 5,800 square feet. As a snapshot of Sainsbury's development activities in the first month of the new decade, new self-service stores were under construction at Stockwell in London; at Upminster and the new town of Basildon in Essex; at Portsmouth in Hampshire; and at Bury St Edmunds in Suffolk. And alongside the development of the new self-service stores, the main thrust of Sainsbury's strategy was to replace the old counter-service shops. No one pretended that this would be an easy task. The deep, narrow-fronted shops on high-street parades were mostly impossible to convert to self-service, and some shops, such as New Malden and Wood Green, could only be partially converted to self-service.

By 1960, the store-development programme was showing signs of becoming a complex activity. In May that year, Timothy Sainsbury – who was now primarily responsible for the development programme and assumed much of the control from Fred Salisbury – told *JS Journal* readers that 'JS seeks about 50 town-planning approvals every year'. By the end of the decade the number of approvals being sought would be less easy to count.

Everyone loved something new on the high street, and Sainsbury's reputation – with a little help from posters and local advertising – was often enough to make a new store the talk of the town. When, for example, Sainsbury's opened a new supermarket branch in Portsmouth on 4 November 1960, with 8,300 square feet of sales area, opening day happened to coincide with the arrival of 20 foreign warships on a courtesy call to this historic naval port. Flags and bunting were going up all over the city near the dockyard. A member of Sainsbury's staff overheard a bus driver asking a conductress: 'What are the flags for?' She replied, 'I don't know,' and then, 'Oh, wait a bit, Sainsbury's is opening today, I expect it's that.'

The new Portsmouth store illustrates another facet of Sainsbury's style, which was the attention that Sainsbury's continued to pay to building and equipping new premises. On the outside, the building was true to the functional modern architecture of the period. Two upper floors were faced in chequer-patterned concrete above the long glass frontage which revealed a brilliantly lit interior. Inside, customers could browse the well-stocked gondolas and the new units specially designed in-house for the bacon and cheese. Six checkouts were placed either side of the central automatic doors. Sainsbury's designers and engineers had searched internationally for the latest and best technology for this store: automatic door mechanisms from Switzerland; main glass door from Belgium; refrigerated meat-display cabinets from Sweden; refrigerated preparation and packing lines from the US; Canadian cedar facings upstairs and Italian mosaic floors and column facings. All the new plant and equipment had been trialled in-house. By contrast, in later years Sainsbury's keenly demonstrated its support and encouragement of British suppliers and sourced most of its shop fittings in Britain. This matched its policy of buying the best of British meat, fruit and vegetables.

As it happened, the Portsmouth store was never a great success, probably because the location was not ideal, but along with the majority of new stores that were successful, this new branch's development was carried out by a small army of painstaking designers and engineers, almost all of whom were on the payroll and supported by external architects.

In October 1961, Chichester became the first Sainsbury's store – although certainly not the first British supermarket – to sell a number of what are known in the trade as 'non-food' lines. Launched under the title of 'Household Goods', these included many of the soaps, detergents, cleaning goods and polishes that are still household brands today. Brillo, Lux, Daz and Fairy Liquid were boldly displayed right next to the Pet Foods section, which offered another form of convenience to the busy food-shopper. Non-food lines in the trade came to be seen as a kind of 'domestic grocery' item. Confusingly for those not in the trade, other domestic goods that were also in time introduced into the larger stores, such as clothing, car accessories, kitchen and garden appliances, were not considered standard 'non-food' items.

Just one month after the opening of the Chichester store, in November 1961, Sainsbury's opened a well-publicised new store in the rebuilt city centre of Bristol, at a full stretch from the central warehouses and depot at Blackfriars. The store sported an even larger range of non-foods, and, where space allowed, these items were soon being sold across the rest of the company's chain of self-service stores. Bristol was the new 'largest store in the chain', with a sales area of more than 10,000 square feet – all of which floor area was painstakingly laid with some two-and-a-half million pieces of mosaic, even extending to the footfall area outside the spotless glass frontage. But in terms of range developments, what was most exciting about Bristol – and unique in Britain as a whole – was the introduction of wines and spirits to Sainsbury's self-service shelves.

Since 1920, Sainsbury's counter-service shop in Weybridge had been the company's only branch with a licence to sell alcohol, which Sainsbury's had inherited with the premises. It was time for a change. The new format was perfect for the sale of alcohol, and JD was determined that shoppers should be able to buy wines, beers and spirits at the self-service branches. But he had an uphill battle to obtain a licence to sell alcohol against what he referred to as 'an unholy alliance of brewers, off-licence shops and puritans'. The most vehement opposition came from the Licensed Victuallers' Association, who rightly perceived that off-licence profits would be eroded if shoppers could buy their drinks from high-street food retailers. There was a long campaign, culminating in a hearing in the Magistrate's Court in which JD and Glynn Harrison, manager of the Bristol store, were cross-examined by a QC representing the Licensed Victuallers' Association, with Sainsbury's represented by Jeremy Hutchinson QC. A licence was eventually granted for the Bristol store and sales began in June 1962.

A new department was born with the initial offer of 24 different beers, 3 ciders and 47 wines and spirits. But local opposition continued, and it was a struggle to obtain licences for other stores: in May 1963 Cowley branch obtained a licence; then Leicester in January 1965 and Reading in December 1965. It took the rest of the decade for the company to obtain just 28 licences, by which time other food retailers were applying their own muscle in their keenness to join the trail that Sainsbury's was blazing.

While Sainsbury's was busy exploring the potential of self-service, Jack Cohen was equally tireless in promoting Tesco's high-street profile and expanding the chain. In November 1961, comedian Sid James, a star of the *Carry On* series of British films, opened Tesco's Leicester store, which the company presented as its flagship. This was huge by any standards of the day, with its sales area of 16,500 square feet many times larger than the average Tesco store at this time. Sainsbury's, the clear leader in average store size among the major multiples, would only have one supermarket of similar size by the end of the decade. The Leicester store was rightly claimed as a triumph by Jack Cohen, who was ambitious for Tesco to become the first food retailer with national coverage. But its launch could do little to disguise the fact that Tesco's fortunes were sliding during this period. Andrew Seth and Geoffrey Randall comment in their book, *The Grocers*: 'Tesco's unruly collection of undistinguished trading locations was seen for what it was – cheap, cut-price, bargain-basement where price was a lone redeeming feature and the only customer buying rationale.'

Compared to Tesco and to other new and established competitors, Sainsbury's was financially sound, expanding surely and maintaining its customers' loyalty; and its development programme did not require borrowing to sustain. Customers clearly believed that 'Good food costs less at Sainsbury's' – the long-serving slogan first introduced by the company in 1959.

By 1962, the family members predominantly in charge of the company had formed a cohesive and determined executive. JD and his brothers, as the Young Turks in the company, had all been fired by the first wave of changes that were occurring in food retailing. The brothers were highly motivated by the accruing success of the company and had every reason to be ambitious. After more than a decade of experience in the firm, working closely with his father Alan, JD in particular had demonstrated his acumen as a trader, and had for some time been assuming a role almost equal with his father in key trading decisions.

On the death of their father in 1956, Mr Alan had become chairman and Mr R J deputy chairman. Mr Alan continued as head of trade, but by the end of the 1950s a gradual handover of trading responsibilities to JD suited him. In 1962, on the recommendation of the Labour leader, Hugh Gaitskell, Alan Sainsbury was made a life peer and assumed the title Lord Sainsbury of Drury Lane. The peerage allowed him to take a more active role in politics, a long-held interest, and devote time to debates and committees in the House of Lords. Simon Sainsbury became increasingly engaged in managing the company's financial affairs and personnel administration, and, in 1962, Timothy joined his elder brothers as a director taking over full responsibilities for Sainsbury's estates and building developments. There was no question that this was going to be a stimulating time for the younger Sainsburys.

Chapter 4

NEW AFFLUENCE
1963–1967

THE 1960s may have been over-mythologised, but most would accept that during this period the style, attitudes and aspirations of the British population changed more than in any other post-war decade. The social and cultural revolution in these ten years embraced the advent of a youth culture, the 'permissive society', a greater desire and opportunity for self-expression, the questioning and often easy dismissal of old traditions and values, the emergence of a mania for fashion, radical experimentation in art, literature, music, dance, sex and drugs, and rebellion. Much was deconstructed, reconstructed or just plain novel. Old concepts wrestled with new, and the 'generation gap' widened considerably. Much of this change involved factors that had only an indirect effect on the progress made by Sainsbury's and other retailers.

Sainsbury's was both able and well equipped to steer its course in a businesslike way through this period of change. It brought 'novelty' to shoppers with its increasing range of food and non-food lines to meet new tastes and changing customer demands. But the key changes that were instrumental in Sainsbury's progress were more economic and functional in nature. In particular, there was growing affluence in the population, and with this came an increasingly widespread ownership of refrigerators, cars and televisions and a new age of foreign travel.

The greater affluence was the result of a fast-growing economy, full employment, low inflation and the confidence that accompanied them. Larger average disposable incomes, spread more equably across the population, meant that while proportionately less of the weekly wage might be spent on food for the family, relatively more was gradually being spent on luxury goods, on quality products and on experimentation with exotic foodstuffs. Food started to become interesting and alluring – for a greater proportion of the population it was no longer just a means of sustenance. Moreover, what you bought and where you bought it conferred status. Sainsbury's had the advantage here, because the company's exceptional emphasis on customer service and quality had made it, in Mr Alan's own words, a kind of 'Fortnum's for the masses'.

By 1965, almost three-quarters of households had refrigerators, up from 24 per cent in 1959. And by the end of the decade, 'fridge' ownership was almost ubiquitous, certainly in the south-east, where the greatest wealth was concentrated and where competition among the supermarket retailers of the new era was consequently the most intense. No longer did the housewife – generally unquestioned and unquestioning as the domestic workhorse – need to visit the high street on a daily basis to shop for fresh food. With a fridge at home she could buy her meat and dairy products less frequently, in greater quantity and in larger portions. However, the frequency of her visits to do the family shopping would actually depend on the amount she could carry home after each outing.

Another statistic pointed the way ahead: by 1964, there were about 11.5 million cars in Britain, almost five times as many as there were in 1950. There were already more cars per mile of road than in any other country in the world.

Television played an important part in broadening the horizons and whetting the appetites of the British public. In 1950, some 382,000 television licences were issued, whereas by 1964, 90 per cent of all homes in Britain had a television. Not only were people exposed to diverse cultures and different food and eating habits in the comfort of their own sitting rooms, but cookery programmes became a popular feature of television schedules. Fanny Craddock instructed viewers imperiously from her BBC kitchen, and was as popular for her sharp tongue and her outrageously bossy manner with her husband and other assistants as she was for her cooking skills. Graham Kerr, whose bi-weekly programmes started in 1969, made cooking seem a pleasure not only because he was continually quipping and smiling as he cooked, but because he almost constantly carried with him a glass of wine and spent much of his time on camera saying 'time for a quick slurp'. The very notion of drinking wine while cooking would have seemed daring to viewers, many of whom were gently being weaned from the habit of buying wine only for Christmas or special occasions. Sainsbury's steadily explored the continental wine market and brought an increasing range of affordable wines to UK customers.

Not least among the important changes that affected food retailing in this period was the dramatic increase in the number of foreign holidays that were taken. In the early 1960s, relatively few people could afford to take holidays abroad; in 1961, just 563,000 British people held a passport. In the mid-1960s, however, the 'package holiday' was introduced, and very soon millions of British people were travelling abroad. In 1971, over seven million foreign holidays were taken. These visits abroad opened up a new world of culinary experience to the British public, which translated into a growing demand at home for Italian spaghetti, pastas and pizzas; French and Spanish wines; continental cheeses, sausages and bread; olive oil from all over the Mediterranean seaboard; luxuries such as macadamia nuts from Hawaii and Australia; even ice cream from the US. Sainsbury's buyers aimed to be first aboard the planes sourcing, negotiating, sampling, and arranging transport and bond to get new products into the Sainsbury's warehouses in optimal condition, and thence to the branches.

As they sought to build the range, responding to these new appetites and trends, the directors continued to make improvements to the self-service approach, so that the whole business of shopping was more convenient for customers. The company's leadership in the sale of fresh meat illustrates this.

Since 1954, following derationing, Sainsbury's had offered customers the choice in most 'self-service' stores of buying fresh meat from refrigerated cabinets or of being served directly from service counters. Following extensive research, the company's first all-self-service fresh-meat department – a prototype of those we see today with a variety of jointed and pre-packaged cuts of meat – became available to customers in Sainsbury's new Basildon branch, which opened in 1960. If customers could not find exactly the cut they wanted, they could press a button to fetch assistance from one of the butchers in the meat preparation area; he would see to their specific needs. The button was no more than an experiment, but it showed the will to please. In the later self-service stores of the 1960s, the meat-preparation areas were generally screened by glass from the sales areas rather than hidden from view as they had been previously. This was transparent proof for Sainsbury's customers that modern merchandising techniques went hand in hand with traditional skills.

In 1963, the advertising agency J. Walter Thompson carried out a survey which revealed that few supermarkets employed self-service methods for selling meat, bread, vegetables or fruit. Unlike Sainsbury's they did not have the same degree of experience in handling fresh foods. Added to this, the survey revealed that housewives were generally suspicious of pre-packed meat; they perceived it as not fresh and somehow second-rate, and tended to have more trust in the traditional high-street butcher. Sainsbury's, by comparison, had been careful to court customer trust and had consistently focused on quality and service. The company ran a daily delivery service of all perishable commodities to its branches. By maintaining strict standards on the shelf-life of their own pre-packed meat, which rarely exceeded two days and was often one day, customers associated Sainsbury's with freshness and quality. Such was the value of this to the company that in October 1967 JD was able to announce to his senior management that the sale of fresh meat accounted for more than 21 per cent of Sainsbury's total gross profits. All Sainsbury's fresh foods at this time – including fruit and vegetables – represented a significantly higher proportion of the company's sales than they did of competitors'. By building its reputation for perishable goods, Sainsbury's not only secured its customers' loyalty and sold high volumes of these products, but the image of freshness and quality attending these perishable commodities actually deepened trust in other products in the stores – which customers were also buying in greater bulk than they were in competitor outlets.

Aside from perishable goods, by the end of the 1960s more than 50 per cent of Sainsbury's turnover would derive from own-label products, comprising more than 1,000 items. On some product lines the ratio was even higher: by 1967, Sainsbury's biscuits enjoyed a 65 per cent share of total biscuit sales, jams 70 per cent and soft drinks 85 per cent. Indeed, as the programme developed inexorably over the next 20 years, the Sainsbury's model was watched with wonder by food retailers all over the world. With Mr Alan's blessing, JD led this development vigorously. He sampled or scrutinised all items personally; no new Sainsbury's-label product would appear on the shelves without his final approval, a process which included agreeing the package designs, all of which were created in-house. Bob Ingham, one of the company's leading buyers during the 1960s, recalls the sense of responsibility to customers that came with the growth in own-label products: 'This set the seal and acknowledged our responsibility for the product; it showed we were standing behind it. We were saying, "This is ours, if you're not happy, tell us." '

Although buying disciplines were followed to the letter in the selection of products and suppliers, the speed with which the own-label machinery was set in motion could be impressive. Within just a few months of launching the company's first self-service off-licence department at Bristol, the company boasted four Sainsbury's Spanish sherries, a Sauternes and a selection of British wines. Soon they added a Bordeaux red and white wine. The programme continued with some slightly experimental offerings, such as British cherry and ginger wines. But the public favoured the cheap but popular Spanish table wines and growing range of French, German and Portuguese wines. After only four years the list included wines and spirits from all over the world. In what is now widely accepted practice, Sainsbury's produced printed labels on the back of wine bottles which unobtrusively educated customers through descriptions of the wine and serving instructions. A Sainsbury's whisky was introduced in 1967 at 45 shillings (£2.25) a bottle, and finally, in 1969, a number of Sainsbury's beers appeared, once the formerly intransigent brewers saw where their advantage lay. This early commitment to off-licence sales, particularly in selling wine, was a strong foundation for the explosion in wine sales that occurred throughout the company's supermarkets in the 1980s.

Sainsbury's buyers also moved quickly to develop own-label non-food lines. These had all been proprietary brands when they were first introduced in Chichester in 1961. The initial offer of soaps and cleaning agents was soon augmented by a whole range of domestic products: Sainsbury's kitchen foils, shampoos, air fresheners and washing-up liquid. Generally these were small products, convenient to carry with the rest of the shopping and designed to meet the needs of the typical housewife. When, for example, a range of own-label nylon stockings was introduced in April 1966, these were an instant success. The trading principle here was not so much seeking to build sales or profits from selling stockings but the mutual advantage gained from offering convenience of this kind to the customer. An early form of 'value-added', this was one more good reason for the housewife to shop for her food at Sainsbury's. By the end of the 1960s, all the larger Sainsbury's self-service stores and supermarkets had an extending range of non-food lines, which greatly added to this convenience – and many of these commodities had better margins than food grocery items, especially if they were own-label.

JD wrote in the February 1965 *JS Journal* about the relative complexity and the commitment to quality and value that went into the development of own-label products compared to the more straightforward buying and quality-checking of manufacturers' brands. The development of each own-label product, he said, involved considerable evaluation of the supplier's own production processes, in addition to cost and quality comparisons, thorough buyer sampling and scientific evaluation in the laboratories. In the article he wrote: 'As always in business, our greatest asset is our reputation.' It was Sainsbury's reputation, and the trust that went with it, that led customers not only to try out new own-label lines but often to stick with them in preference to leading manufacturer brands. JD added: 'We have even found our customers more willing to try new lines under our label than they are new proprietary lines.' Nevertheless, in this article he was modest about predicting the volume of further growth of Sainsbury's own-label products, even suggesting that it would reach a plateau after a few years and tail off in the future, although the reverse was to be true.

Among direct competitors, only Tesco at this stage had started to develop own-label goods at a rate approaching Sainsbury's. By 1964, Tesco had more than 300 own-label lines. But what it offered was generally cheaper goods and inferior quality compared to both the proprietary brands and to Sainsbury's. JD's uncharacteristically modest forecast of growth in own-label probably derived from a general caution about the programme and the desire to maintain only consistently high standards. He was above all determined that his customers would never confuse the quality standards of Sainsbury's own-label products with the kind of offering that Tesco was putting on its shelves in the mid-1960s.

Packaging and design continued to be important elements in the success of Sainsbury's own-label goods. When Beaumont retired in 1962 he was succeeded by Peter Dixon, who took the uncluttered design discipline a stage further. Setting up an in-house design studio, he developed stylised geometric patterns on packaging, drawing critical attention from *Design* magazine, which referred to them as 'austere and even Bauhaus'. Although austerity is too strong a word, there was an economy of presentation which was actually part of the objective, both in the product presentation and the look of the stores.

Under Mr Alan and JD's scrutiny, the Sainsbury's identity was fostered in the new 'supermarkets' as a matter of absolute principle. Expense and ingenuity attended the construction and shopfittings of every branch Sainsbury's opened, and the result was always understated, with clean and functional working surfaces and clearly priced and regimented products. The once highly coloured motifs on the tiled walls and floors gave way to simple white tiling and precise signage: 'Meat', 'Vegetables', and so on. Customers would always know that the cheapest items in a line of goods were presented on the left of the display, the more expensive to the right. This was an unbroken rule in every branch.

Jim Woods, as advertising and marketing manager, wrote in 1965 about the particular importance of maintaining a special identity and image at all odds. He records that as the production of gondolas, refrigerated cabinets and other major shopfitted elements of the average supermarket were becoming increasingly massproduced, this had led to a standardisation in the look of many supermarket stores. It was therefore Sainsbury's committed policy to introduce cabinets and gondolas in 'Sainsbury' colours, and to design new equipment, or commission enhancements, to reinforce the Sainsbury's image. All such extra expense was considered an investment.

The Sainsbury's brand and what it stood for ran right through the company like the lettering in a stick of Brighton rock. In effect, the Sainsbury's name was becoming its main marketing tool. Like its competition, the company regularly promoted lines, either because they were seasonal or because they offered particularly good value. Marketing gimmicks were not considered Sainsbury's style. A rare exception was a campaign in 1961 to boost the Portsmouth store's trade, for the first anniversary of the store's opening. This involved a competition, which drew no fewer than 21,000 entries, to guess the weight of a magnificent birthday cake. The highly valued prize was a new Mini Cooper, which was driven out of the store by the winning family in front of flashing cameras from the local press.

Less than a year later JD was himself in front of the cameras, with another happy family being awarded the keys of a sparkling Hillman Minx de luxe saloon. They had won this in a quiz featured in Sainsbury's new customer magazine, *Family*. This was 'Sainsbury's magazine for every woman', carrying a compilation of 'facts and fancies, fiction, fashion, furnishing and food'. The quarterly magazine lasted three years, and was very popular with customers, selling more copies at sixpence than the then highest-selling women's magazine. It was bought by Roy Thompson – the Canadian publisher and owner of *The Times* – in 1964 and he used it to leapfrog to a captive audience with his own women's magazine, *Family Circle*.

One marketing ploy that Sainsbury's would not countenance was the use of stamps to attract trade. In November 1963, Mr Alan reported to the *Financial Times* that Sainsbury's had just achieved its biggest week's trading in its 94-year history. The timing of the announcement was important because it happened just a week after Tesco had launched its offer of trading stamps in its Leicester store, reporting that housewives had besieged the shop in their rush to lay their hands on the precious new stamps. In the same week as Mr Alan's announcement, Fine Fare launched its offer of trading stamps.

The marketing idea was straightforward – the more you bought in the stores, the more stamps you could stick in your books. Stamps could be exchanged for various goods, from saucepans to television sets (the latter requiring several suitcases full of stamp books), but not for cash. The stamps were issued at a healthy price to the retailers by the two stamp companies that had set up in the UK: Richard Tompkins's Green Shield Stamps, and Sperry & Hutchinson, who issued pink stamps.

Stamp trading was yet another US import. In 1961, the members of the British National Association of Multiple Grocers had agreed among themselves not to introduce stamps without informing other members. But clearly there was pent-up enthusiasm for introducing them. First of all, Fine Fare announced that it would launch its own stamps on 23 November 1963, and immediately there was a scramble among most other multiple grocers to do the same, preferably before that date – with the notable exception of Sainsbury's and Allied Suppliers among the larger chains. Pricerite jumped to pole position, introducing its own stamps in mid-October 1963; Tesco was elbowed into second place, and Fine Fare had to bring forward its own start date by a fortnight in order to get into the race it had started.

Sainsbury's refusal to adopt trading stamps illustrates its general position on competition and fair dealing. The directors believed that stamps were expensive gimmickry that would not ultimately benefit the shopper, who would eventually realise this; they were neither in Sainsbury's interest, nor represented its style. In the midst of the early stampede, Sainsbury's relaunched its 'Star Buys' initiative in its stores on 13 November 1963, to show how its anti-stamp policy would benefit shoppers. JD came up with a new line, 'Honest to goodness', which in combination with 'Good food costs less' fully expressed Sainsbury's approach.

Mr Alan, supported by JD and the other directors, led the fight against stamps from the outset. He argued that an increase of no less than 20 per cent in turnover would be required by retailers to pay for stamps. This would unfairly and unnecessarily push up prices for shoppers, so the only winners would be the saucepan sellers and stamp companies. He made his case determinedly in the House of Lords and argued that it would be fairer on customers if they could redeem stamps for cash. But he sought in vain to get a bill on the statute book to this effect; stamps continued to be collected and traded for the next 15 years.

JD had meanwhile taken charge of a massive anti-stamp campaign, which included a series of full-page advertisements in national newspapers and the production of leaflets for customers explaining the company's opposition: 'Sainsbury's makes no bones about it . . . it would be impossible for Sainsbury's to maintain their high standards of quality and freshness and give trading stamps without raising prices.'

Allied Suppliers was a firm ally of Sainsbury's in the fight against stamps. David Greig, another staunch family firm, was also an ally. The battle reached the courts when Sainsbury's and Greig's issued a joint writ against the two stamp companies in 1965. The writ stemmed from Sperry & Hutchinson sending out a circular letter which suggested that Sainsbury's and David Greig's profit increases, as non-stamp companies, were at a level that was less than a quarter of the true figure. Sperry & Hutchinson was forced to admit the defamatory nature of its error and was bound over to pay damages to a charity.

Sainsbury's well-publicised position on stamps became known to its loyal customers and no doubt served to enhance the company's reputation for fair trading. And the whole issue was excellent publicity for the company. JD recalls: 'We probably never had such national publicity. Our advertisements played a part, but the editorial coverage we obtained was even more important.' For example, Robert Heller, editor of *Management Today*, wrote: 'The 95-year-old firm . . . already had a marvellous reputation for quality. But until the stamp battle broke across the front pages and advertising columns few customers saw Sainsbury's as it really is: an efficient, expanding multiple chain which is fiercely competitive . . . very profitable and very much in the firing line of the food revolution.' Flurries of Sainsbury's customers did move to stamp-trading retailers but most quickly returned.

Stamps apart, the competition offered by other leading food retailers was positively sleepy compared to what it would become. In 1963, within Sir Lancelot Royle's large Allied Supplier group – which remained bent on an expanding empire of relatively small high-street outlets – only 51 of Home and Colonial's 649 shops and 62 of Lipton's 434 shops were self-service. Fine Fare was a newer challenge in the market, a rapidly growing chain with 200 stores, all of which were self-service. This chain was set up by Garfield Weston, owner of Associated British Foods, and, like Allied Suppliers, it was another example of manufacturer turning retailer as a means of extending control – but not always serving the customers' best interests. In 1963, Tesco had 149 self-service stores and only one counter-service store, and with typical entrepreneurial zeal the chain was beginning to add new items to its non-food offer: buckets, brooms, ironing boards and other bulkier household products.

Meanwhile, Safeway set up in the UK in 1962 as a subsidiary of the giant US food retailer of the same name. It started with one large supermarket in Wimbledon, south-west London, where it sold a broad mix of goods, from women's clothing to floor mops, as well as the usual self-service range of food and 'non-food' items. The company gradually expanded in London, but would remain a small chain until 1987, when the Argyll group bought it.

The first sign of what would become serious competition appeared on the horizon in 1965 with the establishment of Asda in Yorkshire by Noel Stockdale of Associated Dairies and Peter Asquith, a butcher from Pontefract. Where Tesco and Fine Fare piled in new lines and frilled the shop windows with stamp promotions in their generally smaller stores, Asda's approach involved straight discounting. It developed very large stores selling only proprietary lines, kept overheads down and prices low. The new company employed a highly successful strategy of converting readily available and cheap former industrial space, including old mills and redundant factory units, into massive sales space.

Asda was based in the north, far from Sainsbury's home ground, but Mr Alan and JD started to watch the company attentively. They took note of all such competition but were seldom unsettled by it.

Chapter 5

PROBLEMS OF SCALE
1963–1967

S AINSBURY'S PROGRESS might be described as implacable, so much so that even in the early 1960s it was actually being challenged by its own success. New stores and developing headquarters operations led to a constant demand for more staff and the need to review training and personnel organisation. The anitquated central depot and warehouses at Blackfriars were under severe pressure to keep products flowing into the stores fast enough to meet demand, and the small army of headquarters clerks could scarcely cope with the pace of daily orders from the branches. The store-development programme was often stultified or obstructed by town planners, and a substantial growth in car ownership threw up the long-term challenge of finding parking space for car shoppers at or near the stores.

Some of these challenges applied to all types of retailer and business in this period; others applied particularly to Sainsbury's. Most required significant organisational changes to provide a platform for future growth.

Sainsbury's continued expansion now depended on its ability to supply the increasingly large new stores with skilled managers and a committed workforce. In the 1960s, the number of Sainsbury's full-time-equivalent staff grew from 15,000 to 23,500. Yet the entire food-retailing sector in the 1950s and 1960s was notably short of staff; jobs in other sectors of commerce and industry tended to be more fashionable and attractive to school-leavers and others entering the job market. Central London was the most difficult market for recruitment, as the competing food-retailing multiples determinedly poached each other's staff to grow their self-service businesses. Sainsbury's growth in the early 1960s therefore fuelled the need to make continual improvements to the company's conditions of work, staffing structures, and its recruitment and training programmes.

While rates of pay during the 1960s were not exceptional at Sainsbury's (and this was true in the sector generally), the conditions of work were exemplary. Earlier in the post-war period, Mr RJ had introduced a shorter working day on Saturdays which, coupled with compulsory mid-week early closing, enabled the company to offer full-time employees a 45-hour working week, as against the more than 50 hours that was often typical. This helped Sainsbury's to compete for new recruits. Nevertheless, for several years there remained pressure to be able to offer full-time workers at least two consecutive days off work each week – the equivalent of the weekend enjoyed by workers in industrial and commercial sectors. In 1961, the company experimented with all-day closing on Mondays, the least busy of the shopping days. By the time the Shops (Early Closing) Act was passed in 1965, allowing retailers to choose their preferred early-closing day, Monday closing had become standard in Sainsbury's and remained so until the late 1970s. The only exceptions to this were five Central London branches that relied on office-workers' lunchtime trade.

Mr RJ and Simon Sainsbury, assisted by senior personnel managers G. W. Smith and Ted Farrell, sought to improve the supply of skilled personnel as future managers in the company. One approach was to promote younger employees to store-management positions much earlier than had traditionally been the case. In tandem, they introduced new training techniques and programmes to broaden the knowledge and capability of more experienced employees. Some of the most talented store managers, well-proven deputies, top tradesmen and recently retired managers with appropriate skills were brought in to instruct at Blackfriars. Experienced trainers were also recruited from outside the company. A range of induction and refresher courses was introduced for tradesmen, salesmen, deputies and managers. Gradually, the exacting Sainsbury's standards became codified in instruction manuals, so that there were solid references to the working procedures of each store department.

At the same time, the business needed young, highly trained managers, less dependent on following the old routines. Greater attention was focused on the skills required to supervise people, to monitor stock levels and determine orders, to schedule staff rotas, to motivate and delegate. There was less emphasis on leading by example as an experienced senior tradesman than on these 'modern' managerial requirements.

In 1963, the personnel department launched a fast-track training programme for A-Level students. By combining instruction at Blackfriars, on-the-job training and day-release at college, the idea was to promote A-Level recruits to deputy-manager position within eighteen months to two years. Bert Ellis, who was later manager of retail personnel, had joined the company in the first small batch of graduates recruited in the mid-1950s and groomed for head-office management positions. He was well aware that fast-track training in these early days of the art might cause ructions within the staff. 'Some of the senior, time-serving staff at Sainsbury's greatly resented the new fast-tracking in the stores,' he comments. 'Quite a few people left because of it . . . But times were changing and these things needed to be done.'

It is perhaps not surprising that there was resentment. The 1960s was a decade of transition in Sainsbury's overall structure. At its leading edge, the company was heavily involved in the development of increasingly sophisticated self-service stores and supermarkets. All the company's innovations – the development of the range, the new shop-floor and back-room technologies – were focused on the self-service sector. On the other side, in uneasy harmony, were the counter-service shops. They were still in the majority for most of the decade, but were completely overshadowed. Not only did the shops inevitably offer a far smaller range, particularly of grocery lines and non-perishables, but as each year passed they became quainter and less fashionable than their bigger, younger sisters. Very few carried fruit or vegetables, with the exception of the traditional offering of tomatoes and cucumbers. And while such items as washing powders, soaps, shampoos and household cleaners soon became a standard part of the self-service offer, no counter-service store could do them justice. It was perhaps inevitable that in 1965 and 1966, for the first time since the war, the turnover in some of the high-street counter-service shops started to become dented by self-service competitor outlets.

The counter-service shops did not represent the future, and could not begin to cater for the changes in consumer buying and expectation that were taking place. Some of the managers in the counter-service stores and those who had already served time in the traditional phased career from trainee salesman to salesman, leading salesman, assistant deputy manager and deputy manager undoubtedly would have felt aggrieved that an 18-year-old school-leaver might leapfrog them and move so swiftly to a top position.

The 1960s also saw a steep increase in the number of women employed by Sainsbury's, particularly married women who mostly needed to work part-time. By 1968, 11,000 of the company's 28,000 employees were part-time, and most of these were women working on the checkouts or as 'gondola girls' whose job was to keep shelves filled. Women were also mostly involved in a new evening shift devised by Simon Sainsbury to help replenish the shelves at the end of each working day, an innovative scheme at the time which greatly improved the efficiency of replenishing stocks before the next day's trade.

The employment of more women was another phenomenon caused by the rise and rise of larger self-service stores and super-markets. And towards the end of the decade, it was in response to the number of women working for the company that one of the few full-time posts purposely offered to women at this time was the new role of branch personnel manager (BPM). BPMs became gradually more involved in local recruiting activities and in other personnel issues, but their main role was the pastoral care of the female staff. BPMs reported to area personnel managers who were themselves appointed and supervised by five superintendents.

Sainsbury's had a long-established supervisory structure cover-ing the branches, which focused on five regional 'areas'. During most of the 1960s, there was a 'superintendent' responsible for branch operations in each area. By the end of the decade, as part of the changes to staff structure introduced by the fourth generation, the superintendents were replaced by 'area general managers', reporting to Blackfriars. Each area general manager had four dis-trict managers reporting to him and took on some responsibility for recruitment, training, administration and staff welfare, as well as keeping a close eye on each of the Sainsbury's branches in his own domain. Over time, the Sainsbury's regions assumed more decen-tralised administrative functions as the company expanded and its operations grew more complex.

In general, the commitment and loyalty of Sainsbury's staff was high, and boosted as each new or converted store opened in the high streets and the volumes of food sold increased. Employees felt they were part of a successful business that offered a structured career and security for the long term. Their loyalty and sense of belonging was continually reinforced through the broader Sainsbury's culture. The directors encouraged and subsidised the activities of the Sainsbury's Staff Association (SSA), which played a major part in this culture. Each store had its own SSA representatives helping to organise local, regional and company-wide social and sporting activities: dances, darts nights, quizzes, fancy-dress parties, summer outings, clubs and hobby interests, even group holidays. The *JS Journal* slavishly recorded headquarters, depot, factory and branch anniversary dances and other events – the name of almost every individual in each spread of photos depicting these occasions was printed in the caption, even those caught mid-throw in an energetic jive. In this way, the staff magazine was the *Tatler* of the Sainsbury's social world.

Year on year in the 1960s, the annual summer fêtes at the Griffin Club became ever larger social jamborees – testimony to this Sainsbury's camaraderie and the growth in employee numbers. Literally thousands of staff attended with their families; they thronged the beer and food tents, or joined in the summer sports activities. Most if not all of the directors would be present, and also many members of the active Veterans' Club of pensioned former employees. Meanwhile, the journal continued to be a source of vital internal communication about the key things happening in the company, the main suppliers, new training programmes and retail developments.

Counterbalancing this slightly rosy view of corporate harmony, there were some differences in attitude between the front-line staff in Sainsbury's branches and those in the less visible distribution and manufacturing parts of the company. Joe Barnes recalls that industrial-relations problems were already brewing at the time he joined the company as a trained accountant in 1956: 'The worst was probably the factory operation, the next was the bacon-smoking at Union Street, and distribution was probably the third most difficult.' In these areas the company dealt with representatives of TGWU or USDAW unions in the negotiation of pay and working practices; head office laid down its own pay scales for the company's shop staff, very few of whom were members of a union.

Naturally, the family members at the helm were keen to promote the belief that all the company's workforce were equally and inclusively important to the success of the company. But the Sainsburys' paternalistic approach actually worked best where the family's presence was strongest and where its leadership had most immediate effect, which was at head office and in the branches. JD admits that he and his father's devotion to the buying and trading aspects of the firm made it easy for them occasionally to overlook or perhaps to turn a partially blind or optimistic eye to what was happening further down the food chain. This said, there was relatively little that any industry captains could do about the unionisation and worker/management divides that characterised the British workforce.

By 1963, customers appeared, quite literally, not to be able to purchase enough of what Sainsbury's had to offer. Ron Yeates recalls one of the new branch openings in 1963:

> Because we were so overwhelmed by customers, we just couldn't keep the shelves filled up . . . Blackfriars couldn't keep us supplied – it just took off, and took a long time to settle down. But we never lost customers' good will, because we were always on the shop floor, right up until closing time. We realised that we weren't giving our customers the service they were entitled to, because we weren't able to keep the shelves filled all the time. But the quality of the products worked for us. People just went berserk about Sainsbury's. Every person you spoke to talked about Sainsbury's and talked about the range. It made you very tired, but so proud to be associated with a company that was so successful.

The sense of excitement and energy is almost palpable, but this recollection pinpoints a major problem – how to keep up with the demand; how to source supplies, check quality, increase range and deliver to shops efficiently and in sufficient volume. The same phenomenon occurred in all types of store. At Guildford, for example, a complex two-stage conversion from counter service to self-service had required the former shop to be completely rebuilt during 1962 and 1963. A local-authority multi-storey car park was built just behind the store, and the estates department took advantage of this by putting some checkouts at the back of the store and installing lifts to the car park. Shortly after it reopened, Guildford experienced a 68 per cent increase in trade. The branch soon became too crowded for comfort, and shelves could not be replenished fast enough.

In fact, Sainsbury's distribution system had needed serious over-haul for a number of years. The depot facilities at Blackfriars had not been able to keep up with the trade because the system employed to supply branches was truly antiquated; indeed, it had not essentially changed, except in scale, since the 1890s. Goods were moved by hand from the specialist Blackfriars departments to the loading-bay areas and then shifted manually into the delivery vans and lorries. Cooked meat pies and sausages had to be loaded at the factory across Stamford Street from the main depot, while meat, butter and bacon were stored and loaded around the corner at Union Street. At full stretch, the company was struggling to supply branches within a 120-mile radius of headquarters. Compounding problems of labour-heavy and time-intensive processes, traffic congestion was terrible, with up to 300 lorries – including Sains-bury's own as well as suppliers' – sometimes waiting more than an hour to load or unload, with others struggling for passage; all this in the heart of London. The system was both inefficient and expen-sive. Constraints on the lorry drivers led to deliveries being made at the last minute, and sometimes missing items had to be sent sepa-rately and expensively by passenger train or any other means possible.

In the early to mid-1960s the situation continued to be close to breakdown, although in 1959 Sainsbury's had embarked on what was to become a radical strategy of decentralising depot operations. In that year, with JD and his brothers pacing anxiously outside their door, the general managers finally agreed to purchase a former Royal Army Ordnance depot at Buntingford on the A10 north of Ware. After converting the premises, the 40,000 square feet of ware-house storage space – about the size of a football pitch – was opened for business in November 1960. Buntingford was well situ-ated to take over the delivery of some 500 non-perishable grocery lines to all Sainsbury's branches in the Midlands, East Anglia and North London. Thus a reasonable portion of Sainsbury's canned goods, biscuits, tea, flour and 'stores goods' such as paper bags could be diverted from Blackfriars to the company's first regional distribution centre. New working systems enabled warehousemen to 'pick' entire orders from the 13 long aisles of racked goods in the warehouse and assemble each branch's delivery in an assigned area. Smart new forklift trucks were used to carry goods directly from incoming lorries to the aisles. With the opening of this new regional distribution centre and the upgrading of technology there was a sense that head office were recognising the importance of depot workforces in the overall business.

Setting up Buntingford was a move that the company should ideally have made three or four years earlier. As Sainsbury's steadily added to its sales area during the early 1960s by developing new stores and carrying out major conversions to existing branches, sales volumes continued to grow. The new regional warehouse clearly offered insufficient space. Not long after Buntingford had opened for business, plans were made for a series of regional depots which would have the facilities to supply the entire product range.

In April 1962, Sainsbury's acquired a new and major regional depot site at Basingstoke. Timothy Sainsbury's brief had been to find a site of ten acres within 20 miles of London; instead he found a site of 20 acres which was some 50 miles from London. The site offered various advantages. In this recently expanded town to the south-west of London there would be housing for those of Sainsbury's own workforce who opted to transfer from Blackfriars. The site would be close to the proposed M3, and the M4, which would help Sainsbury's to service new branches as the company extended its reach to the south and west. Fortunately, the proposed plans were wholeheartedly welcomed by the new town planners, who were happy to attract business investment and considerable employment opportunities. Sainsbury's was the first incoming business to set up after Basingstoke's town-expansion scheme was launched. This was a very promising move, but also an extremely bold and big investment. Construction was a major undertaking. It took two years to develop the entire 25-acre site, eight acres of which eventually comprised buildings with a total covered floor area of 350,000 square feet.

The main building area at Basingstoke incorporated an office block, service station, gatehouse and reception area. The service station had the latest plant and equipment for servicing and electrical repairs and for spray-painting the company's fleet of lorries. Facilities for the staff were also considered top-notch in their day. The Griffin Club at Dulwich was obviously no longer accessible to Basingstoke staff for recreation or regular sporting fixtures, so the plans included two tennis courts, cricket pitches, and indoor facilities for table tennis and badminton. There was also a staff restaurant which seated 300.

The L-shaped main structure contained warehouses for perishable and non-perishable goods, production areas, cold stores and bacon rooms. It had been decided that Basingstoke offered the opportunity for the company to upgrade its bacon stoves and bacon-packaging operation. Unsmoked bacon had hitherto been delivered to Blackfriars, transferred to the Union Street bacon stoves for smoking, and then despatched to the branches as whole sides or prime cuts for preparation on the premises. Basingstoke offered space for modern, more efficient smoking kilns, and Sainsbury's engineers had designed a new packaging line for slicing, wrapping and pricing the product. Facilities at Basingstoke were also engineered for handling chilled and frozen food. Successful experiments were carried out into the pre-packing of New Zealand lamb and fresh beef, breaking new ground because of the perishability of these products. Some years later, JD made special mention of this facility in his annual address to senior executives: 'We have in the lamb-packing line at Basingstoke a production unit which is, to our knowledge, unrivalled in the world.' He also explained that in one of his recent visits to the US he had learnt that 'every chain store was dreaming of the day when beef can be pre-packed either at central depots, or delivered, packed, direct to their shops . . . We really are first in the field in our pre-packing beef pilot scheme'. These important developments required further innovation at Basingstoke, in the form of Sainsbury's own new fleet of 12-ton TK Bedford refrigerated lorries.

On a far smaller scale, soon after work began at Basingstoke the company opened its second operational warehouse at Hoddesdon, Hertfordshire, in November 1962. Fred McManus – who had discovered the original Buntingford site – was placed in charge of Hoddesdon with an initial staff of 25. His exclusive purpose was to receive, store, ripen and distribute Sainsbury's growing range of fruit and vegetables then sold through about 35 self-service branches. Through Hoddesdon, Sainsbury's could ensure the ripeness and freshness of these 'produce' lines, as well as keeping responsibility for delivery schedules in-house. The offer of a range of fruit and vegetables was both innovative and attractive. Most British housewives in the 1960s bought their fruit and vegetables from greengrocers or in the thriving street markets which were commonplace in all parts of the country.

It was not until 24 January 1964, at 8.22 am, that the first

Sainsbury's lorry left Basingstoke to deliver to branches in the south-west. Shortly before setting off, Fred Brown the driver sipped celebratory champagne with Mr N. C. Turner, the company secretary, whose added responsibility was to run Sainsbury's distribution. On this day and for many months to come, the massive racks in the main warehouse required considerable filling, and it would take until the end of the year before the depot was fully operational and staffed. But it was only weeks before the company started to realise the benefits of having proximity to roads that were relatively free of traffic, and access to 350,000 square feet of storage space.

By the time Basingstoke was launched, a major programme of rebuilding was already in process at Buntingford. Sainsbury's was turning out 1,500 tons of concrete a week to supply just the foundations for the extension of the old ordnance depot along the A10 Cambridge Road. On completion in 1967, there were 500,000 square feet of floor space, and in-house engineers had designed or specified advanced plant and equipment to ensure optimum storage and handling of products.

Facilities included temperature-controlled freezer areas and cold stores, the latter capable of storing two million cubic feet of goods – enough according to the company's statisticians to fill 360,000 refrigerators. Engineers had also specified a new style of 'Vierendeel' beam supporting the long roof extensions; these beams not only took the weight of the roof, but a number of them were designed to let in light and allow ventilation. Learning from experience, the in-house team had installed heating elements within the concrete floor of the low-temperature storage areas to prevent damp from penetrating into the ground beneath and freezing up to 12 metres below the surface. This could create earth movement and structural damage. The loading bays could accommodate up to 75 vehicles, incoming and outgoing, and a unique goods-flow system ensured efficient handling and despatch. Introducing such techniques, Sainsbury's engineers were at the forefront of their industry. This vast increase in capacity still left room for a cricket pitch and football field among other recreational amenities provided for the enlarged workforce of 2,000. Apart from Basingstoke there was, in fact, nothing quite like Buntingford in the UK. When it finally came into operation in July 1967, the new depot had cost £4 million.

The extensive reorganisation of the company's distribution was only completed when a fourth regional depot site, at Charlton in South London, opened on the last day of the decade. This was to serve the company's 80 branches in London and the south-east, which were still receiving their supplies from Blackfriars. The depot added an area of nearly 230,000 square feet, half of which was devoted to cold storage, and there were 46 loading bays.

The proximity of Charlton to Blackfriars meant that the company's buyers had readier access to check the goods they purchased. At Buntingford, Basingstoke and Hoddesdon, Sainsbury's had established a number of dedicated quality inspectors to do this and to ensure that the goods brought into the depots were to the required standard. The laboratories at Blackfriars were also involved in regular sampling of batches of goods. But in this ten-year overhaul of the entire distribution system, perhaps the one thing to be regretted was that it broke the previous one-link chain between the head buyers and their goods at Blackfriars. If anything, this placed even greater importance on the directors' unannounced visits to the stores. These continued to be carried out weekly, though stores were usually forewarned, either through solicitous leaks from the centre, or via frantic calls between stores once the top brass was spotted in a specific area.

Once the new depot organisation was in place, Sainsbury's was in a position to maintain efficient supplies across its network of stores, and also to provide a basis for expansion. The former 120-mile supply radius centred on Blackfriars could be extended significantly. Basingstoke could serve an area west of the line that lay roughly between Brighton, London and Shrewsbury; Buntingford could serve the Midlands, East Anglia and North London, while Charlton could serve the southern geographical quarter.

Between 1960 and 1969, Sainsbury's self-service sales area grew from some 100,000 square feet to more than 800,000 square feet, and the volume of sales in this space increased substantially. The development of the distribution system was like a game of catch-up in which the depots only just managed to provide adequate levels of delivery to branches as the programme of decentralisation continued. Yet by the end of the decade Sainsbury's had a total of more than 1.5 million square feet of depot storage space – more than five times the amount that the company had in 1960; this space would vitally assist the explosive growth to come.

Sainsbury's also needed to upgrade its administration system in order to handle the increasing volumes of goods. At the beginning of the decade, processing each branch's sales orders had become an administrative burden that required a growing army of clerical staff; the system was inevitably vulnerable to human error and overload. Systemic change was equally required in order to monitor and enforce the standards set by head office as the retailing operation grew in complexity.

In 1959, the company had begun looking in earnest at the potential of the computer – a novel approach, since no retailer in Britain employed one at this time. An EMIDEC 1100 was duly given thorough consideration and then ordered; in time this was to replace the row of heavy iron Powers-Samas card-punching machines in Tress House at Blackfriars. The new computer took EMI two years to build and customise at Hayes in Middlesex, during which time Sainsbury's own computer programmers devised programs mostly for calculating orders of non-perishable goods.

During a quiet weekend evening in June 1961, the bulky behemoth, with its magnetic reels, printers and control-panel instrumentation, was craned to the third floor of the Stamford Street headquarters and hoisted in through a window. The EMIDEC 1100 was designed to be capable of taking every single Sainsbury's store's branch-stock accounts for a week at a rate of 8,000 coded characters per second – i.e. in only 75 seconds. Not only was this massive number-crunching, but it was also a means of providing up-to-date stock accounts for each store. The EMIDEC 1100 stood sacred in its spotless laboratory-style suite, operated by a new and rarefied breed of technician and programmer. Thus Sainsbury's entered the computer age, the first of the leading food-retailer multiples to do so; of retailers in general, only Boots had adopted a computer system for similar purposes, installing its machine just a few weeks before.

In its day, a computer offering this kind of capacity – actually a tiny fraction of the speed or function of an average desk PC today – was difficult for most office clerks to comprehend. But under the supervision of Bernard Ramm, the EMIDEC 1100 soon became invaluable in the distribution and reordering of supplies. He also harnessed it to produce sales statistics and sales forecasts, and these had gradually more influence on buying policies. During the decade, the computer department was enlarged to cope with growth, with the addition of another EMIDEC 1100 (now called the

The founders, John James and Mary Ann Sainsbury, pictured in their High-
gate house in about 1886. John Benjamin, their eldest son, is in the centre
with his fiancée, Mabel Van den Bergh

Sainsbury's Guildford High Street shop on its opening day, 16 November
1906

The first Sainsbury's self-service shop, at 9–11 London Road, Croydon, soon after it opened in 1950

Checkouts at Sainsbury's second self-service store, at Eastbourne, in 1952

At Sainsbury's Self-service shopping is EASY and QUICK

1—As you go in you are given a special wire basket for your purchases.

2—The prices and weight of all goods are clearly marked. You just take what you want.

3—Are you a fast shopper or a slow? You can be either when you shop at Sainsbury's!

4—Dairy produce, cooked meats, pies, sausages, bacon, poultry, rabbits and cheese—all hygienically packed.

5—Meat is served from Sainsbury's special refrigerated counters. Or you can serve yourself from the cabinets.

6—Pay as you go out. The assistant puts what you have bought into your own basket and gives you a receipt.

'How to Shop Self-Service' at Sainsbury's new Lewisham branch in 1955. Sainsbury's employed retired store managers to help customers who found self-service difficult

Customers by the novel, open-topped refrigerated-fresh meat cabinets at Sainsbury's Southampton store in 1955

An all glass-fronted store – a completely new phenomenon – in Kentish Town in 1955

Messrs Harrison (head grocery-buyer, left) and Matthews. Tea-buyers met every week to sample own-label and proprietary brand teas, as well as teas sold by competitors

Interior of the newly converted town-centre store at Guildford in 1963

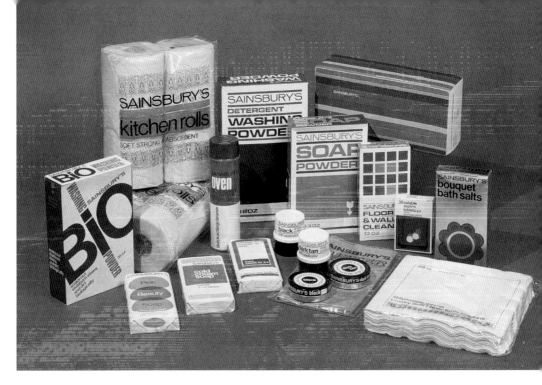

Buyers developed an increasing range of Sainsbury's own-label, non-food goods during the 1960s

Wrapping, weighing and pricing fresh meat on a 'rolling cold' unit, developed for use in the preparation rooms of Sainsbury's 1960s supermarkets

Tottenham High Road, one of Sainsbury's largest new supermarkets in 1968, with 9,400 square feet of selling area

Sainsbury's first regional depot was built at Buntingford in 1962, here viewed following significant enlargement in 1967

Studying new store plans in the late 1960s, from left to right: Geoff Skipper, Roy Linfield, Timothy Sainsbury, Bert Nurthen, Derek Foster

The arrival of Sainsbury's first computer, in 1961; the EMIDEC 1100 was so large that it had to be craned through a window onto the third floor

ICT 1100) and a new IBM 1440. By 1967, when there appeared at last
to be a better balance between the company's retail advances and
its distribution capability, Bernard Ramm was seeking ways of com-
puterising the management of perishable goods – meat, bacon,
vegetables, fruit, eggs and some cheese – which had until then been
treated separately. Another computer, the IBM 360/20, was on
order, and the company was looking further to incorporate the
whole stock-ordering system on one new computer, the ICT 1904.
Bernard Ramm, whose estimations were always carefully reckoned,
was reported by *Management Today* in 1967 as saying, 'Our computer system is about the most advanced in Britain.'

Strategic planning for the growth of the network of stores was a constant organisational headache. In common with all developing
businesses in the 1960s, and for the following 20 years, Sainsbury's
experienced considerable difficulties with planning authorities. JD
and Timothy Sainsbury were often exasperated by what appeared to
be almost Kafkaesque obfuscation and delay. Not infrequently, Timothy's efforts to build new stores in strategically important locations
were hindered by what he considered to be sheer amateurishness in
the local and regional council departments. Early in 1960, Timothy
wrote, 'Planning control stops much that is badly designed from
being built, but it also stops some very good designs. This is particularly true when the local planning committee does not have any
professional advice from independent architects.'

Comparison with the situation in America further inspired
Sainsbury's directors, as it did other British retailers, to want to create appropriate new stores and modern shopping centres, but this
only heightened the frustration. Cheaper and more available land,
lower-cost building materials and faster construction techniques,
combined with almost negligible planning restrictions, ensured a
buoyant, ever-changing scene in the US. It is recorded that in 1959
some 4,000 new supermarkets were established there, while some
4,000 department stores – the rage of the 1950s – went out of business. At the same time there was a trend for supermarkets in the US
to become 'variety stores', with about one-fifth of their generally
huge sales areas devoted to food, and four-fifths offering haber-
dashery, clothes, toiletries, toys, garden tools and man-sized
refrigerators. Many of these mixed-offering supermarkets were
situated in purpose-built shopping centres. One report on the US

retail scene in the *JS Journal* of February 1961 refers to 'huge gatherings of shops built in splendid, orderly array, joined by covered sidewalks, and interset with modern gardens and playgrounds'.

While they were impressed with the boldness of scale and technical innovations in food retailing across the Atlantic, the Sainsbury's directors were equally aware of the extreme unlikelihood of being able to establish such retail communities in their home territories. It was Mr Alan's opinion that what happened in the US occurred in Britain ten years later. He was also inclined to believe that because the US had about 38 times more land area than Britain, with only three-and-a-half times the population, many aspects of US retail activity were totally impracticable in Britain. For his part, JD remained a keen and close observer of the American retail sector. He travelled widely in the US, as he did in Europe, to see what multiple retailers were up to in these countries, how their methods might be applied in the UK and how Sainsbury's might improve on them.

Planning constraints in Sainsbury's heartland areas also provided a good reason to develop the business further afield. In 1960 the County of London published its development plan laying down the permitted use of all land in the various London administrative 'zones' for the first half of the decade. Timothy Sainsbury acknowledged the validity of green belts but wrote at the time: 'If shopping centres like those in America – a number of shops grouped round a pedestrian precinct and surrounded by car parks – are ever to be built in England, they will have to be built on land not now zoned for shopping.'

In 1963 Sainsbury's managed to open 11 new, converted or greatly enlarged self-service and supermarket outlets, including greatly enlarged branches in Nottingham, Leicester and Northampton. Another store in Rugby was an entirely new territory, and together these larger branches gave the company a more dynamic presence in the Midlands. In the same year, the Sainsbury's opened in Chatham and Reading were also in new territory – and the latter of these was built with 11,000 square feet of sales area. In Southampton, another store was built in Shirley, a suburb of the city, to consolidate Sainsbury's establishment in the south of England. The only building in London involved a refurbished branch at Catford and an extension to the Lewisham store to provide a sales area of 11,500 square feet – once again Lewisham carried the flag as Sainsbury's largest store.

Added to the complexity of the planning process, there was inevitably debate about what the 'ideal' size should be for a new store once its location was chosen. Estimating its appropriate size was fraught with imponderables, particularly when so much depended on anticipating demand at a time when society was enjoying an unquantifiable boost in affluence. By the mid-1960s it was becoming clear that 10,000 square feet of sales area, which had so recently seemed to be the ideal, appeared to be insufficient space for the stores that were being planned for opening in the later 1960s. The whole process of seeking locations, acquiring sites and planning permission and constructing the store could take anything up to three years at this period, sometimes longer. Perhaps the ideal size, therefore, was more like 15,000 to 20,000 square feet of sales area, but would this be risky in terms of the commitment of resources, given the long period between acquiring a site and opening a store, and could planners be persuaded of Sainsbury's case? We should also remember that Sainsbury's stores of the period all had a substantial non-sales area given over to staff, preparation and in-store warehousing.

Future development planning was a necessary and constant factor in the boardrooms of ambitious food retailers, even if their survival depended on their ability to respond to customer demands immediately on a day-to-day basis. Store development would continue to be a process of trial and error, each new site acquisition combining science and hope – what JD sometimes called 'the art of the possible'. In fact, by the end of the decade the sheer scale of customer demand, particularly in Sainsbury's stores, would make any forecasts about ideal store size almost futile. It was clear by then that the company's smaller self-service stores were often hopelessly overcrowded, and the wry adage, 'No one shops at Sainsbury's because of the queues,' was becoming something of an embarrassment. It seemed more often to be a case of the bigger the store the better – provided planning permission could be obtained.

The use of cars for shopping, a new phenomenon of the 1960s, had also to be factored into the store-expansion programme. It particularly affected Sainsbury's among the nation's multiple food retailers because the business was concentrated in the southeast, where both the self-service revolution and the growth of car ownership were most in evidence. At a conference of the International Association of Chain Stores held in Nice in June 1964, Mr Alan read a paper on retailing trends in an increasingly motorised community in which he lambasted the British government:

> In Britain the research carried out into this vast problem has been too little and too late, and there is at present no integrated government policy to cope with it. What we can be sure of, however, is that the motor car will alter our way of life to a large extent during the coming decades. Our towns and our roads must be changed and developed to meet this challenge, but we have no definite plan how to do it.

Mr Alan's assessment of the challenge of the new age of motoring and how it would affect retailing was remarkably accurate. He believed there was only a remote chance that the infrastructure of Britain's towns and cities would be anything like equipped to handle the 'Motor Age' adequately by the 1970s – six years away. He foresaw a 'mixed system' in which city centres would remain the focus of business and shopping, although he said: 'A limited number of out-of-town shopping centres are likely to be built at particularly suitable locations within easy reach of a large population.' Most tellingly, he added: 'The retailer who can offer the widest selection, the most comprehensive range of goods, will have an advantage as obviously car shoppers will be more than ever inclined to make all their purchases under one roof.'

During the second half of the decade, the directors applied significant energy to the location and design of new or replacement stores which would suit shoppers using cars, or to siting branches appropriately close to municipal car parks. But Sainsbury's was by no means leading this movement. 'We could have caught on to the importance of car parks a bit sooner,' says JD. Yet in planning terms alone, building a car park adjacent to one's own town-centre store was very difficult, if not impossible, to achieve. The siting of car parks in urban centres was a jealously held prerogative of the county, town or borough councils in charge of planning. In the 1960s, these authorities were generally reluctant to focus attention on car parks in the older town- or city-centre areas until the pressure of traffic became intolerable. By that stage, limitations on space usually meant that retailers and shoppers in the newly built high-street shopping centres of this era would have to share the general inconvenience of a multi-storey parking facility, above or below ground level. This had its merits for high-street browsers, but was generally exasperating for shoppers trundling their weekly or fortnightly family food and domestic purchases up and down crowded lifts or stairs. And when it was possible to build a customer car park, the car-space allowance tended to be smaller than ideal, or would quickly become so.

For the Sainsbury's directors, determined to build larger stores with more lines of both food and non-food products, all the while improving the general shopping experience for customers, it was difficult enough to obtain planning permission to extend an existing premise over two shop widths, let alone to build on a newly acquired site in the town or city centre. On the list of proposed facilities for a new branch, a car park would often be met with a blank stare from town planners.

Reflecting the society it served, Sainsbury's was in constant transition during the 1960s. By 1967, the public face of the company was represented by a remarkable mix of branch formats, sizes, styles of service and degrees of modernisation. Leading the gradual expansion into new territory in the Midlands, the east and the south of England, the new Sainsbury's supermarkets shouldered their way into the high streets – with aesthetically abrupt frontages of concrete, brick and glass. Another tier of branches were the older, first wave of self-service stores, now requiring refurbishment, such as those at Kentish Town, Stevenage, Debden and the pioneering store at 9–11 London Road, Croydon. In their own league, but still waving the Sainsbury's flag, were about 140 counter-service shops.

On 2 January 1967, Mr Alan retired from the chairmanship of the company and was succeeded by Mr R J, while JD took over from his father as head of trading. Taking over so many developments midstream, it was now the fourth generation's responsibility to steer Sainsbury's future course.

Mr Alan, as the company's president, later reflected on the dynamic of succession in the company: 'My brother and I accepted the fact that the third generation could not and would not wish to run the business in the same way as the second. The same law will no doubt apply to the fourth. But the combination of keeping traditional values at the same time as welcoming change will continue to be the cardinal feature of the firm's policy.' No better words could describe the approach that the fourth generation would take.

Part Two

SEA CHANGE
1967–1992

Chapter 6

THE FOURTH GENERATION
1967–1969

O N BECOMING CHAIRMAN, Mr R J wrote to senior executives, paying tribute to his brother and making it clear that he saw his own holding of that position as a brief period of transitional government: 'My pride [in becoming chairman] does not spring just from the past achievements of JS, but also from my knowledge of the present vitality of the business and my conviction of an even greater future, which now lies largely in the hands of a generation of Directors and Staff younger than myself.' This confidence was well placed. JD was now heir apparent to his uncle, and had been a highly visible and energetic director for almost ten years. Quite apart from his knowledge as a retailer, particularly in driving own-label developments, he was already well known for his determination and decisiveness.

Simon had been a director almost as long as JD, and Timothy had five years' experience on the board – both were well versed in their particular responsibilities. David Sainsbury, Mr R J's son, was the last of the fourth generation to join the company, in 1963. Initially, he was placed in charge of the management-development section. Subsequently, he studied for an MBA at Columbia University in New York before joining the board in 1966 to take on gradually increasing responsibilities in the financial department.

The one addition to the Sainsburys-dominated board at the beginning of 1967 was a newly appointed director, Gurth Hoyer Millar, also in his prime at the age of 38. He had boxed for Oxford University and been capped as a Scottish rugby international. A man of broad talents, he had trained as a lawyer following a commission in the army, then travelled internationally, negotiating oil concessions for BP before joining Sainsbury's in 1964. Hoyer Millar was well prepared to succeed N. C. Turner, who was approaching retirement, in the position of director responsible for the company's distribution – the warehouse and transport departments and the motor-engineers departments.

Apart from Hoyer Millar, the only non-family members on the board were Bernard Ramm, the company's chief statistician, who had become a board director in 1962, and Max Justice and Arthur Trask, who became directors responsible for buying in 1959 and 1965 respectively.

The fourth generation were eager to impress their own signatures on the future development of the company. According to Simon, 'Even though it was a tremendously healthy business when we took over, we were all fired by the ambition to run it better than it had ever been run before.' Sainsbury's was indeed a 'healthy business'. The company's investment programme in new stores had run at an average of between eight and nine openings each year up to this point. Only government building and licensing regulations had the temporary effect of restricting store openings to just six in 1967. This was a temporary dip, for the next year the number was up to 12. At Sainsbury's year-end in 1967, the company had 249 stores in total, of which 64 were defined as supermarkets, 39 were mostly or partially converted self-service stores, and 146 were counter-service. This was virtually the same number of branches in total as the company had in 1960, but with an average sales area in the supermarkets approaching 6,000 square feet – about 50 per cent larger than the average size of competitors' supermarkets at this time.

What competing companies lacked in store size, they more than made up in overall numbers. Compared to Sainsbury's, they grew their businesses at a ferocious rate, mostly through acquisition. Tesco, driven by quantitative principles of cheap goods and cheap prices, believing that 'almost any outlet will do as long as it adds to the number', opened more than 40 stores in 1966 and more than 50 in 1967. Measured by the 4,000 square-foot rule, Tesco now had 180 supermarkets in total and 300 other stores. Another growing name, Victor Value, had 100 supermarkets out of about 400 shops, all offering what Seth and Randall in *The Grocers* have called 'a pathetic shopping experience'. In 1968, Tesco bought Victor Value, adding this to its purchase of the Cadena Cafés, to become the nation's largest chain, with more than 800 branches. Fine Fare, in 1967, had a total of 300 supermarkets and as many other shops. And under the Allied Suppliers group, Lipton and Home and Colonial had more than 230 supermarkets and about 900 other shops.

Meanwhile, Co-op and a large number of independent high-street food retailers between them took a 25 per cent share of the market.

But successful food retailing could not be measured in branch numbers. Sainsbury's now had a range of more than 3,000 separate products in its leading supermarkets, and each week it is estimated that about 1.7 million customer transactions were made at its branches. The company's ability to drive volumes of sales through its shops left its competition well behind. Each week Sainsbury's was turning over an average of almost £4 per square foot of selling area, while the best of its competitors could generally achieve no more than 30 shillings (£1.50). And these were relatively early days in the supermarket revolution, when customers in every high street in the country were eager to see more and better choice. By 1967, when the new distribution structure was better positioned to support Sainsbury's expansion to the west and south-west, and some way further to the Midlands, fewer than 20 per cent of the population of the UK had access to a Sainsbury's store. There was plenty of room to continue to improve the Sainsbury's offer and for the company to expand within its traditional territories, while moving the boundaries further afield.

Close food-industry watchers noted various factors that contributed to Sainsbury's success. Robert Heller, editor of *Management Today*, wrote a lengthy article about the Sainsbury's business model in July 1967, extolling the virtues of a business that was so closely controlled by the family. This control allowed the Sainsburys to take the long view and 'not necessarily turn in bigger profits today or tomorrow'. Heller refers to other advantages, including 'continuity of management, an awareness by the staff that things are not going to change overnight, a relative freedom from "office politics" and the very marked atmosphere of family business that is immediately noticeable in the company'.

Sainsbury's business model worked admirably, but there were occasional mistakes. For example, one of the few stores that the company opened in 1967 was at Aston in Birmingham, where the City Council had planned a massive new development, including housing, shops and schools. The 6,000 square-foot supermarket did so little business that it was unceremoniously closed after just ten months. According to Joe Barnes, Aston was 'a classic mistake', but an untypical one: 'Unfortunately, we built our store before the project was anywhere near completed and then the development was drastically curtailed.' Aston was perhaps the exception that proved the rule.

As head of trading, JD now had full responsibility for the front line of the business, a role which embraced the company's entire buying and selling strategy. Head of trading also meant head of marketing. Whereas in the highly 'corporatised' structures of the service industry of the 1990s and later no large company would be without its corporate marketing director, there was no such position in Sainsbury's in the late 1960s. Marketing and food retailing were considered one and the same thing. Working closely with JD, the senior buyers in each central department were effectively senior marketers too, because they handled all the many processes from sourcing supplies to suggesting the retail prices of the goods for which they were responsible. At the front of the operation, they were energetically assisted by Jim Woods, who continued to organise external press advertising, occasional television adverts and in-store promotional literature.

Although it would be two years before JD took over as chairman from his uncle, his position as head of trade had already placed him in the operational driving seat. It is perhaps not surprising, therefore, that the articulation of company policy and the communication of strategy to external audiences usually fell to JD rather than to his uncle as company chairman in this interim period. On 30 October 1967, for example, Sainsbury's was one of four companies awarded the Presidential Medal for Design Management by the Royal Society for the Arts. The prestigious award was presented to JD by the Duke of Edinburgh. The citation aptly summarises Sainsbury's achievements to this date and gives some idea of the company's place in the public eye:

> It is no mean feat in this age of multiple competition for a family grocer starting with a single shop to have grown in four generations into a chain of over 250 stores and still to remain a family grocer, but that is the story of the Sainsburys, a story brought about in a very real sense through their consistent adherence to a family handwriting, to a planned housestyle that has missed no detail while relating every part to the whole. This instantly recognisable public face has been the outcome of good design

management from buildings to packaging, from shopfront lettering to counter ticketing and from store layout to advertising. Such attention to every detail of design has greatly contributed to the Sainsbury reputation for cleanliness and quality.

In a brief address before the actual presentation was made, JD took the opportunity, as he often would on such occasions, to reinforce Sainsbury's key principle of trade, 'that the finest quality food served in the cleanest and most hygienic manner can also be priced at the keenest and most competitive level; that those who look for and need low prices, also value and appreciate quality'. This was not only deeply ingrained within the family and throughout the company, but was something that JD believed in strongly as the key to the firm's continuing success. In the development of own-label products, he had always promulgated the Sainsbury's mantra concerning quality, attention to detail and the pursuit of value and choice for the customer.

JD was quick to establish his own style of leadership, one which combined tenacious focus on this trading principle with a passion for innovation and day-to-day vigilance of the conditions affecting the company's trade. This vigilance concerned not only merchandising – the development of the range, supply and distribution – but also involved a critical and detailed review of the company's strengths and weaknesses.

The annual meeting of senior managers in October 1967 was an important early opportunity for JD to make his own vision of the company's purpose and future strategy crystal-clear to subordinates:

Our prime motivation in the business is the search for perfection. We have no ambition to be the largest food retailers in this country, but we are totally set and determined on the course of being the best. By best we mean essentially giving our customers the best value that is possible, not only in the quality and price of the goods, but in the manner and style of the service. In achieving this, our trade not only will grow, but must grow to make it possible.

JD went on to draw attention to the strength of the company's leading self-service stores (even in 1967 it was still customary to refer to these stores as 'self-service' stores or shops rather than 'supermarkets'), and he also outlined what he then considered the main competition to be. As a snapshot of the period, his analysis shows how much the competitive profile would change. His opinion was that with its large chain Tesco appeared to be the keenest rival, but he considered Pricerite and Wallis really to be closer competition 'purely from the price angle of groceries and non-perishables'. Tesco were trying to improve their perishable offer, which was a significant strength in Sainsbury's stores, but Tesco's standards and volume of sales were far lower than Sainsbury's. Fine Fare had adopted a policy of lowering prices, but their shops were not busy. Meanwhile, Safeway appeared to JD 'to be going downhill . . . In some of their branches there has been a noticeable lowering of standards'. In sales of perishable food, JD reckoned that Caters, followed by David Greig and Key Markets, presented the keenest competition to Sainsbury's. Allied Suppliers were mentioned but dismissed as not being in the same league, and International Stores were considered 'rather moribund and ineffective'.

Activities at Marks & Spencer, on the other hand, were noted with interest. Directors at Sainsbury's had always respected M&S because their principles of trade were not dissimilar to their own. At this period there were notable dynastic similarities between Sainsbury's, Pilkington the glassmakers, and Cadbury, among major family concerns. In each, the elder son had usually succeeded elder son as chairman. But industry-watchers most often compared Sainsbury's with M&S. In his July 1967 article, Robert Heller of *Management Today* had observed: 'Lord Marks, the late chairman of M&S, and Lord Sainsbury were admirers of each other. With roughly the same number of shops and employees and the same passion for quality, the two groups occupy roughly the same prestige position in their respective sectors of the retail trade.' There had been press reports that M&S's turnover from food had reached £66 million, representing a substantial increase. Nevertheless, while JD praised M&S for the quality of their produce, cake and biscuits, he did not consider this respected rival to be a real threat: 'Their entry into the provision trade in our areas has not, in general, appeared to have met with any considerable success, by our standards,' he said.

Essentially, JD considered that Sainsbury's modern stores – those carrying the full range and which were not too overcrowded – were able to hold their own against any of this competition. But the counter-service shops were increasingly vulnerable. The company was more than ever determined to step up the rate of converting counter-service stores and building new supermarkets.

Setting a course for the future, JD wanted Sainsbury's to focus on three areas in the years ahead. The first was management and leadership style. He said that Sainsbury's needed to push decision-making further down the line; more grooming of one's subordinates was needed, as was a more systematic way of communicating information and more understanding about company objectives at lower management levels. At the time, Sainsbury's management had some way to go to achieve these ideals. Top management was a cone-shaped hierarchy in which all decisions and relevant information were closely contained by the family. Angus Clark was one of a new breed of young professional managers who had been recruited in 1966 to help run the Basingstoke distribution centre. He recalls the poverty of communication within the upper echelons of management when he arrived:

> When I came into the company, one of the biggest surprises I had was the absence of information. I didn't even know what it was costing me to run my operation because I didn't receive any management accounts. Information was held close to the family. You didn't have much idea of what was going on; what sales were or sales forecasts, what new store-opening plans were. All this fairly basic stuff was just not in the common pond.

According to JD, the second area to tackle in the medium term was productivity in the branches. The family's obsession with quality had led to a generally larger workforce in the branches than in competitor companies. There were also more junior managers relative to sales staff in Sainsbury's. Branch productivity had been greatly assisted by more centralised packing of beef, lamb and bacon, and the pre-wrapping of produce. But Sainsbury's was also well known in the industry for its large overall branch size compared to its selling area. Its emphasis on fresh meat was partly responsible, requiring far more preparation space compared to competitors. By further reducing the amount of work in the branches and improving techniques, the company could increase efficiency. Apart from keeping costs down, this could help to tackle the continual problem of staff shortages while maintaining high trading standards. Most of Sainsbury's competitors did not have the same standards, so they could generally achieve lower labour costs.

The third area of focus for the future was the company's computers and the brave new world of electronic data processing. Sainsbury's had been something of a pioneer in computerisation, but as the company became more complex so its overall efficiency would depend on making optimum use of sophisticated technology. At the close of his address in 1967, JD left the imaginations of his senior executives whirling with a prophecy of how electronic data processing would completely transform retail efficiency in the future:

> The checkout would be automatic; the customers would place their purchases on a moving belt and, as the products went along the belt, a code would be read from the label by the mini-computer at each checkout, which would be sufficient for this to be able to total the customer's purchases and pass the information automatically to the customer's bank, initiating the necessary transfer of funds. At the same time, it would be able to pass the information to the depot computer to calculate the order to our supplier.

It is hard to believe that this vision of the future dates from 1967, the best part of 20 years before the radical new technology of scanning was completing its roll-out to all Sainsbury's stores, in the company that pioneered it in the UK. In fact, all three key areas outlined in JD's first address to senior managers – management skills and structure, branch-productivity improvements and the adoption of advanced computerisation – would remain key elements of Sainsbury's strategy for the next 20 years.

JD's enthusiasm for computerisation reflected a traditional Sainsbury approach to the use of data. Mr Alan ruffled through the papers at his buyers' meetings, eager to learn how each department's trade was doing. JD equally required the latest data so that he was aware of current performance and could be informed about orders, stocks and prices – and also productivity in the stores. His determination to have useful data ready to hand was to some extent learnt from his father, but was boosted by his awareness of how comparatively backward food retailing was in the UK compared

with the US, where management information was more sophisticated. Since the late 1950s, he had travelled many times to North
America and to Europe to explore new retailing ideas. In the early
1960s he had struck up a relationship with Mike O'Conner, head of
the Supermarket Institute of America (SMI), who had a passion
for sharing knowledge and new ideas about food retailing. Mike
O'Conner had originally asked Mr Alan whether he would like to
join the SMI, but the offer had been politely declined. Not to be put
off, O'Conner had quietly approached JD and said he would like to
keep in touch and would be prepared to send over copies of any
information that he required – and that the invitation to join the
SMI would always remain open. JD promptly joined the Institute
when he succeeded his uncle in 1969.

Mike O'Conner recalls that his approach to Mr Alan had perhaps
not been right for an older generation of European food retailers,
but he saw in John Sainsbury someone with whom he could work
and share ideas in the future. For his part, JD recognised that Sainsbury's could make significant improvements to its business by
learning from best practices in the US. He had kept in close touch
with O'Conner throughout the 1960s, and often took his counsel as
the company broadened its operations in the 1970s and 1980s. It was
O'Conner who had introduced him to findings from the early US
trials with scanning technology in 1967.

There was real value in this relationship. In the US, food retailers
tended to be regional rather than national operations, which
meant that while companies were wary of providing commer-
cially sensitive information to local competitors, there was a well-
established tradition of sharing general ideas and data at a national
level. Sainsbury's thus found itself in the enviable position of being
able to access ideas and knowledge from numerous American
retailers who were more than happy to share this with a company
across the Atlantic. In time, Sainsbury's would be able to benchmark its own performance against these American companies,
and would monitor the progress in many areas, such as ordering
technology, distribution and methods of evaluating labour productivity.

Keen to develop a network within leading European food retailing and manufacturing companies, in 1968 O'Conner invited JD
and other younger-generation captains within the European food
industry to learn about recent computer advances in America. The

group met in Zurich, where professors from the Harvard Business School unveiled the mysteries of basic computer programming and decision theory. JD learnt that computers could be used not just to record and analyse existing stock more efficiently but, with the right information and programming, to assess future orders and determine optimum stocking levels with great accuracy. O'Conner remembers being struck by JD's response, which was to see the potential of such advanced technology primarily in terms of benefits to customers. The Americans at the meeting tended to be preoccupied by the potential cost savings of such systems, whereas JD was enthused by the prospect of having a system that could ensure that the right goods in the right quantities were always available when customers needed them. Such a view fits squarely with JD's diktat about being the 'best' rather than the 'largest' food retailer in the country. It also matches the Sainsburys' belief about taking the long view: please customers first and the money will follow.

Following the visit to Zurich, and with the SMI's assistance, the company found and appointed Ned Harwell, an American consultant, to advise Sainsbury's how it might improve the efficiency of the branch-ordering system and merchandising, and also how the business might benefit from the next generation of computerisation. The development process looked as though it might take two or three years, as there were marked differences between the retailing environments in the US and in the UK. For example, US suppliers had a different relationship with retailers and different responsibilities in relation to keeping supermarket shelves filled.

While Ned Harwell was busy trialling and developing a new ordering system for Sainsbury's, Bernard Ramm's team was preparing the ground for the next-generation mainframe computer at headquarters. In April 1969, the new ICL 1906E computer was installed, taking up nearly 4,000 square feet of the second floor at Stamford House. This was faster by a factor of ten than previous versions, which meant that the computerised stock-control cycle for non-perishables would now take four hours to complete, as against 40 to 50 hours; for perishables the cycle would take only half an hour.

For Sainsbury's, it was not a difficult financial decision to commit to these new technologies. Compared with the cost of building new supermarkets, the capital investment was relatively small.

Besides, it was a family trait to set down objectives and to invest both time and money in their pursuit to secure the right eventual result. It was more typical than remarkable that Sainsbury's pioneered these new developments in the UK.

As Sainsbury's approached its centenary, it was a difficult time for the food-retailing trade in general. One recurring problem was the extent of government intervention. The introduction of Selective Employment Tax (SET) in July 1966 was a worrying example of this. SET was imposed solely on the service industries, reflecting a doctrinal belief in government that services were growing at the expense of manufacturing. It represented an additional tax burden that Sainsbury's estimated would cost the company 0.75 per cent of turnover. The government also introduced National Insurance contributions and State Graduated Pension schemes to add to the tax burden which, in 1968, Sainsbury's estimated cost the company more than £2.5 million. The company's net profit margins could not afford to shrink lower than the 1.75 per cent of turnover recorded that year. Moreover, food prices were beginning to edge up, and would climb dramatically in the early 1970s. Care was also needed to curb rising head-office expenses and distribution costs.

As the increasing volume of sales constantly drove the business, Sainsbury's buyers were continually urged to increase the range in their departments to keep attracting and pleasing customers old and new. Compared to the independent traders, the larger stores were becoming a feast of choice, with approaching 4,000 different products. In the typical modern stores of the period, enormous growth was recorded in both non-perishable lines and non-food lines. Sainsbury's own-label products included new breakfast cereals, crisps and all types of biscuits and cakes, and every home-baking product – in the days when home baking was still extremely popular – had a Sainsbury's label. The pet-food lines sported plenty of own-label products too, and the Sainsbury's name festooned the growing non-food lines, including new medicated shampoos, washing-up liquids, cleaning and bathroom products. The largest stores also outran competition in the range and quality of pre-packed fruit and vegetables. There was an abundant selection of fresh meat, and customers could select from poultry that included pheasants, patridges, grouse and other seasonal game. Added to these traditional offers and innovations, the off-licence department's trade was hugely boosted, with 16 new licences granted between 1967 and 1969. Confectionery sales tripled in the same period – perhaps an impulse buy as customers waited at the checkouts.

As planned, there were productivity gains too. Sainsbury's introduced a new time-saving method of pre-packing individual items on special trays, 'outers', surrounded by shrink-wrapped polythene. The outers could be readily slotted into the gondola shelves, and this successful labour-saving device was soon copied by competitors. Sainsbury's had been able to develop the technique because of its control of own-label lines. Helped by such innovations, there was now a marked difference between the cost of labour relative to turnover in the larger, modern stores and that in the older service branches. This reinforced the directors' determination to step up the company's store-conversion and development programme.

Sainsbury's truly did have something momentous to celebrate in their centenary year. Nineteen branches were opened in 1969, the largest number for one year in the company's 100-year history. A new supermarket in Balham High Road became Sainsbury's hundredth self-service outlet, and the propitious combination with the centenary was marked by a visit from Princess Margaret.

The formal centenary events were held on Tuesday 15 April. There were celebration lunches, dinners and dances for staff, a party for the company's pensioners, and a huge centenary banquet held at the Savoy Hotel attended by suppliers, leading figures in the trade and foreign and civic dignitaries. The centenary motif was a four-candle logo, representing the four generations. The Sainsburys did not forget their loyal customers; more than a million slices of birthday cake were handed out in the branches. An illustrated history entitled *JS 100* was published as a record of the company's achievements, and the Sainsburys announced that it would entrust £250,000 (just under £3 million at 2005 prices) for the advancement of research in food science over the next ten years.

The year-end results for 1969 showed that during the 1960s Sainsbury's sales had tripled and profits had doubled in real terms. Only the Co-op and the independent sector as a whole were selling more food than Sainsbury's, an astonishing achievement considering that only 20 per cent of the population lived within reach of a Sainsbury's store. The Sainsbury's chain comprised 82 supermarkets and a total of 162 other outlets, of which 122 were counter-service shops, and 40 were self-service outlets smaller than 4,000 square feet or partial self-service branches. The supermarkets were responsible for about 72 per cent of total sales. At the same time Sainsbury's were able to offer a range of more than 4,000 lines in their largest supermarkets as against 2,500 ten years before. The new supermarkets had grown significantly; the average selling area in 1969 was more than 8,000 square feet, a figure no doubt boosted by the opening of the new branch in Croydon's Whitgift Shopping Centre. This had some 16,500 square feet of sales area and was a spectacular success from the day it opened. Colin Harvey was there as a deputy manager and remembers: 'No matter what we put on the shelves it sold. We just couldn't keep the shelves filled.'

On 12 June 1969, when the centenary partying was done but the glow of success remained, Robert Sainsbury retired and JD stepped into the ring as the company's new chairman.

Chapter 7

THE CHAIRMAN
1969–1972

WITH ALL THE ENERGY of the new broom, JD set about developing Sainsbury's strengths in an increasingly competitive market. In this mission he was supported by his brother, Simon, who took over as deputy chairman, and a board which for the first time in the company's 100-year history comprised as many non-family as family members.

In March 1969, there were three appointments to the board: Roy Griffiths, Joe Barnes and Peter Snow, who was the first branch manager in the company ever to be appointed a director. Griffiths, who had joined the company in 1968 to assist Simon in his personnel role, now became a director in charge of personnel and administration. He had been headhunted from his former position as director of personnel and legal advisor at the American company, Monsanto Chemicals; his skills as a thinker, negotiator and communicator were quickly noted. Griffiths would be a major architect behind the future success of the company. In 1969, both he and Gurth Hoyer Millar represented a new strain of professional managers who had not grown up in the firm. The board was strengthened by these changes, its members reflecting true diversity of background and talent.

An important call on the new board's attention was the need to build profits to support the company's expansion, and so to develop the company as the best in its field. Although Sainsbury's profits had doubled during the 1960s, profit margins were relatively low: in 1969, the figure was 2.7 per cent, about the yearly average for the whole of the 1960s, whereas the average for the top 20 food multiples was about 3.5 per cent in that year. The entire food-retail sector operated on relatively low profit margins, but Sainsbury's had long accepted that this was a high-turnover, low-profit business. Moreover, Sainsbury's directors had always taken the long-term view where profits were concerned: 100 years of successful trade had proved that provided they focused sufficiently on customer needs, profits would follow.

An improvement in margins was a strategic objective to consolidate the company's strengths and ensure the continuation of store expansion without borrowing: the development programme was funded almost entirely out of profits. The older counter-service shops that could not be converted to self-service stores provided additional cash when they were sold; this usually happened when a new supermarket could replace them serving the same population. Occasionally, a supermarket was located suitably to enable the closure of two or three counter-service shops in the area.

The key to improving productivity and making other efficiencies was selling increased volumes, building larger, modern stores and continuing to develop the range and quality of products for sale. From the moment the fourth generation took the baton, the store-development programme therefore received its full attention. In an interview in *Campaign* in September 1969, JD said: 'Our plans are to build stores far bigger than we have ever built before . . . [although] our policy is to expand our business only at the rate at which we can maintain our standards. This means that the whole programme of staff training, of the purchasing of quality goods, has to be scaled up in a planned way.'

Behind this measured statement there remained, of course, JD's unremitting drive to make Sainsbury's 'the best'. Pursuing these objectives required considerable thought to what customers needed and expected, and also to how Sainsbury's developed its offer. In the first new style of annual report for 1970, in which JD provided Sainsbury's first-ever written account of the company's progress, he commented: 'Our present policy is to try and provide our customers with true one-stop shopping but not to diversify into what are sometimes described as discount stores or a supermarket-type department store.' What 'one-stop shopping' meant here was the development of the best possible choice under one roof of high-quality, best-value food and basic household items to meet the weekly shopping needs of customers.

By this year, a more mixed offer of food and other products was already emerging in competitor stores: Tesco with its early attempts at a DIY and clothing range; Asda with its increasingly large discount-style 'variety' stores in the north of the country. Most supermarkets with the space to experiment were diversifying, or experimenting with range in some form or other. But Sainsbury's was determined to stick to what it understood and did best, which was predominantly a growing range of food. It just needed the supermarket space to sell its food, which meant continual scouting, planning applications, frustrations and sometimes compromises in what it was possible to build. Among the company's other glaring needs was to make the shopping experience more comfortable. Some of the older self-service stores cried out for wider aisles and more checkouts.

Of course, what the one-stop shopper wanted above all else was ample and easy car-parking space. Unfortunately, only a third of Sainsbury's supermarkets in 1970 had what the company at the time considered sufficient car-parking space – although even this would soon be inadequate as car shopping steadily increased. The local planning authorities still suffered from occluded vision about facilities for more cars; many appeared to believe that cars were a luxury item and therefore the province of the wealthy. The addition of seven million family vehicles on the roads in the 1960s – a high proportion of which were in the wealthier southern part of the country – failed to convince many planners that this had changed, and would totally alter the townscapes of the near future.

JD and Timothy Sainsbury were well rehearsed in the constraints exercised by planners. Quite apart from the time delays, the drudgery of having to deal with different bureaucratic styles of application process in each planning authority added to the general frustration. In 1969 – a year of optimism and ebullience about the future, the height of the swinging sixties, when Armstrong and Aldrin landed on the moon, and just as the miniskirt was starting to give way to hot pants on British high streets – Timothy made a speech to the Royal Institute of Chartered Surveyors that illustrates how little planning attitudes had shifted in that decade: 'In this country,' he said, 'we are very backward in providing information which would enable planners and retailers alike to make better decisions, both as to the siting of shops and to their size and number . . . We have a planning system which is designed to prevent bad building; unfortunately it also acts as a deterrent to imagination and to design and innovation.'

In a speech on 'How the grocery store is likely to develop' at the Marketing Society annual conference in October 1970, JD argued strongly for the development of regional centres or shopping complexes, 'serving a large area and designed for the car shopper, with as comprehensive a range of large and small shops, department stores and supermarkets as most important high streets'. He envisaged edge-of-town shopping districts which had sufficient ground-level car parks and amenities for consumers such as play areas for children, self-service restaurants, places for customers to relax and cloakrooms where people could leave shopping baskets and parcels. He felt that the UK was thoroughly backward in its approach to developing such schemes, and said, 'Planners are talking about them, but the trouble is they usually talk for seven or eight years and more before anything happens. You think I'm exaggerating, but the development of a shopping centre at Brent Cross in North London was first mooted nine years ago and they haven't started building yet.'

He went on to report that on the Continent, modern shopping centres were far more advanced, particularly in France. JD had long been interested in the phenomenon of French hypermarkets, which were mostly successful because the supermarket revolution had not happened in France. French retailing had leapfrogged from traditional food outlets in the towns and villages to the abundant modern hypermarkets established on land that was far more readily available than in the UK. And the hypermarkets had completely different distribution arrangements, avoiding central depots and ordering in sufficient volume to justify direct deliveries from suppliers. The British were just getting used to the idea of the real convenience of large modern supermarkets, whereas in France Carrefour's hypermarkets were leading examples of the enormous continental one-stop shops. These hypermarkets could be anything up to ten times larger than a typical British supermarket, and would carry a vast range of household and garden goods as well as food and drink. And Carrefour would soon start exporting its brand to the UK.

Part of the planners' resistance to building on commercial land on the fringes of towns and cities was the fear that town centres would become vacuums devoid of shops, or even derelict in the way that was being reported at this stage in parts of the US. But the retailers, including JD, argued the need to provide areas where one-stop shopping by car could be sensibly offered, mainly for food but with perhaps a few other specialist items that constituted a weekly bulk-buy. Meanwhile, the overcrowded town centres would be a more pleasant location for all other shopping, browsing and community needs. This debate continued for many years.

In an attempt to appeal to planners, Sainsbury's organised a special two-day seminar at St John's College, Cambridge, in September 1972, on the topic of 'Retail store location in the 1970s'. This was chaired by Professor Peter Hall of Reading University, and the speakers included JD, Timothy Sainsbury and John Alpass of the Copenhagen Institute of Centre Planning. As part of his presentation, Timothy Sainsbury showed the assembled audience of local-authority planners a short film, one scene of which showed an elderly disabled woman struggling down some stairs in a multi-storey car park where lifts were installed only at landings between the floors of the car park. The sight of this caused some laughter, which later drew a fierce rebuff from Peter Hall who told the audience that they should be ashamed of themselves as they were responsible for the sort of difficulties that the film was highlighting. Kelsey van Musschenbroek of the *Financial Times* reported his reaction to the laughter also; he wrote that it was 'a vivid indication of a lack of identification with the needs of the consumer'.

JD and the buyers at Sainsbury's had good reason to consider themselves closer to the consumer pulse than town planners. The social and cultural changes of the previous ten years had transformed shoppers' expectations. A new generation of customers was accustomed to an ever-growing range and choice. Farming had undergone a revolution in post-war Britain, improving production of cereal crops in a bid for greater self-sufficiency, and leading supermarket chains had developed more direct links to suppliers. Sainsbury's was a past master at this.

For the first time, Sainsbury's offered fruit and vegetables out of season, such as salad items grown in Spain in February, March and April. Sainsbury's was among the leaders to experiment with this range. At the beginning of the decade, the avocado was still considered exotic, although it became a staple in many households within just a few years. There was no end to the potential; in the early 1970s Sainsbury's introduced courgettes, globe artichokes, aubergines and peppers to curious buyers. Some customers were not pleased. One elderly gentleman is reported to have returned some mange-tout peas on the grounds that 'once you've podded them there's nothing left'. Exotic fruits were added to the list, including pomegranates and passion fruit. Adopting an American retailing technique, from the early 1970s onwards the fruit and vegetable departments provided a bright and plentiful welcome close to the entrances of the stores. Their bold displays of oranges, grapefruits and other fruit combined the sense of an abundant street market with the contained efficiency of the modern supermarket. Beyond the 'produce' range, the extending lines of non-perishables also demanded substantially more sales space. But such space was either unavailable or scarcely affordable in the town-centre sites, which was why there was such pent-up demand now for developing in edge-of-town areas.

While responding to this perceived demand for more products and greater choice, few opportunities were missed to demonstrate Sainsbury's wider responsibilities. If there was any matter of local or national importance that affected the interests of customers, Sainbury's would position itself as a source of information, advice or education. The decimalisation of the currency illustrates this.

For most of 1970 and the beginning of 1971, decimalisation, which occurred on 15 February 1971, caused general concern. The government saturated television and radio with a series of public information broadcasts complete with till-clashing ditties and shop-assistant voice-overs: 'That'll be 31 and a half new p, and a half makes 32 . . .' People sung these lines in their sleep.

Sainsbury's sought to make the transition to decimalisation as easy as possible for both staff and customers. A special training shop was set up at 9–11 London Road, Croydon, which had been closed following the opening of the large new store in the Whitgift Centre. The shop was reopened and laid out to provide a modern self-service area on one side and counter service on the other. Between 10 February and 27 November 1970 both parts traded in decimal currency but using plastic coins – and over 1,500 members of staff were trained to use the new money. Groups such as the Townswomen's Guild and Women's Institute were also invited to gain first-hand experience of the new currency, and were shown a purpose-made film called 'Quick Change' presented by television cook Zena Skinner. The last day of the demonstration was for pensioners, who were each given a pound to spend in the store and helped in their shopping by local schoolgirls.

To allay customers' fears that prices would be rounded up on the day of conversion, Sainsbury's made it clear that its policy was to round down when an exact equivalent price could not be achieved. Every store carried a massive conversion board demonstrating that prices remained the same or lower than before. Come the day, the transition to decimal currency went so smoothly that JD referred to it as 'the biggest non-event of the year'. Perhaps of more moment, if only in nostalgic terms, the historic 9–11 Croydon branch was closed down and sold after the demonstration period.

Another example of tuning in to customer's needs, this time of a local kind, was the opening of the Folkestone branch in 1970. This was advertised in the port as *une ouverture à ne pas manquer* (an opening not to be missed). Establishing its own cross-channel shopping style, Sainsbury's accepted French, Belgian and even American currency in this branch. Mike O'Conner, head of the Supermarket Institute of America, was visiting England and attended the opening with his friend, JD. The American could not believe the contrast in styles between his 'stateside' experience of store openings, complete with brass bands and majorettes, and Sainsbury's thoroughly British approach. O'Conner arrived about 20 minutes before the designated opening time to find no celebrity and precious little brouhaha, only a substantial queue of eager but orderly customers waiting to do their shopping.

Although there was no such term in the early 1970s, another illustration of Sainsbury's own style of 'customer-relations management' was the publicity department's initiative to hire five women, all home economists, to act as 'counsellors' in each of the company's five regional areas. Their job was to carry Sainsbury's messages direct to regionally based consumers and opinion-influencing groups, whether the Women's Institute or the then flourishing Young Conservatives. They gave presentations about Sainsbury's trading approach and received feedback about new products, facilities and the contents of new supermarkets.

Such feedback was always useful when testing customer reactions to new retailing ideas. In 1971, Sainsbury's made the bold move of reintroducing an element of personal service through delicatessen counters in new supermarkets at North Cheam and Wandsworth. The latter was part of the new Arndale Shopping Centre, which provided unusually well for car shoppers; it had 16,350 square feet of sales area close to under-cover parking with

1,500 spaces. In the delicatessen, specially trained staff provided advice and service, selling about 80 products – pâtés, salamis, olives, continental sausages as well as pastries and baked goods. The most expensive item was best smoked Scotch salmon at 60p a quarter-pound.

JD also realised that his customers were becoming more educated about and interested in their food, and that Sainsbury's was in a good position to encourage this further. In 1972, ahead of any statutory requirement to do so, Sainsbury's made it policy to declare the ingredients of all own-label products and to include clear statements of weights and descriptions of contents. The company also introduced unit-pricing – for example, by printing the price per pound on the package and therefore giving customers ready information with which to compare the cost of different sizes of product. This was another idea imported by JD after a visit to the US.

The collection of information about the markets that the stores served was another increasingly important means of deepening the relationship Sainsbury's had with its customers. JD used plenty of intuition and practical observation in his trading decisions, but he was never far from appropriate market information. The statistics department, which had been the long-term responsibility of Bernard Ramm, was responsible for gathering a range of demographic and other data. In the 1960s, this would have included some reasonable idea of the wealth profile of local populations and who the effective competition were, how they were doing and, importantly, what they were doing. This knowledge was mostly used to support decisions about the siting of new stores. Sainsbury's was determined to develop an even more sophisticated source of in-house information to provide accurate details about the market potential of each new location. More thorough analysis would be useful, including, for example, data about the number of refrigerators bought in various regions of the country, or how many cars; and not only what competition was there already but who else was interested in the area.

In October 1971, Sainsbury's duly appointed Ivor Hunt as its new chief statistician. His role was to bring sales forecasting, site analysis and the company's general inforamation-gathering machinery into the new decade and beyond. Bernard Ramm continued as a board director with overall responsibilities for the company's computerisation. As he augumented the scope of his department, Hunt not only provided analyses to support decisions about prospective sites for development, but assembled wide-ranging and probing information about Sainsbury's competitors. The thoroughness of this department's market analysis reflected the increasing professionalism that characterised the company as it progressed.

Despite the rapidly growing opportunities, the political and economic climate of the early 1970s presented the entire retail sector with plenty to worry about, and food retailing was among the hardest hit. Inflationary pressure grew and would remain a problem until the last years of the 1970s. The annual rate of inflation in food prices rose from 6.7 per cent in 1970, to 11.5 per cent in 1971, after which the curve steepened at an alarming rate. Wages rose rapidly, at times exceeding food inflation and driving the spiral upwards. The government's attempts at controlling inflation were heavy-handed from the start, including a statutory freeze on prices in late 1971. As a snapshot of worse to come, by 1974 inflation measured 18.4 per cent, and in July 1975 it peaked at 29 per cent. In 1973, the government established the Price Commission and reintroduced price controls, while also limiting the gross margin that retailers were allowed to make on the sale of most foodstuffs.

Industrial unrest was also hitting all sectors that had a unionised workforce. Gurth Hoyer Millar, director of Sainsbury's distribution, had inherited a very difficult situation in the depots. When the workforces relocated from Blackfriars to Basingstoke, Buntingford, Hoddesdon and Charlton in the 1960s, increasingly militant unions had also relocated. Sainsbury's management had dealt with them weakly. At least when the main depot workforce had been based at Blackfriars there had been daily contact between headquarters and depot management. But after the new regional depots opened, communications between senior management and staff in the depots became more difficult and strained. When the unions felt they had a grievance, they began to circumvent local depot managers and communicate directly with senior managers at Blackfriars, who were expected to intervene in disputes about which they had little adequate knowledge or information. Regional depot managers were thus placed in an invidious position, and found it difficult to control their workforces while the union shop stewards gradually became more powerful.

As a result, some of the improvements to work practices and other benefits that the company had sought through decentralisation were not achieved. For example, one of the benefits of the Basingstoke site had been its proximity to the M3, which was being planned at the time the site was acquired. But when the motorway was finally opened in 1973, the drivers refused to use it. Unions argued that because the journey times to the stores would be quicker, their members would lose money as a result of the way their pay was negotiated. The company was forced to back down, keeping pay rates and running times to the stores the same as they had been before the motorway opened.

Union solidarity also meant that a dispute in one depot had an almost immediate ricocheting effect across the distribution system. Depot managers struggled with a complex system of bonuses and incentives to keep the deliveries going. But when any of the board members attempted to solve labour disputes, they often discovered they lacked the experience to deal with them adequately, however good their intentions. For example, in the early 1970s, during one dispute at Haverhill Meat Products, which continued as a successful meat-processing subsidiary, Simon Sainsbury visited the plant personally to try to help resolve the problem. When he entered the cutting hall he was confronted by 300 angry butchers who began banging their cleavers on the tables, forcing a quick retreat and convincing Simon that he should avoid personal involvement in such disputes if at all possible.

Yet throughout the first years of the 1970s, the number of Sainsbury's branches grew, the range of products broadened and confidence in business strategy and trading principles was absolute. In March 1972, Sainsbury's reported a particularly successful year: 14 new stores opened with an average selling area of 12,500 square feet, so that the company now had more than 1.26 million square feet of sales area. Turnover was up by 18.4 per cent on the previous year, and the net profit margin, at 3.84 per cent, was above the 3 per cent mark for the first time in more than a decade. And Sainsbury's was running its own race in the volumes that it could sell per square foot, outperforming its nearest rival by at least 40 per cent. Eighty-five per cent of the company's turnover now came from supermarkets, and the new or extended ones among them had been entirely responsible for the company's growth. Conversely, there was a continuing decline in the sales achived in the older self-service, partial self-service and counter-service stores.

In his annual report for 1972, JD welcomed the government's decision to halve selective employment tax during the preceding year; Sainsbury's were passing the savings made on to customers in the form of lower prices – or relatively lower, given inflationary trends. Along with economies of scale achieved through the larger sales area, the company's success owed to reductions in retail operating expenses as a ratio of its turnover. Contributing to this, JD emphasised the importance of new methods of handling goods within supermarkets and, above all, the introduction of a radical new system of supply and stock control: Ned Harwell's work in developing an innovative branch-ordering system, based on electronic data, was finally bearing fruit.

The product of Harwell's development work over nearly three years was the Store Labour Inventory Management (SLIM) system, better known simply as 'branch ordering'. This was introduced to all branches during 1971 and 1972. The system relied on a new piece of equipment in each store called the Plessey Data Capture unit, an electronic machine which could be wheeled around the store to record the amount of non-perishable stock – which now represented the majority of the Sainsbury's range. The system was a precursor of today's supply and distribution technology, and represented a sea change in industry practice. Bar codes, each identifying specific products, were attached to shelves and were read by a light pen. The single operator, normally working on an early evening shift, entered the number of cases required for delivery, and the information was recorded on magnetic tape inside the data capture unit. Once all the bar codes were read, the operator plugged the unit into a transmitter attached to a telephone line at the back of the store, and his or her work was done. When they were ready, staff at Blackfriars called the line, and the complete order was automatically transmitted. The central computer system then produced 'debit notes' (warehouse picking lists) which were sent to the warehouse in the early hours of the morning. Each order was assembled and delivered to the branch before 5 pm the next day, completing the cycle within 24 hours.

As if saluting the good financial year, a mighty supermarket with

25,450 square feet of sales area was opened on 25 April 1972 at Bretton, near the old city of Peterborough. This was Sainsbury's prototype edge-of-town supermarket, although the town it edged was still largely to be built, and there were sceptics within the retail industry who considered that both its size and location might be a mistake. Bretton was one of four new townships being built to create the new City of Greater Peterborough. In time there would be some 30,000 residents in the immediate area, but when the store was built there were few shoppers in the vicinity. The success of this store, believed to be the largest dedicated food store in the UK, depended on car shoppers, and a 600-space car park was built to accommodate them. A massive publicity campaign employing signs, local press and bus adverts was mounted to generate awareness before the launch. As a result, huge numbers arrived on opening day, and local papers reported that there was a mile-long queue to get into the car park on the following Friday evening. The sales space at Bretton was more than enough to take the entire range of Sainsbury's goods, so that unusually large volumes of the most popular lines were represented. Customers were doubtless overwhelmed by gondolas that, for example, sported 24 bottles of Sainsbury's ketchup in a row, each six deep, with other ketchup brands set out above and below in similar phalanxes – and that was just the ketchup.

Thus, in the first three years of JD's chairmanship, to mid-1972, the company's turnover had risen from £166 million to £262 million. Sainsbury's was consolidating its strengths in the affluent south-east, but also extending its territory with supermarkets such as the one at Bretton, and others in Kings Lynn, Norwich and Gloucester, while new stores were under construction in Telford and Taunton. This was a high-voltage start to the fourth generation's leadership of the company, and it was also a reflection of the new chairman's style, characterised by an unusual degree of attention to detail in both the day-to-day running of the business and in its forward planning. This approach permeated senior management. All the board and the departmental directors understood that Sainsbury's took pains to differentiate itself from the rest of the market by setting and ensuring high standards for the long term. Customer good will and the future of the company depended on this.

In order to ensure that growth continued to be planned 'only at the rate at which we can maintain our standards', JD and his leading board members, particularly Roy Griffiths, were also making various changes to the company's management processes and structure. While such reforms were necessary because the company was growing larger and more complex, they would also prepare Sainsbury's for another chapter in its development, as it drew towards flotation as a public limited company.

Chapter 8

GOING PUBLIC
1972–1973

THE POSSIBILITY of floating Sainsbury's on the stock market had been occasionally discussed within the family since the end of the 1960s, at which point the idea was low on the list of priorities. Sainsbury's was doing well as a private company; no one questioned its management strengths, and the company did not require a war chest of new money from shareholders to sustain its programme of growth.

In the early 1970s, 3 per cent of the company's shares had been placed with institutions on the stock market simply to establish a value of the family's shares for tax purposes. The only other 'public' shareholding related to the property subsidiary, J. Sainsbury Property Ltd, was set up to buy or lease the sites for the stores; the ordinary shares of this company were wholly owned by the main business, but its preference and debenture stock were owned outside the family, and had raised about £9 million by 1970. This money contributed to the store-expansion programme.

Then, gradually, the prospect of a flotation started to have more attraction. The family considered that it meant little to lose and much to gain. They would realise some of their paper wealth and could offer a generous proportion of the shares to the staff. By making shares available to private investors, customers – if they bought shares – could also benefit from the success of the enterprise to which they were contributing. The board therefore decided to float the company, but only when the time was right.

Simon Sainsbury, who played a central role in the financial governance of the business as it approached flotation, remembers that he and his brothers and David Sainsbury 'all felt the same, all wanted to share some of the good times with staff and customers, recognising that it would also be good for business and good for motivation'. Mr Alan was certainly won over by the idea of sharing the bounty in this way, although his initial reaction, as the

company's president, had been, 'What do we need to do this for?' JD
was above all determined that in the event of going public it should
never be in question that the family would continue to retain control, or that their style of leadership and trading principles would be
jeopardised.

In order for Sainsbury's to go public, certain reforms were
needed to meet the protocols required of a public limited company,
such as more transparent information flows and greater streamlining of operations at departmental level. But such reforms – mostly
of the kind that JD had already outlined to senior management
back in 1967 – were necessary at this stage of the company's growth
whether it floated or not. For example, Roy Griffiths began to introduce a number of internal changes to the company's management
organisation. Its extremely hierarchical structure had previously
worked well when trading decisions could all be taken centrally and
needed to be implemented quickly and without question, but it was
less effective for a company of Sainsbury's rapidly growing size – it
now had more than 23,000 employees – which was determined to
grow much larger still. It was known throughout the food trade that
Sainsbury's was run with a kind of military precision, and indeed
had recruited former military personnel for certain supervisory
roles, particularly in the depots. But now that the fourth generation
were in harness, this style of management was anachronistic, and
increasingly disliked. Angus Clark, who joined the firm in 1966 and
was later one of the company's directors, has likened the Sainsbury's of the 1960s to 'an effective army. Give them executive
instruction and they'd do it – but don't ask them to think too much.
That was particularly the case when all the store managers were
selected from the shop floor.'

Since becoming personnel director, Griffiths had dedicated
much of his time to modernising this structure. He pushed for the
increased recruitment of graduates who could be fast-streamed
into both head-office and store-management jobs; he introduced
performance measures, work analysis, job descriptions, job-grading
systems, management-appraisal schemes and procedures which
are common today but were not in vogue during the first half of
the 1970s. More people with outside management experience were
sought to boost the company's programme of internal development
and promotion. The original training centre at Blackfriars was
closed at the end of 1972 and replaced by five regional training

centres; in-store facilities for store-specific training were established, for example cashier training and trade skills, particularly for perishables. A new management centre was also set up at Dulwich, where managers could be trained in the techniques and skills required to run a large, complex organisation.

To encourage more initiative among store managers, significant energy went into better communication, at this level, about company objectives and plans. The biennial retail managers' conference became a true focus for this. This was the company's very own 'Brighton conference'. In 1972, for example, it involved 165 supermarket managers, board directors, area and district managers, and a number of office departmental managers. JD addressed the firm about the company's progress and future plans; Griffiths led a workshop on personnel matters; Peter Snow led another on branch-productivity issues. The workshops encouraged frank, uninhibited discussion and a valuable exchange of ideas.

Griffiths also focused attention on decision-making machinery at the apex of the company. Within the executive board a system of committees, such as the Directors' Trading Committee which dealt with trading developments and strategy, and the Directors' Branch Committee which handled the operation of the branches, had for some time been in operation as a means of dividing decision-making responsibilities. In order to cope with the growing demands of the business, Griffiths, with JD's support, sought to take the delegation of board-level decisions one step further, through the creation of new directors' committees that were established progressively through the 1970s.

Part of Griffiths's skill in personnel and, later, in administrative roles within the company, was his pragmatism and sensitivity to the management of change. He understood that there were advantages in the paternalistic style emanating from the top of the company. It was important, therefore, to maintain this character while professionalising management structures lower down. Like JD, he never lost sight of the company's primary aims, and made sure that the procedures he introduced from the top of the company down were the most efficient in terms of serving the customer, guaranteeing high quality and offering value for money.

Through the offices of Bernard Ramm, and subsequently Ivor Hunt, Sainsbury's was becoming a repository of increasingly detailed management information – this was a resource without equal in most other companies, even at the beginning of the 1970s. But this information, or relevant parts of it, had not been widely shared down the line. Another of Griffiths's reforms was therefore aimed at creating an improved means of disseminating information downwards. He made sure that appropriate information was made more generally available to the middle managers who needed it. The company started to produce divisional budgets, budgetary control systems, improved management accounts and more accurate sales data. As a result of Griffiths's new systems, the kind of criticism voiced by Angus Clark, shocked by the lack of budgetary and other information, no longer applied. Visitors to the company were often truly impressed by the breadth and depth of professional support available to all levels of managers.

Another significant change was the introduction in 1971 of a new tier of top management, known as 'departmental directors'. They were the brainchild of JD, devised on a flight to the US. It would be the responsibility of this new level of senior management to oversee the buying, set prices, ensure the quality of the products sold and be accountable for marketing and innovation in their departments. As JD put it, 'the departmental directors were introduced to ensure we had attention to trading detail at a senior level of management.'

It was important that there was a division of responsibility between a departmental director and his buyers whose job it was to purchase goods for that department. Buyers would focus on sourcing the best-quality products while the departmental directors ensured that these were offered to customers at truly competitive prices. JD's thinking was that if buyers were able to influence unduly the selling price of the goods that they bought, there was potential for complacency and the covering up of buying mistakes. He was determined that if there were such mistakes, the customers should not have to pay for them through higher prices. This new tier of management was therefore a control mechanism that underpinned the company tradition of offering the best possible value for customers. This was especially needed as the business grew larger and more complex. The new level of directors also had a beneficial effect on the ever-important relationship between the company and its suppliers, who now felt they were being appropriately respected by having personal and frequent communication with a Sainsbury's director. Over time, departmental directors were introduced across all areas of the business as well as the buying departments.

The streamlining and modernising of the company's operations necessitated one particularly difficult decision – the closure of the Blackfriars Factory. Sainsbury's had manufactured its own pies and sausages since its very early years, but, by the late 1960s, the demand for increasing volumes had led to the need to source supplies from other manufacturers – a policy that had not gone down well with James Sainsbury. Buyers had consequently learned that products of the standard specified by Sainsbury's could be purchased elsewhere. This had not been the case when the factory was first built in 1936 and for many years afterwards when Sainsbury's pies and sausages were considered the best available. But since the closure of the Blackfriars depot operation, the factory was no longer ideally located, and continual industrial-relations problems, including several strikes, only served to raise the factory's profile as a liability. Its closure, with the prospect of making many of the 2,000 workers redundant, would be painful, but it was clear that the factory no longer served the company's needs.

Staff had been warned about the impending decision to close as early as 1968, but the formal announcement was not made until 1971. It fell to Joe Barnes to handle the negotiations and organise the winding down of the operation. Workers were offered the opportunity of transferring to Haverhill Meat Products but few took up the offer, partly because they did not wish to move from their home communities, but also because they would have had to transfer to a different union and were persuaded by their existing unions against such a course. The factory finally closed in September 1972 at a cost of about £1 million in redundancy money. As a result of the closure and significant improvements in labour productivity in the stores, for the first time in the post-war years the number of Sainsbury's workforce fell, from nearly 24,000 full-time equivalent employees in 1972 to a little over 21,000 at the year-end reported in March 1974.

Flotation was increasingly discussed by directors during 1972, and it was decided that the chain of management below board level should be given early advanced notification of the change in the company's status. The managers were called to a special meeting held at Dulwich in June that year. Ron Yeates was a manager at

Northampton branch at the time, and describes the central moment of the event:

> It was strawberry time when we were called to Dulwich – ostensibly for a review meeting. We all turned up – district managers, branch managers, everyone at grade 12 and above. There were strawberries and cream and JD got up on his podium and announced that the company was going public. He explained to us what this meant and told us that each of the managers there would be given shares. People walked out on air. On air. They were being given a stake in the company. This was one of the defining moments in Sainsbury's history. I've still got those shares; they're worth a tremendous amount today. It really demonstrated the company's commitment to us; it was a fulfilment of all those personnel policies that had been laid down in the 1930s and 1940s by earlier generations of the Sainsbury family.

In public, Sainsbury's approach was cautious. In October 1972, there was a formal, public announcement that the company was 'considering' flotation on the stock market 'in the latter part of 1973'. Then in his March 1973 annual report, JD underlined a key reason for flotation: 'It is no longer appropriate for the ownership of the company to be almost wholly confined to the Founders' family.' Soon afterwards, a memorandum was circulated to all the staff to assure them that the flotation would not affect the company's trading principles or style of management. The memorandum also promised that this was going to be an opportunity for staff to share in the company's future success by owning shares. When the company floated a certain number of shares would be specifically reserved for the staff.

The solid support and high morale among Sainsbury's managers permeated down through the company's workforces in the stores. Although the closure of the factory had been a bitter pill for the unions to swallow, labour relations in the depots were also reasonably stable. As the director in charge of depot operations, Gurth Hoyer Millar was optimistic about a cost-improvement programme that depot management and the unions – heavily represented by both USDAW and TGWU – were now cooperating in taking forward. As Roy Griffiths then wrote in the *JS Journal*, labour-relations problems could always be overemphasised, 'since any company that has to get £1,000,000 of goods into the shops every day naturally lives on a knife edge'.

Simon Sainsbury was not only in charge of all the financial details of the flotation but also largely responsible for the communications exercise, which involved informing and reassuring staff about it. In the same issue of the *JS Journal* he said: 'Life will go on as before and the actual occurrence of going public will be a nine-days wonder that will soon be forgotten.' He also noted that what he called the 'commercial and personal psychological barriers' had all been overcome in preparation for flotation: in particular, the regional depot system was fully up and running and the company's centenary was well out of the way.

At this critical juncture, were the conditions in the trade ideal for such a change in the company's status? On the one hand, the March 1973 accounts offered more than reasonable promise that the business was strong. The average supermarket sales area had increased by 45 per cent from 6,680 square feet in 1969 to 9,690 square feet at the year-end in 1973, during which time sales per square feet had remained relatively static at around £4. This represented a lower taking per square foot in real terms, but only because of Sainsbury's policy of providing wider aisles and thus more shopping space for customers in the new stores. The figure still far outstripped any competitor's achievement. And for any prospective shareholder who might criticise Sainsbury's for clinging to the southern half of England, the annual report disclosed that sites had already been obtained for large new stores in Doncaster and Sheffield, while other sites in the north were being sought. The report also announced the development, in the coming year, of at least 16 more stores and three major extensions, which would generate a net expansion of some 300,000 square feet.

But there were some counterbalancing arguments. Trading conditions at this time were far from ideal. Between early 1972 and early 1974, the price of staple food commodities went through the roof. The most serious market rises were wheat, rice and beef, which went up by 160, 290 and 90 per cent respectively. The situation was further complicated by the falling value of the pound following its flotation on 23 June 1972, Britain's dependence on foreign food imports, and government subsidies on staple foods like bread, milk and butter. Increases in national purchasing power caused by dramatic wage rises and inflation had not kept up with food prices. A national building strike had already inhibited the company's development plans, so that at least three new stores were prevented from being opened in 1972–3, while several others were delayed.

Meanwhile, the battle with the planners, which had to be won for the company to achieve its long-term goals, remained a constant source of friction. A year after the opening of Sainsbury's first major edge-of-town supermarket at Bretton, a review of its operations showed the new store to be reasonably if not spectacularly success-ful. But it was now proving difficult to find further edge-of-town sites; when they were located, planners were not easily persuaded to accept their proposed development. Inevitably there were compromises, and some Sainsbury's branches continued to be extended or developed in city-centre locations where the increasing number of car shoppers were mostly dependent on the multi-storey car parks built by the local authorities. In his annual report in 1973, JD was typically acerbic about the planners' resistance to improv-ing parking facilities:

> It is remarkable how uninterested some local authorities are in making life easier for the shopping public. We and our competi-tors have even experienced occasions when local authorities have attempted to prohibit customers using trolleys to take goods to their cars, demonstrating a lack of sympathy or under-standing of the ordinary housewife who, if shopping for the family, has the task of getting home about 56 lbs of goods per week from a supermarket.

The very oldest supermarkets continued to suffer serious over-crowding and were not able to offer anything like the full range of goods. Some of these stores recorded sales of £5 or more per square foot per week, which actually indicated uncomfortable shopping conditions rather than successful trading. These shops were losing custom to competitors, and the rise in their takings was not keeping pace with inflation. At the bottom of the convenience league only 26 counter-service shops remained in March 1973, most with a loyal local following but representing an antiquated image of the com-pany.

Sainsbury's most closely watched competitors were Asda with its superstores and the new hypermarkets set up by Carrefour. Asda's food sales were growing substantially, and as the company extended its territory southwards it was starting to present strong competition to Sainsbury's supermarkets in the West Midlands. JD believed Asda was the nearest that the UK had to continental hypermarkets – apart from Carrefour. Asda had enormous stores in comparison with any other supermarket chain, with between 40,000 and 100,000 square feet of sales space. With far fewer outlets than Sainsbury's, it had almost exactly the same amount of sales space – some 1.3 million square feet in total – and offered a large range of products, including food which was sold at significantly cheaper prices than at Sainsbury's. Carrefour's success was less easy to judge. The French hypermarket had only one outlet at this stage, in South Wales, although it was planning to build a large new store in Telford, right next to a new Sainsbury's store proposed to open there at the same time.

As Sainsbury's prepared for flotation, it was clear that its competitive success depended on its larger modern stores, which not only continued to trade vigorously but were designed to respond to customers' changing buying habits. By 1973, consumers were spending significant amounts of their disposable incomes on durables such as cars, washing machines, freezers and television sets, and relatively less on food. The statistics department could show the figures. But housewives were reacting to rapid food-price rises by looking for cheaper alternatives. They sought greater economy by buying bigger packs and more frozen goods. Here Sainsbury's large supermarkets could accommodate their wishes. The company recorded significant increases in the sale of goods for home freezing. Sales of fruit and vegetables, fresh chilled turkeys and wines and spirits were also increasing. By now, in mid-1973, more than 70 per cent of Sainsbury's supermarkets had managed to obtain off licences.

With over 90 per cent of turnover achieved by the supermarkets, as recorded in March 1973, the directors were confident that Sainsbury's could ride the challenges of the trading environment and the interventions of government. The latest of these involved a price freeze on all foodstuffs except perishables, upon which the Price Commission had imposed gross margin limits. The board remained determined to plan even larger supermarkets to hold the growing range, including some experimentation with textiles and other non-food products, and a wider choice of brands to complement Sainsbury's own. There were challenges for sure, but none of them was insuperable, 'as long as we maintain top quality standards, a friendly helpful service and keep costs under strict control', said JD.

The big day came. On 3 July 1973, Sainsbury's was floated on the London Stock Exchange. Ten million ordinary shares were sold, amounting to 12.4 per cent of total issued shares; 85 per cent of the shares remained in family hands, and several institutions held the remaining 2.6 per cent. As the company had pledged, one million shares were set aside specifically for staff who wished to buy a stake in the company, while customers were made aware of the pink share application forms distributed across the branches.

The response was overwhelming. Sainsbury's was the biggest flotation in terms of capitalisation ever mounted by the London Stock Exchange. Shares were oversubscribed 34 times. Some £495 million in cheques were received for the £14.5 million of shares on offer. The issue price of 145p gave the company an immediate market capitalisation of £117 million, which quickly rose to £132 million once trading started, representing a premium of about 20p per share.

Sainsbury's was one of the first of a series of major flotations in the next few years that specifically targeted small private investors. An institutional investor who tried to buy the whole share issue was duly disappointed. Sainsbury's customers received 43,500 allotments of shares via the pink form applications, of which 24,000 were for just 100 to 200 shares each. Customers went to great lengths to try to ensure they were successful in their bids. One woman wrote a covering letter with her application which read: 'I love Sainsbury's. My mother and I have always shopped with you. She died last year aged 94 and I am 68. I know it won't make any difference to my application, but wish me luck.' Another customer telephoned Blackfriars to say that she had fallen over while shopping and the manager had said that the company would give her preferential treatment in the allocation of shares as a result.

The media were equally excited by the event. The *Daily Express* referred to the 'sale of the century'; the *Daily Mirror* to the 'chance to buy some quality'; *The Times*'s banner read, 'A battlefield as Sainsbury's deals begin'. The national press also heaped praise on what they considered to be a strong fourth-generation family team at the helm of the company. One comment in *The Observer* went:

'Most family businesses are happy to find one man in every generation to carry on the tradition. To have produced four able business managers in the most competitive sector of the retail trade seems to be just another part of the Sainsbury mystique.'

The sale of shares made members of the family very wealthy, but they were also delighted by the boost that flotation gave to morale and motivation from the top to the bottom of the company. For many staff the 'nine-day wonder' that Simon Sainsbury had referred to proved to be a lifelong event; as Ron Yeates has testified, shares issued and saved in the long term made enormous gains. Jim Woods has added his own enthusiastic voice concerning the effect on senior employees' financial security: 'We were now able to own Sainsbury shares. That changed my life entirely ... At my level I was allocated 9,000 shares which soon doubled and then trebled in value.'

Warburg, Sainsbury's advisers for the flotation, had predicted that the take-up of reserved shares among employees would be low, but they were wrong. Almost 5,000 staff subscribed to the offer, applying for more than the one million shares that had been set aside; applications from new staff had to be scaled back, but everyone received something and most got all they applied for. 'Workers in the depots knew more about the daily share prices than I did,' recalls JD. 'I remember visiting Buntingford and found that the latest share price was marked up on the union noticeboard for all to see; more prominent than all those notices about union activity. These workers, or many among them, had a strong vested interest in the success of the company.' The vested interest of 43,500 customers was another valuable bonus. Retired staff were not eligible to apply for the reserved shares, but the family were keen to acknowledge their contribution to the business, and they all received a personal cash gift.

JD now had to take shareholders into account when he reported company progress at annual general meetings, but he was not unduly bothered by the City. According to Barnes, 'The one thing that was perfectly obvious was that the chairman was not going to have the City, the bankers, the analysts, the brokers running the business.' In any case, Simon Sainsbury found that the City was highly supportive of the company throughout the flotation and beyond, and that there was great confidence in the capabilities of the management. JD adds, 'It was well understood throughout the

business that our commitment was first and foremost to the customer. As far as I was concerned that would not change and it
didn't.'

As Simon had predicted, it was indeed 'business as usual' after the
event. With nice timing, no fewer than three new stores opened
before the end of the month of the flotation, at Swindon, Wood
Green and Hitchin. The Swindon branch in the new Brunel Shopping Centre was the company's first in Wiltshire. About 200
shoppers waited for the doors to open on the first day, including
young mothers who were delighted to find special baby carriages
fitted to a number of trolleys. Designed in-house, the baby carriages
were an answer to mothers' fears about a spate of baby-snatching as
well as to the problem of leaving their youngest at home while they
shopped. Having given banner headlines to Sainsbury's flotation,
the media gave almost as much attention to this innovation. Along
with national newspaper coverage there were interviews on the
BBC *Today* programme and *Nationwide* television show. Competitor supermarkets were soon coming up with their own versions.

At the beginning of October 1973, Sainsbury's unveiled its largest
and latest store at another new town, Telford in Shropshire. The
store had almost 26,000 square feet of sales space. The pressure to
open on the planned date of 2 October had been enormous, and
preparations were frantic. Staff scarcely had the time to acquaint
themselves with the geography of the building before the first day of
trading; some goods for sale only arrived on that morning. There
was another cause for apprehension about this particular opening.
The new store was located right next to Carrefour's second British
hypermarket. Both 'superstores' were due to open on the same day,
and would be the first premises in Telford's shopping centre, a construction so new that the roads surrounding it were barely finished,
and the detritus of building work was everywhere to be seen. In
time, Sainsbury's, Carrefour and the other retailers established in
the centre would be serving a population of some 300,000 planned
to live in this new rurally sited conurbation.

When the automatic doors leading onto the generous 1,200-
space car park were switched to 'go' on day one, the usual queues
were notable by their absence. JD was among the welcoming committee who took a walk across the car park, from which vantage
point they discerned a general milling of customers at the opening

of Carrefour, next door. Carrefour sold televisions, hi-fis, refrigerators and items of furniture as well as food, and placed right next door to Sainsbury's the rival company was now offering effective competition as a food retailer too. 'Never mind,' JD comments, 'we had plenty to offer at Telford and business picked up soon enough.'

Like Bretton, the Telford store carried the full Sainsbury's range and a large counter-service delicatessen. A novelty was the company's first in-store bakery, where customers could watch loaves, cakes and pastries being baked virtually before their eyes. The aim of this department was not to sell a single loaf more than an hour old, and they accomplished this by having part-baked bread at the ready. Hardware and kitchenware were added to the standard non-food lines in the store, but by far the greatest innovation was the trial of Sainsbury's own-label clothing. This was a small range of purpose-designed, affordable but good-quality clothes intended for all the family and presented in 'shop within a shop' style in the store. There were about 750 different items in total, taking different colours and sizes into account.

The launch of Sainsbury's own clothing brand in the new large supermarkets seemed right at the time. Customers were mostly women, and all were potential buyers of the new range; it was estimated that these shoppers were far more frequent visitors to Sainsbury's stores than to dedicated clothing stores. But although the clothes continued to sell reasonably well and were offered in several new stores during the next few years, the move into textiles was a relatively short-lived experiment, managed without the same conviction and confidence that Sainsbury's buyers had always applied to the development of traditional lines. Moreover, food and standard non-food lines in Sainsbury's stores always took priority if space was an issue. However popular and successful the supermarkets became, Sainsbury's would not become famous for its fashionwear.

Back at headquarters, as the prices of food commodities and oil not only rose but almost looked as if they were taking flight, and as the government imposed restrictions on the gross margins that food retailers were allowed to make, there was inevitable concern about the effects on the company's progress. JD remained convinced and convincing about long-term prospects, but it would be a little galling to a family as fiercely proud of their business if Sainsbury's first year as a plc were to prove disappointing to the company's new shareholders.

Chapter 9

SURVIVAL OF THE FITTEST
1974–1975

T HE MIDDLE YEARS of the 1970s were a bumpy ride for British industry, and multiple food retailers were forced to negotiate some of the deepest ruts. In 1973, Prime Minister Edward Heath had led Britain into the Common Market, an event which divided opinions among the British population, some of whom erroneously believed that it was the main reason for inflation. Then, following the 1973 Arab-Israeli conflict, oil trebled in price, and a protracted coal-miners' strike in the winter of 1973/4 aggravated the problem, so that households were often reduced to sitting round the table in candlelight. As an energy-saving ploy, the government imposed a three-day week on industry from 1 January 1974. Strikes in all sectors of industry were commonplace, and union muscle was crippling the government's room for manoeuvre. The coal strike also forced the prime minister to call a general election in February of that year, when Harold Wilson's Labour government was returned to power with a wafer-thin majority. Wilson decided to confirm his mandate by calling another election later in 1974 which Labour won by a majority of just three seats.

Sainsbury's progress has to be understood in this political and economic context. Like other food retailers, the company had to contend with the vicissitudes of a global economic downturn, which hindered its ability to source important supplies and, domestically, to fight to maintain its progress in modernising food distribution in the face of continued government intervention. It was perhaps inevitable that as the fourth generation leading the company grew more prominent, and as their responsibilities for the well-being of Sainsbury's staff and shareholders extended, they became more involved in the political fray.

Timothy Sainsbury took the most direct approach by putting himself up as a Conservative candidate. His selection to fight a by-election in November 1973 caught him by surprise, and he was

JD hands out cake to a customer in the Drury Lane store, flanked by Mr RJ (left) and Mr Alan as they celebrate Sainsbury's centenary in 1969

Sainsbury's at the new shopping mall at Poole in Dorset in 1969, described at the time by JD as 'the only really well-designed enclosed shopping centre in Britain'

An operator using the new Plessey electronic branch ordering system introduced in 1972; this enabled products to be delivered to each branch within 24 hours of ordering

Sainsbury's first delicatessen, in the new supermarket opened in the Arndale Centre at Wandsworth in 1971

In the new supermarkets, there were constant improvements in the display
of the range, including the height and capacity of the gondolas

Simon Sainsbury had the main responsibility for the flotation of the company; here he is seen with customers at the opening of a new supermarket at Hemel Hempstead

No. 9–11 London Road, Croydon, the first shop in the nation to use decimal currency; it was employed for training and demonstration a year before formal decimalisation in February 1971. JD is with Jennifer Jenkins, chairman of the Consumer Association and wife of the Chancellor of the Exchequer. She later became the first woman on the Sainsbury's board, in 1982

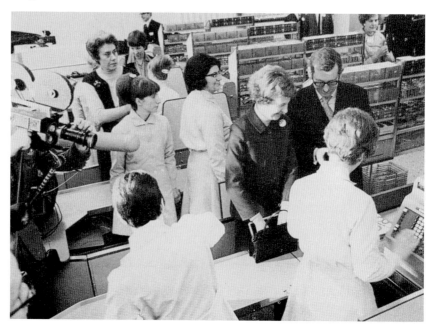

The Stock Exchange on 12 July 1973: within one minute, £495 million was offered for £14.5 million worth of available Sainsbury's shares

The 24,000 square-foot 'superstore' at Coldham's Lane – the ideal edge-of-town supermarket, built on disused land at the edge of Cambridge and the first Sainsbury's store to sell discounted petrol

The fresh-meat counters at Coldham's Lane: choice and quality proves attractive

RECOMMENDED FOR BRAISING/STEWING/BOILING

Coldham's Lane opening day: JD amid customers

JD talking to a customer on one of his frequent branch visits

elected as the Conservative MP for Hove in Sussex. Soon after-wards, in February 1974, he campaigned successfully to retain his seat. Although keen to pursue a career in politics, he had not expected to become an MP quite so soon. He had been the prime mover behind Sainsbury's property-development programme since the early 1960s and had played a major role in doubling the com-pany's sales area in the previous five years alone. Remaining on the board, he passed on this key responsibility to Gurth Hoyer Millar.

Hoyer Millar was aware that his new job would be a challenge, but relished a change from running distribution – a job which bore the brunt of the parlous state of British labour relations within Sainsbury's organisation. The depots were 100 per cent unionised and the unions were increasingly quick to flex their muscle. 'Actu-ally,' says Hoyer Millar, 'I think I spent more of my time dealing with the unions than thinking through distribution strategy.' In response to both needs, he occasionally drew on contract suppliers. This not only made it possible to keep up with delivery schedules as new stores opened, but provided some leverage on depot staff when trouble brewed. The unions disliked the use of contractors intensely; occasionally contractors themselves would come out on strike. 'You have to remember', reflects Hoyer Millar, 'these disputes and intermittent strikes were widespread in the 1970s; they affected every business and industry sector – and of course consumers. It is hard to give contemporary audiences an idea of what union power meant to the economy at that time. It's so different now. I know industry has other types of problem to contend with but we are really spoilt in terms of labour relations.'

Roy Griffiths was keenly aware that, replacing Hoyer Millar, the distribution job needed someone who was both experienced and streetwise. In October 1974, Len Payne, who had significant back-ground in transport and in negotiating with the unions, was duly appointed to the board as Sainsbury's new distribution director.

Apart from strikes, another factor that may be unfamiliar today is shortages, both of staple foodstuffs and domestic items that most people in the UK take for granted. The three-day week in the fac-tories, and the global oil crisis which lasted a lot longer, were part of the reason for this, but the situation was aggravated by panic-buying. For example, when paper and packaging shortages became acute in early 1974, one commodity that everyone insisted on stock-piling was toilet paper. The humble loo roll became national news, and no pun was left unturned in reference to it; headlines included: 'Toilet roll stocks hit rock bottom.'

Cecil Roberts, as departmental director in charge of grocery-buying, had the onerous task of keeping this and other supplies, such as detergents, flowing into the stores: 'People will have to stop buying soon – garages and spare rooms can only hold so much,' he commented drily. One lady was politely persuaded by the store manager at Sainsbury's in Fulham that 120 toilet rolls were perhaps more than her immediate needs; the same manager spotted customers buying up to 80 packages of detergent at a time. When Sainsbury's opened a new store in East Grinstead, customers appeared to have one main purchase in mind. The store sold a staggering 24,000 rolls of lavatory paper on its first day. Later that year, sugar shortages achieved an even higher profile, and such was the scarcity at its worst that some shoppers started to believe the quite unfounded rumours that food retailers were sitting on their very own sugar mountain.

Recalling the contribution made by Sainsbury's buyers when the food shortages were acute, Joe Barnes said: 'During the three-day week in 1974 we did not have to be one, but four steps ahead,' such were the snowballing effects of small changes on the supply chain, even in distant markets. By way of illustration, he explained: 'The shortages of Peruvian anchovies used as a high-protein fish meal in animal foodstuffs, resulted in a rise in feedstuff prices, this was one factor behind a rise in meat prices and a slackening in demand.' Another example was the poor soya bean crop in 1974, causing the price of margarine to exceed that of butter, which in turn caused a run on dairy products and a shortage of them.

Despite all these problems, Sainsbury's annual report in May 1974 opened with the promising line 'Record sales and profits in first year as public company'. Sales of over £362 million were 22 per cent up on the previous year; and profits of £13.6 million were up by nearly 20 per cent. JD reported that this success was the result of 16 new stores opening during the year, plus four refurbished stores, and the sustained growth in volumes of goods sold. But, as he also disclosed, the figures disguised a struggle. Food prices had risen by 18 per cent, and Sainsbury's had kept its own average increases to only 15.5 per cent. Against a background of exceptional inflation, the growth in the company's sales in real terms had declined. At 3.76 per cent, the net profit margin was still good, but was also slightly down on the previous year. Sainsbury's considerable volume of trade in the stores, coupled with the drive to improve productivity, had helped to maintain some slow progress.

Sainsbury's share price dipped a little following the announcement of the results, after which it resumed what was to become a long upward journey. But the small dip came as a surprise to the board at the time. The Lex column in the *Financial Times* had referred to 'strikingly good results', although the *Guardian* judged Sainsbury's 'glamour tarnished a little'. Whatever the reception in the press, this was the first time that Sainsbury's had ever submitted to external scrutiny in such a measurable way, and the board decided to take whole- or half-page space in most national newspapers to explain the year's first trading results since flotation to Sainsbury's shareholders. The adverts made the point that continued success in serving customers depended on continuous reinvestment, which in turn depended on being able to earn a reasonable profit. In his address to senior managers JD said: 'We are certainly living more than ever in an age of the survival of the fittest. If it's any consolation, many retailers will be in more trouble than we are or will be whatever the rigours that may stem from the Whitehall diktats.'

The instruments of government intervention in trade in the mid-1970s were certainly clumsy. Despite hard lobbying from the food-retail industry, the newly elected Labour government remained convinced of the efficacy of tightening the screw on the profits and gross margins of food retailers. Food inflation was travelling upwards at a rate well above the general inflationary trend. The Price Commission, which was independent of government, was now calling for an even greater reduction of food retailers' gross margins. In fact, the effects of competition had ensured that most food retailers, including Sainsbury's, were managing to keep their margins lower than the level demanded by the Commission, which was a little below 20 per cent. But in 1974, the whole trade was faced not only with rising food costs but with even faster-rising labour and running costs. Utilities and rates were going up by about 30 per cent, packaging material by 50 per cent and diesel by 80 per cent. The trade wanted the freedom to improve their gross margins to make allowance for such costs, not to cut them further. The Price Commission was asking for a further 10 per cent cut on retailers' gross margins on food sales. Non-foods, wines, cigarettes and milk were exempt. But the government wanted more than this. Shirley Williams, Minister for Consumer Affairs, laid down that the 10 per cent additional cut should apply to all retailers, thus affecting all aspects of Sainsbury's and other supermarkets' trade.

More than any barrier to trade in the mid-1970s, it was the manacling effects of this kind of intervention that frustrated the chairman most. In his first annual general meeting as a public company, in June 1974, JD readily took up this theme. He said that the word 'profit' had been turned into 'an emotive term of abuse' and that 'the true nature and need for profit is not widely understood'. He added that it was 'equally unacceptable that state interference is growing to the level that enterprise, innovation and progress is being thwarted. We are having to spend quite disproportionate time and energy with the government and government agencies explaining the facts of our business to those who, if not biased against them, are unaware of the complexities and difficulties we face.' He pointed out that the recent imposition of VAT on various products, including soft drinks, confectionery, drink and tobacco, itself added 1.75 per cent to the cost of living – and that food costs in the UK would be far higher were it not for the way that the food trade had modernised and innovated 'on a most ambitious scale in the last 20 years'.

While Timothy Sainsbury took a more conventional approach as an MP, Sainsbury's itself had become JD's own political platform from which he railed against these 'Whitehall diktats'. Whether they liked it or not, his senior managers, his shareholders and anyone else who would listen, heard JD's strongly held views about his trade, trade in general and the politics surrounding it. His annual report statements and AGM speeches were among his most public opportunities to vent his frustrations not only concerning government intervention, but the short-sightedness of planning authorities. Above all, he propounded the message that market forces should be freed to do their own proper and effective work. He consistently argued that the competitive structure of the modern food-distribution industry in Britain had a direct and beneficial effect on the economy, that expansion improved productivity, and that economies of scale kept food prices down and improved the cost of living. Price-freezing and price codes were bureaucratic fiddling; they stifled competition and worsened unemployment.

JD was making these points not only to drive home the importance of improving modern food-retailing methods, as epitomised
by Sainsbury's, but to raise the flag for the retail and service industries in general, which had long been considered of secondary
importance to the manufacturing sector. His strong opinions
also reflect the tenacity with which he kept Sainsbury's on its ambitious course of expansion, however poor the economic forecasts
appeared to be.

Whatever its external problems, Sainsbury's continued to forge
ahead. The board considered it was essential to continue a regime
of cost-cutting and seeking greater efficiencies. But JD was
adamant that no reduction in cost should affect standards. He told
the AGM in 1974, 'Savings that risk quality and therefore our reputation . . . are false and dangerous. Nor must we be tempted to be
short-sighted. Nothing must be done which has the effect of
inhibiting the progress towards greater long-term efficiency.' The
company's achievements in branch productivity reassured Sainsbury's board in the wake of the 1974 results. The company's
achievements even became a matter of academic record.

An extensive survey conducted by the Manchester Business
School for the Institute of Grocery Distribution found that Sainsbury's was more efficient, more profitable, made better use of staff,
traded at a higher intensity while still managing to sell goods at a
lower gross margin than the rest of the grocery trade put together.
The survey noted that Sainsbury's had a particular advantage in the
increase in productivity in its larger shops.

Productivity improvement was also one of Roy Griffiths's pet
subjects. His contributions as an astute thinker and organiser, and
the way in which he complemented the more passionate tempera-
ment of JD, earned Griffiths the position of joint deputy chairman
alongside Simon Sainsbury in January 1975. In this role he maintained responsibility for personnel activities, but now supported JD
by taking over much of the administrative and operational aspects
of the company. Ever eager to improve the company's productivity
and efficiency, Griffiths set up and chaired the Directors' Administrative Committee (DAC) in October 1975. This had various roles: it
aimed to eliminate waste, such as the duplication of departmental
activities; it would ensure that divisional budgets, performance
comparisons and other management information were properly

and effectively delivered; and it approved every new staff appointment, while a board director's authorisation was needed to replace
staff in existing posts.

But the greatest improvements to productivity were achieved by
increasing economies of scale which demanded an aggressive pursuit of new and better sites. On 3 December 1974, Sainsbury's
opened a total of 58,405 square feet of new sales space in one day,
with three new stores at Coldham's Lane in Cambridge, Chingford
in Essex and Woking in Surrey. Between them the three stores
recorded probably the biggest shopping spree that the company
had ever known on any opening day. When David Sainsbury
opened the doors at Chingford's new supermarket of nearly 20,000
square feet, it took 15 minutes for customers in the original queue to
enter. The combination of novelty, access to goods that were in general short supply, and preparations for Christmas, quickly turned
each store into a riot of noise and excitement. The queues swelled
most for sugar, bread, yeast, flour, syrup and bread. At Woking the
opening-day crowds proved too much, and by 10.30 in the morning
the shop had to close for half an hour to let the queues subside at
each of the 22 checkouts.

Of the three new stores, Coldham's Lane was the blueprint for the
ideal Sainsbury's store for years to come, and probably the most
important branch to open since the company moved into self-
service in 1950. It was in the perfect location. Unlike the other 1970s
new-town stores at Bretton, Telford and Bletchley, this store – now
second-largest with 24,000 square feet – was built on the edge of a
historic, densely populated urban area. The store had also been
built on a derelict industrial site and therefore was not taking up
precious green-belt land. The large, edge-of-town site not only provided space for car parking and a substantial sales area but also for
store operational areas, including preparation space and warehousing, all built on ground level. By comparison, the town and city
stores were built on two or even three levels, and the Coldham's
Lane design was a major factor in reducing the operating costs of
Sainsbury's modern supermarkets. The cost of the derelict site itself
was another bonus for the company. It was acquired for £135,000,
which was less than a quarter of the price achieved for the Cambridge city-centre store that it replaced. Bargains such as this were
unheard of once supermarkets and other retail businesses caught
on to the real value of edge-of-town locations.

Coldham's Lane specifically targeted customers travelling by car, and there were soon plans to extend the 376-space car park from which shoppers followed a covered walkway into the store. Coldham's Lane was also the site of Sainsbury's first petrol station, with six electronic pumps capable of delivering petrol at six seconds per gallon, at the discounted price of 59p per gallon (about 14p per litre). Although Sainsbury's was not the first supermarket chain to offer it, the sale of petrol at a discounted rate was a sure attraction to the car shoppers of the 1970s, and, wherever possible, a Sainsbury's petrol station would be added to the list of proposed requirements at subsequent development sites.

Alongside the fullest possible supermarket range, including an in-store bakery and delicatessen, Coldham's Lane offered a range of clothes and some additional lines of domestic household and garden goods not previously sold at other Sainsbury's stores. The new store was a fitting tribute to Timothy Sainsbury, for he had been primarily responsible for the site's acquisition and development before passing over the reins of the estates department. Almost without exception, Sainsbury's new stores were opened by leading family members, but the directors knew Coldham's Lane was special, and invited Jim Prior, former Conservative Minister for Food, to be present at the opening. He was an appropriate choice since he would later become one of the company's first non-executive directors.

Coldham's Lane and the 'three-stores-in-a-day' seemed to cap the year's retail successes for Sainsbury's, and helped to redress the frustrations of the economic and political climate, perhaps even making up for the frantic price-changing needed to keep up with food inflation. Coldham's Lane itself represented Sainsbury's of the modern era; this was where the company wanted to go. As Hoyer Millar comments: 'John Sainsbury believed the future lay in significantly larger stores. Even if we hadn't the range to fill them adequately I think he realised that we could do in time and that this was the way forward.'

Hoyer Millar's comment about the company's range is apt. By 1975 the largest stores contained about 5,000 products, almost half of which were Sainsbury's own-label. Sainsbury's range in food terms was significant, but by comparison to competitors operating larger stores, the overall range of products was relatively modest. For example, whereas Asda inevitably had to fill its 40,000 and more square-feet stores with a massive product range – including food – Sainsbury's had a more limited range, concentrating on food but gradually enlarged by more standard non-food products and occasional experimentation with heavier household goods and clothes. This range grew steadily with each passing year. Seth and Randall in *The Grocers* make an interesting comment about customer reaction to Sainsbury's range: 'Customers, increasingly persuaded by the store's growing reputation for the best food quality and control, appeared simply not to notice the limited range. Quality was emphatically preferred to width.'

For Sainsbury's to maintain its reputation for quality was an enormous commitment which fell squarely on the shoulders of its buyers. Each buyer learnt his trade thoroughly, tutored by senior buyers and learning a range of skills that had no equal in scope in the rest of the food retailing industry. Unlike their competitor equivalents, buyers at Sainsbury's were responsible not only for sourcing supplies and developing new products, negotiating and dealing with suppliers and constantly checking quality, but also for ensuring that all the products they bought reached the appropriate warehouses in the right quantities. Buyers might have to order more than 1,000 tons of potatoes at a time, or ten million bananas from the Caribbean, or five million oranges from Israel. With each passing year the quantities grew, which meant that the demands for quality control increased.

The development of each new product or new line – even that of a different flavour of a particular cereal – could be a complex task. Where supplies were imported, buyers would make frequent visits overseas, and they would often have to handle legal and bureaucratic negotiations surrounding the import and bond of goods. But wherever the product was sourced, there was an endless round of product-sampling and scientific analysis within the laboratories. As well as introducing the occasional novel product, buyers would argue for new sizes, colours and flavours to develop the range, and their antennae were constantly attuned to new trends.

As increasing numbers of British people took foreign holidays, Sainsbury's buyers would satisfy newly acquired and developing tastes for every type of continental cuisine. But they also launched new styles of own-label products of a more traditional type, such as the hugely popular Sainsbury's cholesterol-free, spreadable margarine, which became a best-seller, and Sainsbury's yoghurts, including Champagne rhubarb, strawberry and apple, lemon and lime, Victoria plum and peach melba flavours. Buyers explored and experimented freely, but the factor that everyone adhered to religiously was the observance of quality in every product that made it to the shelves.

Bob Ingham, whose long career as a buyer at Sainsbury's covered a great deal of ground, from dairy to bakery to wine, records that the buyers in the company took on the pursuit of quality almost as second nature and propounded the drive for high standards as an essential part of their daily work. Sainsbury's management of the buying process, in which the pursuit of quality was so intrinsic, set it apart from its competitors. Since his accession to the chair, JD placed great emphasis on the role of the buyers. He had already strengthened their position through the new role of the departmental directors; later he would promote the most talented senior buyers, such as Cecil Roberts and Bob Ingham, to board positions.

Joe Barnes's appointment as the company's new director of marketing in 1973, the first such title on the board, was recognition of the importance of developing the range to suit new and varying tastes. Barnes comments: 'At that time, the new larger stores were coming into their own; we were able to introduce many new lines, especially on the non-food side – textiles, household goods, cosmetics. Our bakeries and delicatessens were adding an extra degree of customer service. As well as being very aggressive with our own brands, the larger stores gave us the opportunity to market an increasing range of proprietor brands.'

Helping to underpin buying decisions, buyers were fed the latest market data gathered by the company's statisticians. According to Ivor Hunt, close monitoring of customers had revealed a gradual but distinct move from the social aspiration to 'keep up with the Joneses' – typically measured by the ownership of one's own car, fridges, televisions and other material goods – towards a desire to be different from the Joneses. Customers expected higher quality, more value for money and greater choice; alongside this, in fashion and in culture generally, there was greater pursuit of individuality and a taste for novelty. In the motor industry, Ford reflected this trend by producing so many different models of, for example, the new Ford Fiesta, that customers were able to buy a car that appeared almost individual. Sainsbury's acted on this – particularly in its range of food and standard non-food items – more quickly and successfully than competitors.

The wine department was one of the most important growth areas. Sainsbury's had made the decision to purchase wine bottled at source in 1972, and the move had paid off handsomely. In July 1973, a new range of French wines included Gaillac Perlé at 63p, Anjou rosé at 73p and Beaumes de Venise at 83p a bottle. By introducing these and many other provincial wines Sainsbury's contributed in a substantial way to a major change in the nation's drinking habits. Sainsbury's was also the first British retailer to bottle Spanish wines and sherries at source, and customers were introduced to unfamiliar wines such as Manzanilla, Vino do Catalonia and Arruda. Added to the description labels on the bottles were indicators of the dryness or sweetness of white wines, and leaflets provided information about regional wines. Such information, commonplace in modern supermarkets, made Sainsbury's off licences attractive to a population that was fast gaining a taste for wine. By the end of the decade Sainsbury's had the largest wine sales of any British retailer.

An altogether new growth area was frozen food. During early 1974 there was a marked growth in the number of people buying freezers and filling them with as much bulk-packed food as they could find. The result was a new style of freezer-food outlet on the nation's high streets, a trade led by Bejam in front of Alpine Everest, Cordon Bleu and Dalgetty. It was estimated in 1974 that 11 per cent of households, that is about two million, had freezers, and that the number was growing steadily; shoppers were buying in considerable bulk and taking advantage of the substantial price reductions possible from large pack sizes. This presented an opportunity for Sainsbury's, not only in terms of developing the range, but also of making propitious use of some of its older outlets. Sainsbury's had several shops remaining in good high-street locations that might convert well to freezer centres.

The directors planned to develop 40 new Sainsbury's freezer centres within the next three years, with no fewer than ten opened by the end of 1974. Some would replace existing shops not suitable for other purposes; some would be built in areas where there were no other Sainsbury's stores; others would be developed in premises close to the main store. Sainsbury's would start with proprietary lines and build up its own-label frozen goods. The venture, headed by Derek Salisbury, son of former director Fred Salisbury, looked promising.

The freezer venture did not start well owing to an unusual lack of insight in the siting of the first outlet, opened in a former counter-service branch at Southbourne near Bournemouth on 25 June 1974. The store was closed after only ten months because few of the town's largely retired population actually owned freezers. Subsequent stores were more successful. Gradually, Sainsbury's built up its own lines of bulk freezer packs, such as 5lb packs of vegetables, peas and crinkle-cut chips; bulk packs of meat and fish; and many different puddings, including an own-label version of the widely popular 1970s hit, Arctic roll. Just as the mainstream stores were catering for the taste buds of increasingly adventurous consumers, the freezer centres offered frozen continental specialities such as lasagne, pizzas and 'chicken espagnole'. There were even packs of uncooked frozen 'Dinnodog' for the family canine.

Freezer centres did not represent a significant labour overhead, requiring an average of about six staff per shop, but the idea of an 'independent' freezer operation soon lost its sparkle. The new supermarkets being planned were perfectly capable of accommo-dating larger freezer-cabinet sections, and the ordering for and supply of these sections would be integrated with other store prod-ucts. The decision to develop freezer departments more fully in the main supermarkets was made in early 1975, although the planned openings of independent centres continued for the next two years while further mainstream supermarkets were constructed. Eight independent centres were established by the year-end in 1975. In 1980 there were 21 independent Sainsbury's Freezer Centres still trading, but these were eventually sold to Bejam in 1986.

The buying role and range development were essential parts of an increasingly complex, expanding supermarket organisation. At the front line of this were the store managers, who were gradually under more pressure as the stores grew larger and the volumes of sales rose. In early 1975, at a conference specifically devised to apprise deputy managers – 'the future of the company' – of the opportunities and challenges that lay ahead, JD pointed out that Sainsbury's expansion required a new store manager every fort-night. This focus on the deputies was typical of the company's continued emphasis on developing and training its staff. And, with an overall programme now costing well over half a million pounds a year, Sainsbury's had every reason to believe that they continued to offer the best food-retail training in the country.

Given the economic and political constraints, shortages and union problems, Sainsbury's advances during these difficult mid-decade years are all the more remarkable. The directors and senior managers were often surprised by the degree of success to which they were contributing. 'We must have had the trading formula right,' says Ivor Hunt, 'because, at that stage, before the competition for new sites really stepped up and we had to pay significantly more for new properties, we would find that sometimes the trade we managed in a new store would exceed our expectations by as much as 50 per cent.'

In order to get their forecasts right, market information was systematically sought from all quarters; there was also more need for information covering all aspects of the company's business since flotation, and greater emphasis on target-setting and performance-monitoring. This data was also useful to Sainsbury's in assessing its performance relative to competitors. By 1975, Asda was achieving a very impressive 3 per cent of the country's share of grocery sales from only 46 stores and trading mostly in the northern half of the country, which covered a little over half of the population. Tesco had higher takings than Sainsbury's but a far larger percentage of its turnover resulted from sales of non-foods. Waitrose and M&S were gaining a solid reputation for their own good-quality food, even if their prices were less competitive than Sainsbury's. But what were the factors that really attracted customers most?

A large-scale survey at this time, produced for Sainsbury's by Gordon Simmons Research, provided the following summary statistics:

> There are 77% of housewives in reach of a branch of a Co-operative Society store, 36% in reach of Tesco, 32% in reach of Fine Fare and 23% in reach of an Allied Suppliers' shop as compared with 20% in reach of a JS branch. However, only 57% of those who can actually do shop at the Co-op, 56% at Tesco, 65% at Allied and 47% at Fine Fare, against 80% at JS.

This was a resounding thumbs-up as far as it went, but further analysis of shoppers' opinions about the leading retailers – this time including Waitrose and Asda – allowed no room for complacency. Sainsbury's came top for 'quality' and 'cleanliness'; Asda for 'prices', 'efficiency' and 'premises'. Sainsbury's were second for 'prices', while Waitrose scored seconds for 'quality', 'prices', 'efficiency' and 'premises'. Tesco were last under three headings, 'quality', 'cleanliness' and 'efficiency', and Sainsbury's achieved a definite last place for 'crowding'. Reputations take a while to change, and although Sainsbury's had a growing number of more spacious stores with fewer queues at plentiful checkouts, the crowded stores remained, both in reality and in people's perception. However, as the editor of *The Grocer* had once remarked of this commonly reported Sainsbury's phenomenon in the late 1960s, 'It was a problem that many of Sainsbury's competitors would like to have.'

Nevertheless, this study underlined the company's need to seek greater comfort and space for its customers in its store-development programme, as well as more room for increasing the range and choice. In several sites, the estates department had adopted the policy of building stores in which some parts of the new construction could be sub-let to other traders when the store opened. As pressure for space grew, Sainsbury's would reabsorb the sub-let space to enlarge its own selling area. Such ploys were useful but not always possible. Mostly, Sainsbury's took up all the space it could acquire, and the company was now more than ever determined to continue its ambitious development.

In 1975, the Price Commission yet again demanded a lower gross margin, at a time when there was virtually no room for manoeuvre and when food prices were rocketing towards an all-time high of 29 per cent. In his 1975 company report JD stated that it had been 'the most difficult trading year in the last 25 years, with the greatest rate of inflation in food prices and operating costs that we have ever experienced'. Added to which, he noted that competitors such as Asda, Morrison and Kwiksave – all of whom were unheard of only ten years before – were taking the laurels for providing the cheapest food in the north of England. These difficulties made Sainsbury's cumulative achievements more conspicuous. By its 1975 year-end, the company had invested more than £74 million in the five years since 1970. Of its 164 supermarkets, 70 had been opened in this time and a further 33 modernised or extended. During the same period sales had risen 26 per cent in real terms while the numbers of staff in the branches had only grown by 1.7 per cent.

The board now planned 17 new stores with an average sales area of 19,500 square feet. It was also contemplating the launch of a subsidiary hypermarket company which could be operated as a joint venture and which would offer even greater economies of scale. However, a hypermarket company in the UK posed specific challenges, particularly as regards planning, since applications for stores larger than 50,000 square feet had to be referred to the Department of the Environment. The application process took a long time and often failed. The directors also realised that a hypermarket should have a strong clothing range, and that it would be useful to find a partner with the appropriate experience and reputation in this field. JD turned to British Home Stores (BHS), a high-street retailer he particularly respected, and worked with Colin Paterson, the managing director, to develop the joint venture.

In May 1975, JD duly announced the enterprise in which hypermarkets of upwards of 50,000 square feet would be built with BHS. The new company would be run independently by its own management team but would be supported by the financial, management and buying resources of its parents. As in Sainsbury's stores, high standards of quality and lower prices would apply for all the many food and other supermarket lines, while BHS's quality standards and good-value approach would apply to textile lines. In two or three years' time, the largest of Asda stores and the Carrefour hypermarkets would have serious new competition resourced by thoroughly experienced retailers. This was the vision for Sava-Centre, Sainsbury's first major diversification.

Chapter 10

INFLATION AND STRIKE
1975–1977

WHILE SAINSBURY'S appeared to be able to take the nation's economic problems in its stride and was determined to build more new supermarkets, trading conditions steadily worsened for the rest of 1975. Inflation caused a massive rise in local government expenditure during that year which forced up rates as well as building, electricity and other utility costs.

In the same period, a new wage settlement fanned the flames. Although labour amounted to about 55 per cent of its costs, Sainsbury's had improved its productivity – as measured in relation to sales per employee – by more than 50 per cent in real terms since 1969. This was a fundamental achievement which placed the company in a stronger position to withstand the serious pressures of inflation on the one hand and the artificial constraints on margins demanded by government on the other. It also underpinned the directors' confidence in maintaining the long-term strategy of acquiring more and better sites for expansion. A more immediate boost was the knowledge that, despite a decline in consumer spending from about May 1975 – both in total and on food in particular – Sainsbury's volumes of sales continued to rise.

Some competitors, however, were forced to curtail their expansion for the time being, and realised that Sainsbury's seemed to have got its trade formula right. Sainsbury's was becoming that yardstick to follow in its buying skills and range development, its own-label programme, its quality-control methods, the way it inspired a loyal and committed staff, head office organisational disciplines – all the factors that ultimately led to high sales intensity and growth in volumes sold. In his autobiography, *Tiger by the Tail*, Ian MacLaurin, who became managing director of Tesco in 1975, writes: 'Since John Sainsbury opened his first store in Drury Lane, the company had been a dynamic element in British retailing, the benchmark by which Tesco judged its own performance.'

Despite a very poor first half reported in May 1976, with delays to the building programme resulting in only four new stores trading, Sainsbury's managed to complete all its planned 17 new stores while, in the second half of the year, sales and profits picked up dramatically. Turnover was well over half a billion pounds. The company now had a strong property portfolio, which continued to include a high proportion of freehold premises. This was good security if the need arose to borrow to support long-term plans. Sainsbury's expansion, which in the previous year had cost just over £30 million, had been paid for mostly from retained profits supplemented by a limited policy of sale-and-lease back and the sale of counter-service shops in valuable high-street locations.

In his statement to shareholders JD made clear that, in the face of reduced consumer food spending, the Price Commission's fiddly price codes were an irrelevance. He stated: 'There is no more effective discipline in holding down prices than competition. There is no better protection for the consumer than the simple fact that if you don't look after her interest you will lose business to your competitors.'

The profit margins of all food-retailing multiples were being comprehensively squeezed and, in 1976, Sainsbury's fell below 3 per cent for the first time since 1971. Cost-savings were urgently sought right across the company. Every aspect of Sainsbury's revenue expenditure came under the close scrutiny of Roy Griffiths's Directors' Administrative Committee (DAC). Divisional directors set their own targets for cost reductions, but the exercise covered all aspects of administration – Xerox copying, telephone use, the examination of wasteful or duplicative systems in every office. Griffiths urged staff to get their priorities right with the tongue-in-cheek announcement that 'the emphasis is not on saving the paper clips whilst the sacred cows go on eating the grass'. After less than a year of setting up the DAC, head-office savings already amounted to hundreds of thousands of pounds. By tackling the problem of waste and high return levels in the branches – such as damaged goods and unsold perishables which were costing well over £5 million a year – significantly more savings and organisational improvements were possible. Since the oil crisis, there was a raised awareness about the importance of saving energy, and stores unofficially competed for the honour of achieving the greatest cuts in their electricity consumption. But keeping the refrigerator cabinets and storage areas cool in the exceptionally hot summer of 1976, when tarmac in the customer car parks frequently melted at the seams, did not make this easy.

Improvements within Sainsbury's reach were going well, whereas the bugbears beyond its control persisted. Planning delays and government intervention continued; food shortages eased but remained a problem – for example, the price of tea quadrupled in 1976 and that of coffee trebled. The partial removal of government food subsidies pushed up the price of other staples, including bread.

The next government anti-inflation measure was a freeze on weekly wage increases to a maximum of £6, part of an attempt to fetch inflation down from a high of 25 per cent in 1975 to an ambitious target of 10 per cent by the end of 1976. Although the Sainsbury's board found most government tactics tedious, they were happier to comply with this than the continuation of price codes and institutional restraints on margins.

Yet at local-government level the planning delays continued to grate. Some stores were taking as long as five-and-a-half years from planning concept to store opening. A happy exception to this was the development of Sainsbury's Kempston store, outside Bedford, which had opened in November 1975 with a massive 37,608 square feet of sales space. Here the development programme had been unstoppable, and the huge store, complete with basement car park for 600 cars and standing on a platform into which 30,000 tons of concrete had been poured, had taken just 20 months. At almost double the latest annual average-size-supermarket, Kempston sported the full Sainsbury's food range, an in-store bakery, a large delicatessen, an integral freezer centre, a new-loose bacon counter and a wider selection of textiles, hardware – including additional lines of glassware and crockery – and other non-food lines than any other Sainsbury's supermarket. New lines were added in an attempt to fill the space: garden tools, toys, cosmetics, wallpaper, stationery. Soon after opening, rows of Sainsbury's own-label gloss and emulsion paint were introduced. New, larger trolleys with locking devices were designed to avoid accidents as customers returned to their cars down the 'autowalk' conveyors.

Despite the enormous potential of this fine modern store, hailed initially as the next ideal and somewhere between a superstore and a hypermarket, Sainsbury's found it could not fill such a mighty space adequately. Significant areas of the sales floor felt either empty or were taken up with repeated goods. It was a salutary lesson, and one that pointed to the need to balance range and size in the forthcoming store-development programme. In due course, Kempston's sales area was cut back by some 5,000 square feet. The company planned for a more modest ten stores in total for 1976/7, and the average size of these would be around 19,000 square feet, marginally smaller than the previous year. The replacement or upgrading of the oldest stores remained a top priority. The oldest of Sainsbury's supermarkets, mostly in city- and town-centre locations, were becoming more crowded and uncomfortable and therefore much more vulnerable to competition; they were in dire need of replacing.

Meanwhile, buoyed by the continued good will of customers, whose numbers had grown steadily with the opening of the newer stores, the company continued to push out into the west and north of England. Expansion also provided an incentive to the company's staff, creating more opportunities for the managers of the next generation, apart from which it ensured an exciting and ever-changing environment. But JD did not, as he put it at the senior managers' meeting in 1976, 'seek the god of growth for its own sake'; he believed growth was absolutely necessary if the company was to continue to improve the service to its customers and fulfil its potential.

In Sainsbury's strongest trading areas, which were still mostly in the south and south-east, Tesco had now become the main competitor to watch. Ian MacLaurin, the new chief executive, working with a strong executive team, was determined to upgrade Tesco's image, improve its structure and unashamedly follow Sainsbury's lead by making improvements in service and value for customers. Tesco had a larger overall turnover, although its trading performance in sales per square feet, in common with every other competitor in the country, was nowhere near Sainsbury's. Like Sainsbury's, it had suffered downturns in its profit growth in real terms in the previous two years. But with some 900 stores, and many more than Sainsbury's in the north of the country, Tesco had a substantial property base to build upon. Sainsbury's had always maintained a lead in the average size of its new supermarkets, but Tesco now had plans to create no fewer than ten stores, each of which would be larger than Kempston, with an average sales area of 38,000 square feet. Heavy borrowing would be needed to achieve this, but it was unlikely that Tesco would suffer the same ranging problem as Sainsbury's in such large stores considering that its non-food lines – over and above normal supermarket 'non-food' – were contributing about 30 per cent of the company's turnover.

By the year-end in 1977, Sainsbury's own 'non-traditional' non-food lines were also beginning to build: there were health and beauty products in 68 stores; kitchenware, glass and china in 57 stores; car-care items – including Sainsbury's own-label motor oil – in 18; and a limited range of household textiles and clothing in 13. These lines were boosting sales, but the proportion they contributed to total turnover was insignificant compared to Tesco.

The ideal store format – edge-of-town or out-of-town with good parking space – was clearer than ever now, and Coldham's Lane remained the blueprint. The latest city-centre stores at Nottingham, Northampton, Derby and Sheffield were proving to be a disappointment, partly because they depended on unsatisfactory multi-storey car parks as part of the city-centre redevelopments. They also suffered strong competition from Asda's superstores and other modern supermarkets in the suburbs and edge-of-city sites – with excellent ground-level parking for shoppers. Sainsbury's had also experimented by setting up a store on two levels at Barkingside, with food on the ground floor and an extensive range of non-food lines above. Tesco had been employing this approach in a number of its stores for some time. But the Barkingside format was not popular; customers did not relish moving upstairs having filled up their trolleys on the ground floor. In due course the upper floor was unceremoniously closed to shoppers, and later this space was redeployed for district training sessions or additional storage space.

Deciding to add to its more northern stores in Doncaster and Sheffield, Sainsbury's placed advertisements for sites in local newspapers. Hundreds of replies flooded in, some from councils offering land they wanted to put to good use, some from landowners and others from loyal followers who had moved north and missed their former local Sainsbury's. A number of people even offered their own small back gardens as potential sites, while one landowner suggested Sainsbury's could take up to 37 acres of land next to her equestrian centre. The optimistic ploy proved beyond doubt that Sainsbury's reputation preceded it in these potential locations.

A typical Sainsbury's development followed a programme of thorough market analysis. Ivor Hunt's responsibility as chief statistician included studies of new sites which were both strategic and tactical. The former examined how the sites would fit the company's geographical aims modified in the light of the competition already in place and local demography. The statistical department had divided the country into market-planning areas, each representing a population of shoppers profiled according to such factors as wealth and car ownership. The tactical analysis sought to forecast as closely as possible, through the annual results of comparable stores and other information gathered about the local market, what takings could be expected from a Sainsbury's store in a given location. This was the basis for assessing how much Sainsbury's could afford to pay for the site. Ivor Hunt remarks: 'As competition got tougher this forced property costs up and sites became harder to obtain. We therefore clearly needed to be much cleverer in our forecasting in order to maximise what we could afford, otherwise we would miss the best sites.'

Provided management continued a disciplined approach and cost control remained tight, Sainsbury's business model in the second part of the 1970s could be described as a virtuous circle: greater efficiency led to keener prices; keener prices led to more customers; more customers led to better profits; better profits financed investment in more stores, wider choice, sustained quality and greater efficiency. The pursuit of quality lay at the centre of this model. The May 1977 results showed that the model was working. Sales were up by more than 22 per cent on the year before, while profits before tax had improved by 70 per cent – in real terms this was an increase of 46 per cent on the year before. Real-term profitability was now well above 1974 year levels. Over the previous year, another 190,000 square feet was added to the sales area via ten new stores, including three large modern stores replacing smaller, older supermarkets at Bexhill, Maidstone and Poole. Thankfully, inflation was beginning to climb down from its exceptional levels, as the government had planned, although the wage restraints had lowered general living standards and reduced disposable incomes considerably.

In such conditions the price of food was more than ever a factor in customers' minds. At Tesco, MacLaurin was critically aware of this. It was also dawning on him that stamp trading was both out of date and expensive to maintain. With Tesco's profit margins barely scraping 2 per cent in 1977, and with the burden of heavy borrowing, MacLaurin needed an effective fix to pull the company out of a quagmire. In *Tiger by the Tail*, he records:

> Tesco, in fact, was caught in a double whammy, for while the economics of scale allowed operators such as Asda to discount prices in their large stores, Tesco was lumbered with the escalating costs of trading in Green Shield stamps from pocket-handkerchief-sized stores. And the more of the sticky little things we offered the less attractive they appeared to become.

Like JD, MacLaurin was also a friend of Mike O'Conner, who in 1977 was president of the US Food Marketing Institute. O'Conner advised him with the words: 'Hell, Ian, what planet are you living on? Stamps are yesterday's news.'

MacLaurin made the bold decision to abandon stamp trading altogether and to initiate a massive price-cutting campaign to stimulate trade. Tesco's 'Operation Checkout' was craftily planned to launch on the Wednesday after the Queen's Silver Jubilee weekend in June 1977. Disinformation was provided to make competitors think the actual launch date of the generally mysterious campaign would be a day earlier. Tesco's timing could not have been better – or worse for Sainsbury's. The problems of industrial unrest in the depots which had been brewing for years came to a head in the very same week that Tesco launched what proved to be an exceptionally successful campaign.

While millions of people were attending Silver Jubilee street parties, of a kind not seen since VE-Day, staff in many Sainsbury's stores were battling to ensure there was at least a reasonable supply of goods for party-minded customers. That bank holiday marked Sainsbury's greatest fight with the unions – a struggle that would ultimately lead to significant reforms in the company's distribution methods.

In the 1970s, unions had become progressively more demanding, and industrial action had become more painful for the company as a whole. As sales volumes grew, a reliable distribution service was essential for the business, but it was very difficult to maintain harmony in the depots, the source of Sainsbury's distribution network.

Three years before the Silver Jubilee, Roy Griffiths had recognised the importance of employing someone with the right experience to take control of distribution strategy, and recruited Len Payne. He had previously served as finance director and managing director of British Road Services, then as vice-chairman of the National Freight Corporation.

From the outset Payne worked closely with Griffiths, who also had considerable experience in dealing with unions in his former career at Monsanto. The strengths and characters of the two men were admirably matched. JD observes of Len Payne: 'He was street-wise as far as the unions were concerned. Really was. But then Len would not have been so good without Roy, who was a real thinker. They complemented each other brilliantly.'

One of the first changes they introduced was to extend the number of contract distribution firms that Sainsbury's used. Previously, contractors had been used at times when the company did not have the capacity to meet short-term peaks of demand on its own. From 1975 onwards, contractors were brought in on a permanent basis, and Payne tried to ensure that if they were themselves unionised, it was not by the same unions that represented Sainsbury's own staff. Inevitably, Sainsbury's unions protested, and Payne had to maintain a tough line. He remembers: 'We stood up to all the threats and the short-lived industrial action that came when we began to contract out. Our own depots went on strike for a bit but they didn't stay out for long because they saw that it would only accelerate the speed with which we went outside.'

The very process of contracting out made Griffiths and Payne realise how uncompetitive Sainsbury's own depots and distribution system had become. This strengthened their resolve to improve this side of the business and, in particular, to take a much firmer line with the unions. Payne was particularly concerned to address the problem of shop stewards bypassing their local managers. At all hours, the stewards telephoned head office at Blackfriars and made demands such us 'Give us two more hours' overtime or tonight's sausages won't go out.' He recalls how 'The union leaders, not the depot management, were dictating how the business was run. The trouble is the trade union stewards had nothing else to do. They were full-time shop stewards and they knew a lot about the nitty-gritty of the agreements.' Payne's solution to this problem was to cut the shop stewards' telephone lines, forcing them to speak directly to the depot managers who were usually able to respond more informatively and constructively about issues and grievances than managers at Blackfriars.

Len Payne soon became recognised for his negotiating ability among the shop stewards, and describes a Christmas-time visit to Basingstoke to look at the plant which was then processing and packing nuts:

> It was extremely noisy. As I walked in the shop steward came up to me and said, 'Governor, this noise is very bad for us. It's injurious to our health.' I said, 'I agree with you, that noise would drive me round the bend.' So he said, 'Just for you, we'll carry on working as long as you give us another £3 a week.' I said, 'Okay, fine, but what good is £3 a week for you – you can hardly stuff the notes into your ears. So what I'll do instead is buy you all mufflers to keep the noise out. That'll be better for your health.' This began to set the tone.

Payne and Griffiths tried to make depot staff more aware of the consequences of strike action. Occasionally, the board were so despondent about how uncompetitive the depot operation was becoming that there were discussions about totally reforming, and possibly even closing the whole depot system. Each time union leaders threatened to strike, they would be told in no uncertain terms that it was not the shareholders or management alone that suffered when a customer decided to go to Tesco or Asda because she could not find a particular product on the shelves at Sainsbury's. Staff in the depots were putting their own jobs at risk.

The unions resented losing some of the power they had previously enjoyed, and government-imposed wage restraints aggravated their mounting sense of grievance. Intermittent strikes continued to cause friction. In the run up to the Silver Jubilee bank holiday, Payne had learnt that the unions were planning to stage a massive strike, so JD called an extraordinary meeting of the board specifically to discuss what the response should be. The board was by now determined to risk a confrontation with the unions in the hope that by maintaining supplies by whatever possible methods they would force the unions to back down once and for all. Payne was asked by the board how long he thought the unions would stay out on strike if the company stood firm; he considered this might be three weeks, and the cost was estimated at some £7 million. The board decided to take the risk and make their stand.

The directors prepared for the strike as meticulously as time allowed, warning each store manager of possible disruption to deliveries and advising him to minimise it as best he could. In the week leading up to the Jubilee holiday, the stores took extra deliveries to ensure maximum stock levels; suppliers were also asked to make urgent direct deliveries to the larger stores if called on. Payne managed to secure an agreement from the company's drivers that they would not join any strike that broke out in the depots. Sainsbury's also hired an extra 800 vans and rented various barns and stores across the country to use as temporary storage facilities.

On 2 June 1977, the Thursday before the bank holiday, staff at Hoddesdon and Buntingford depots went on unofficial strike after management had rejected a claim for payment for meal breaks. Workers at Basingstoke joined the strike immediately after the bank holiday, while staff at Charlton resolved to work as normal. Sainsbury's management refused to concede to any of the strikers' demands, but referred the matter in dispute to ACAS, the conciliation and arbitration service.

With the main depots blocked by strikers, suppliers began to deliver direct to supermarkets. Strikers responded by sending secondary pickets to suppliers' depots, so the company brought on stream its temporary storage sites. The lines were drawn clearly between the strikers and staff in the stores, with the latter adopting highly ingenious methods of obtaining supplies. Some branch managers smuggled goods out of supplier depots in their own cars, while others organised the collection of fresh fruit and vegetables direct from the fields. One branch manager who had rented a farm barn for storage space outside Bury St Edmunds codenamed the store 'Glasgow' to prevent pickets from finding it. Staff from Coldham's Lane branch set up a regular rendezvous to transfer goods from a suppliers' lorry into vans in a lay-by some two miles from the store. Occasionally, store managers took deliveries from supplier lorries at their own homes. In a complete overturn of normal trading disciplines, some local managers were even allowed to set their own prices – in agreement with district managers – for goods for which they haggled at cash-and-carry wholesalers.

The board met daily to review progress and discuss tactics, and the company's resolve held. On 16 June, a fortnight after the start of the strike, following ACAS's ruling that the payment demanded was not within agreed procedure, workers at Hoddesdon returned; a few days later staff at Basingstoke and Buntingford followed.

Extraordinarily, Sainsbury's managed to trade at approximately 88 per cent of its normal levels during the strike. A survey carried out soon afterwards found that half of Sainsbury's customers were not even aware there had been a strike. Those customers that did learn of the lengths to which Sainsbury's had gone to maintain normal service were deeply impressed. Yet the biggest impression was made on the unions, who realised that this was a company more determined than ever not to yield to their demands.

The way the branch staff, whom JD calls 'the real heroes', had faced the Jubilee strike was a momentous achievement. The result of the strike allowed Sainsbury's to pursue productivity improvements within the depots which had formerly been inhibited by the recalcitrance of the unions. And no one needed persuading about the benefits of maintaining and improving the existing depot system. The board set about introducing more flexible working practices. Delivery scheduling was immediately reviewed. Before the strike, queues of lorries waited to get into the depots at Buntingford and Basingstoke, since the unions had determined how and when they should be loaded and unloaded. Subsequently, computerised systems enabled delivery times to be synchronised with suppliers in advance; Sainsbury's could guarantee to unload a lorry within a certain time provided it arrived within its allocated slot. Depot managers were therefore able to adjust the work schedules of the staff, and this brought significant cost savings to Sainsbury's and its suppliers. Gradually, as Sainsbury's could be more certain that supplies would arrive on schedule, it was possible to order and store lower levels of stock. Buyers were able to request delivery in stages and to particular locations, significantly reducing storage costs. Suppliers, in turn, had greater control of their manufacturing schedules, again reducing their own costs.

A far more important change for the long term was the greatly increased level of outsourced distribution after 1977. Gradual improvements to ordering and stocking systems enabled contractors to become more closely integrated in the company's distribution system. Over time, more contractors became linked directly via the Blackfriars computer, enabling the same responsive delivery schedules as the company's own depots. In effect, the dispute was a catalyst for change, which led over a number of years to the creation of a far more competitive and flexible distribution system which could support a dynamically changing and growing company in the 1980s.

The resolution of the Jubilee strike was not a fairy-tale ending to the problems of industrial relations – nothing is ever that simple. But it did allow Roy Griffiths and Len Payne to get to closer grips with productivity and systems improvements. The successive decline in man-days lost through disputes in the depots testifies greatly to the success of a changing regime: 11,116 in 1977/8, 1,585 in 1978/9 and 1,007 in 1979/80. In 1980/1 there were only 27 lost man-days recorded in the company, and only five in 1981/2. The very dramatic reduction in the last two of these years was only partly the result of Sainsbury's own significant efforts, and mostly because of Margaret Thatcher's and Jim Prior's new legislation to curb union power.

Later still, there proved to be increasing value in retaining Sainsbury's own depots, because, among other benefits, they gave the company a benchmark against which their contractors' performance could be judged. Sainsbury's could make its own improvements and pass on new ideas and best practices to contractors who were never able to become complacent. If one did become unreliable or uncompetitive, Sainsbury's had the means to supply itself. The system proved so effective, as it was refined over the years, that during JD's period as chairman of the company and for some time afterwards the company did not build another depot; by 1994 it had an additional 17 contractor depots serving its supermarkets.

Although Sainsbury's struggle with the unions would, in the longer term, prove to be a godsend, back in Blackfriars in the immediate aftermath of disruptions, the focus was on restoring trade to full levels and ensuring sufficient deliveries to meet what continued to be a steady demand. At the time of the strike, Sainsbury's had hired Saatchi & Saatchi to produce a series of television advertisements for an autumn campaign focusing on the company's traditional virtues of competitive pricing, freshness, quality and choice. This was reasonably successful, but the board were ever conscious of the sustained success of Tesco's Operation Checkout, and what most of the trade and the media were calling a 'price war'.

Such was Checkout's success that Tesco's lamentable distribution capability at the time almost broke at the seams. MacLaurin wrote: 'In our wildest dreams we'd never imagined that Checkout would generate such an astronomic lift in sales, but without being able to get supplies into our stores in sufficient quantities to meet demand, there was a very real danger that we'd become the laughing stock of the trade for promoting cuts that we couldn't deliver.' Tesco scrambled desperately to set up new warehouses in an attempt to rationalise their distribution, for all its 900 stores were logjammed with up to 120 supplier deliveries a week, each one having to be unloaded by hand and humped into first-or second-floor storerooms.

In November 1977, Sainsbury's announced another steady rise in sales and profits during the previous half-year. JD and the board continued to exude a sense of the company's strength, undeterred by competition. But by this time the board was already planning to launch Sainsbury's own campaign; one that would be a major milestone in the company's fortunes.

Chapter 11

DISCOUNT 78
1977–1980

A T THIS POINT, Sainsbury's and Tesco had to struggle both against each other and the adverse trading conditions. Food-price inflation had come down from its exceptional high point, but in July 1977 it was still hovering at around 20 per cent over the previous year, while the growth in average national incomes loitered at 12 per cent. Reduced living standards inevitably drove customers to find the best deals, and price had become a funda-mentally important factor. As competition increased, the key to success was more than ever the ability to sell larger volumes of goods while keeping overheads as low as possible. This was a game for big players. The pressures of the past three or four years had taken their toll on smaller high-street chains, and during the last quarter of the decade several well-known names either sold up or went out of business: farewell David Greig, F. J. Wallis, MacMarkets, Cater Bros, Cee-n-Cee and Cartier.

The success of Operation Checkout told, in particular, on inde-pendent traders from whom Tesco was winning significant numbers of customers. Checkout may also have snipped a corner from Sainsbury's own market share, although a temporary dip recorded in the three months after the Jubilee strike was most prob-ably the result of the strike itself. The measurement of 'market share' was not an exact science, but industry-watchers found the figures useful as an indication of the position of the front-ranking companies. The two most quoted measures for market share were those recorded by market research company AGB and the Depart-ment of Industry (DOI). AGB's figures were based on a proportion of the grocery market, whereas the DOI's represented total sales in all grocery outlets. JD and Sainsbury's record-keepers trusted the latter more; in July 1977 the DOI market share for the company was 7.9 per cent, while Tesco was placed only one or two percentage points in front.

Once Sainsbury's had fully recovered from the effects of the strike, the board decided it would fight back by devising its own substantial discount operation. Peter Davis, a new face on the board, was given the job of creating Sainsbury's campaign. Davis had been recruited from Key Markets, a small UK food-retailing chain where, as marketing director, he had introduced a discount campaign called '160 Knock Down Prices'. He had joined Sainsbury's as departmental director responsible for non-foods in 1976, and, in 1977, was promoted to the board as marketing director. It was now his brief to devise a campaign that would offer significant price cuts and reinforce Sainsbury's value-for-money reputation.

The idea that Davis proposed was to make 'permanent' reductions of as much as 15 per cent in the prices of about 100 carefully selected and predominantly staple items, with some seasonal changes to the list of discounted lines. Even if the prices themselves were to be changed as a result of food inflation or other variables, Sainsbury's would maintain a very low margin on the discounted lines to ensure this level of competitiveness. Examples of reductions when the campaign was launched include 8p off selected cuts of bacon, 4p off own-label cornflakes and 20p off a quarter-pound pack of instant coffee. The plan was to launch the campaign at the beginning of the New Year; hence the decision to call the campaign Discount 78.

On the evening of 9 January 1978, a large number of branch staff in every Sainsbury's store stayed on to work through the night. They were supposedly carrying out a massive stocktaking project, but were actually re-dressing sheleves and repricing the products selected for discount. All these products were provided with new labels which showed the old price appearing with a cross through it and the new, lower price emblazoned next to the 'Discount 78' logo. To publicise the launch of the campaign, the next day Sainsbury's ran a major advertising campaign in newspapers, magazines and on television – the first time the company employed such widespread advertising for a single promotion. The broadsheets and business media picked up on the event. One report in the *Daily Telegraph* could have been written by JD himself, so close was it to his own oft-repeated views about the benefits of competition: 'Such vigorous competition between the supermarkets must be good for the housewife. How irrelevant and ineffective this renders the whole bureaucratic flummery of price controls and monitoring.'

The campaign was an instant success; so much so that even the directors were taken by surprise. Customers flocked to the stores and, in the first 12 weeks of 1978, there is an AGB record showing an increase in Sainsbury's grocery market share from 8.5 per cent to 9.8 per cent. Tesco was still building its own share but at a far more modest rate; Sainsbury's was fast closing the gap on its main rival.

Figures for the first half-year of Discount 78 showed that Sainsbury's had rung up the biggest ever increase in volume of trade recorded in a six-month period. Food prices had risen by 7.3 per cent in the previous six months, while Sainsbury's sales had risen by nearly 20 per cent. If we compare this to activity in the rest of the sector during the same period, the sales gain in all food shops was 3.8 per cent and in food multiples it was 8.8 per cent. A price comparison in mid-1978 covering 150 lines (including own-label and proprietary, perishable and non-perishable goods) shows Sainsbury's to be nearly 1.5 pence cheaper in the pound than Tesco and nearly 2.5 pence cheaper than the average high-street competition.

At the end of 1978, it was recorded that Sainsbury's sales had increased, in real terms, by more than 14 per cent over the period of the campaign – more than the company had achieved in the previous six years combined. As Discount 78 drew to a close, it was followed immediately by a relaunch of the scheme, in the form of Discount 79. At the annual general meeting that year, JD described Discount 78 as 'without doubt the most important new marketing strategy since we established our unique range of own-brand products many years ago'.

The success of this operation was mostly the result of reducing prices in the stores while maintaining quality, but other factors contributed. In the six months after the Jubilee strike and before the start of the campaign, JD had made sure that the senior managers throughout the company were aware of certain strategic priorities that would strengthen the company's competitive position.

First, the store-development programme would continue at an ambitious level, as long as planning allowed, but there would be greater focus on achieving the right balance between the ideal size of store and the range of goods on offer. JD reported to shareholders that Sainsbury's had spent 20 years developing stores that were too small followed by two years building some of them too big. With hindsight, of course, that was not true, but at this stage there was a growing concern within the trade generally that the market was becoming saturated, or was likely to become so. It was surely unsustainable for all the leading competitors to push forward building bigger and better food stores for a relatively static, price-conscious population. At mid-1978, the ideal Sainsbury's size appeared to be around 23,000 square feet, sufficient therefore to take the full food and standard non-food range, to allow comfortable shopping and to leave some room for developing the range. Sainsbury's could also maintain its high level of sales per square foot in this size of store. The acquisition of larger sites up to about 29,000 square feet – when and if their purchase was possible – would be considered on their merits. In such stores the company would have the option to offer an extended range including hardware, textiles, cosmetics and other more recently introduced lines.

Second, as part of the general thrust to improve productivity, the directors sought to reduce branch storage areas as a proportion of the overall floor space in the stores. This would provide more selling space for the same property overhead. Sainsbury's earlier self-service stores had generally much larger preparation and storage areas than competitors. But even as these areas had diminished, with most of the pre-packaging work now carried out by suppliers themselves or at Sainsbury's depots, the more recently built stores still needed large storage areas because of the demand to replenish the shelves quickly – a factor directly relating to the company's primacy in sales intensity, as measured by sales achieved per square foot of sales area. No matter the pressure on store managers and staff, keeping the shelves filled remained an unshakable priority and was one of the keys to maintaining customer loyalty. In practice, for the time being, there was no easy way to reduce the size of in-store warehouse areas; adjusting the balance would have to be an evolving process.

A third strategic element – and one that could more readily be achieved – was the renewed energy and vigour applied to the development of Sainsbury's own-label products. These continued to be a hugely successful part of the sales equation. For example, approximately two-thirds of Sainsbury's grocery sales in 1977/8 were own-label. There was occasional debate among trading directors as to whether Sainsbury's was even putting too much emphasis on its own-label programme, to the detriment of some secondary brands and thus to customer choice. But the fact remained that Sainsbury's own-label goods were immensely popular and highly competitive; they were an essential element in the company's trading success. As the average size of the stores increased, it would become possible for much of the extra display space to be devoted to widening the choice of proprietary brands, while maintaining the vigour of the own-label programme.

Customers were becoming aware that they could almost always find a Sainsbury's version of their favourite product. In 1979, for example, among numerous own-label lines that Sainsbury's intro-duced were additional breakfast cereals, new styles of conserve, lager in new wide-mouthed bottles, biscuits, cream cakes, new champagnes, cassis and Italian wines, and a range of prepared chicken meals. The new breakfast cereals, including bran flakes, reflected a gradually emerging demand for healthier natural prod-ucts. In 1980, a further 189 own-label goods were added, and in 1981 the number of new products increased to 240. The pace of innova-tion remained unrelenting. All the while, Sainsbury's upgraded its labelling policy, offering more information about the nutritional values and calories of its products.

JD told his senior managers, 'We must have greater recognition of the advantages that come to us by being ahead of the game, by anticipating changing customer tastes and habits, by being there before others.' The clarion call for sustained effort and the obser-vance of traditional principles of trade would be made by JD frequently and in various ways, from board level down. All the directors acted on it, and it was heard by a highly motivated work-force to whom it became apparent that Sainsbury's was set to assume the dominant place in the market.

Everything was geared for further progress, but the supermarket-development programme was increasingly constrained by the difficulty of finding suitable sites. For some years now, effort and expense had been put into the second tier of the development programme, which involved replacing or upgrading stores that Sainsbury's had either outgrown or that were not ideally located. Directors were now resolved not to accept compromises of this kind in the location of new stores: they wanted only the sites that offered the right combination of space, car-parking facilities and accessi-bility for pedestrian shoppers. It was partly because of this – and the continuing difficulty of obtaining planning consent – that only seven new stores were opened in 1977/8 and then again in 1978/9, adding a relatively modest 256,000 square feet of sales space in all. Fortunately, the relentless pursuit of sites for new stores had, by 1979, borne good results, and the company announced plans to open no fewer than 50 stores in the next three years.

Considering the low number of new stores, the trading results announced in May 1979 were exceptional. Turnover exceeded £1 billion and profits before tax approached £33 million, up from £27.5 million the previous year. These figures reflected the phenomenal growth in trade that had resulted from the discount campaign and, of course, the hard work of all staff in making this work. As with the distribution of shares to staff when the company floated in 1973, the family were particularly keen to involve staff in the success of the business. In 1974, the company had introduced a save-as-you-earn share scheme enabling employees to take options to buy shares at a reduced price. In the 1979 annual report, JD announced the start of a profit-sharing scheme for staff which was now allowed under new legislation. Whenever the profit margin exceeded 2.5 per cent per year, staff would receive a share of profits. Employees may not have fallen over with excitement at the time, but within just a few years they would certainly notice the annual bonus, particularly those who accumulated shares rather than taking the cash alternative.

The year's volume growth in 1979 was the highest the company had recorded in any one year since the end of wartime control, and passing the billion-pound mark was an achievement that flagged the general successes of the company since its centenary. Department of Industry figures showed Sainsbury's market share of trade at 8.6 per cent, up from under 5 per cent in 1969. Over this period the company's profits had grown sevenfold, and Sainsbury's was serving about two million more customers each week and selling twice the volume of goods. The development programme had cost Sainsbury's more than £175 million, all of which was self-financed. This money had been spent on opening 127 supermarkets with a total of nearly two million square feet of sales space – the equivalent of about 80 per cent of the total sales space in mid-1979. In ten years, the 110-year-old company had undergone a sea change in its size, its structure and its fortunes.

In 1979, it also looked as if SavaCentre, the new joint-venture hyper-market company, would shortly be adding to the company's overall profits. Trading at Sainsbury's and BHS's first 76,600 square-foot SavaCentre, which opened at Washington, Tyne and Wear, in November 1977, was showing promise. More than 10,000 customers had passed through its doors on the first day, and the interest was generally sustained at a high level, so that the volume of trade was only outstripped by two or three hypermarkets in the whole coun-try. Deploying a brand new computer, Washington SavaCentre was one of the first stores to be able to provide hourly reports of the tak-ings, the numbers of customers through the checkouts, the average spend and even the rate of sale of individual items. SavaCentre became the only British retail store to rely on a computer for so much of its management information.

In October 1978, the second SavaCentre had opened in Hemp-stead, near Gillingham in Kent. About one-third of the 65,000 square-foot sales area was allocated to supermarket food and trad-itional non-food lines; two-thirds was allocated to space-hungry ranges of clothing and an extensive selection of household and gar-den goods. This balance of products became a template for further SavaCentres in the chain. It was always expected that food would contribute at least 60 per cent of SavaCentre's turnover. Sales at Hempstead were also well above the company's expectations. JD commented: 'These stores have outstripped our most optimistic forecasts. The volume of trade being achieved by the first two hypermarkets has caused us to review the systems necessary to handle an intensity of sales per square foot that is rarely achieved in hypermarkets anywhere in the world.'

In the establishment of SavaCentre, Sainsbury's and BHS had been significantly influenced by Carrefour in France and had adopted some of this leading hypermarket's methods. One of the notable differences in trading style between the early SavaCentres and the Sainsbury's supermarkets was the autonomy the former enjoyed. Each departmental manager was responsible for nego-tiating with suppliers, placing orders, pricing, evaluating local competition, controlling his own stock and managing his own sales team – a far cry from the approach at Sainsbury's, where such oper-ations were all centralised. The initial intention was for each new SavaCentre to operate this degree of autonomy, but in due course it was recognised that the disadvantages of this very different system outweighed the advantages. In another departure from Sainsbury's mainstream stores, each SavaCentre initially organised direct deliveries from suppliers, which reduced distribution costs, while the hypermarkets' size generated certain economies of scale. But one drawback, which would be closely monitored, was that early Sava-Centre stores lost out on the favourable terms that the centralised buying teams negotiated with suppliers for the mainstream supermarkets.

These hypermarkets were not simply conceived as massive supermarkets with an extended range. They were aimed at attracting customers who wanted to do all their regular food and non-supermarket shopping including clothing and household goods under one roof. They were moving toward the realisation of the true 'one-stop shop' that JD had spoken about in his marketing paper back in 1971. SavaCentres were thus designed for lengthy shopping trips which might involve the whole family. They had enormous car parks, generous aisles, large trolleys and attractive restaurants. Not least, SavaCentres offered lower prices than other supermarkets in the area – the prices of both Sainsbury's own-label lines and proprietary goods were about 1.5 to 2 per cent lower in these hypermarkets than in Sainsbury's mainstream supermarkets. Wherever possible, the plan was to locate the hypermarkets close to excellent transport links, ideally to the motorway network – although neither the Washington nor Hempstead locations were ideal in this respect. Further SavaCentre stores were under construction at Basildon and Oldbury, and planning was being sought for the first 'free-standing' SavaCentre on the edge of Reading, close to the M4. The Reading site was far closer to the ideal, but such sites were not easy to find.

To consolidate what had clearly become an effective management team at Sainsbury's, a number of board changes were made in the last two years of the decade. Timothy Sainsbury had relinquished his executive duties in 1974 to pursue a full-time career in politics but he was nominally an executive until 1978, after which he would remain closely involved as a non-executive director until 1983. Also in 1978, Tom Vyner was appointed as an additional buying director in charge of the grocery and non-food division; he brought with him what would prove invaluable experience, having come from the board of the Allied Suppliers Group. In 1979, Simon Sainsbury retired after 23 years with the company, having worked closely with

JD as deputy chairman since 1969. In his chairman's statement that year, JD paid a warm personal tribute to Simon's contribution to the company's success: 'No one could have helped me more to forward the growth and development of the Company,' he commented. 'His knowledge and depth of understanding of the business have been unrivalled and these, together with his financial acumen and vision, have brought great strength to the Board.'

Roy Griffiths now took over as sole deputy chairman, and in September 1979 became managing director. This was a key appointment. Everyone within the board and across the company's management had come to admire Griffiths for his particular gifts as an administrator and for his unstinting pursuit of improved productivity. As he worked increasingly closely with JD he became widely recognised as a perfect complement to the chairman. According to Joe Barnes, 'Roy was extremely level-headed and diplomatic, a superb thinker. He was the calm, reflective right-hand man, a perfect foil to John who was the passionate, intuitive retailer.' The temperamental balance between JD and Roy Griffiths was an important one. Ivor Hunt comments: 'The relationship worked particularly well because each greatly respected the other's abilities, and Roy became adept at sensing JD's mood and responding accordingly.'

In the same month, September 1979, JD appointed Peter Davis as assistant managing director, specifically responsible for directing and coordinating company trading in the buying and marketing areas. Angus Clark now joined the board as the company's personnel director and Derek Henson, also from Allied Suppliers, was appointed financial controller.

Alongside the newcomers, stalwarts on the existing board included Joe Barnes, who had been retail director since 1976; also Gurth Hoyer Millar, David Sainsbury and Len Payne, well established as development director, finance director and director of distribution respectively. And alongside Tom Vyner, who had come from a different milieu, the board already had two highly experienced buying directors who had in effect 'grown up' with Sainsbury's: Bob Ingham and Cecil Roberts. Bob Ingham was responsible for off-licence, frozen foods, dairy and produce-buying departments with the added role of overseeing the company's scientific services. Cecil Roberts was responsible for the fresh meat and all other perishable-buying departments. Sainsbury's top management reflected considerable breadth of experience. JD continued as chairman, and assumed the new title of chief executive.

Both new and existing board members were soon making improvements in their own areas of responsibility. As assistant managing director, Peter Davis remained in charge of marketing activities, and, following his key role in the discount campaign, focused on strengthening the marketing department by bringing together all the marketing-related operations from other divisions. Thus, the advertising department was brought under his wing, as was the public-relations department which had previously reported to Nigel Matthews, the company secretary. A new Directors' Marketing Committee was formed, chaired by Davis, which focused on the leading marketing issues in all the departments.

These developments changed the scope and activity of Sainsbury's marketing during the early 1980s. The monitoring of competitors was taken to new levels. Like his father, JD took keen note of the relative performance of other food retailers, not only in the UK but around the world. But what had once been close observation of competitors was now extended into rigorous benchmarking of their performance and regular data about a number of their operational activities. The scope of the data generated by the statistical services department was probably more wide-ranging than anywhere else in the trade. Ivor Hunt and his team would, for example, ensure the board had access to frequently updated knowledge not only of competitors' prices – which continued to vary as inflation slowed while competition increased – but also their stock levels, customer-service problems, display methods, anything that offered an insight into their performance, innovation or likely success.

Added to this, the marketing department started to develop more sophisticated tools for measuring Sainsbury's own customer expectations and perceptions about the stores; these were used to inform new-product development, store layouts and advertising campaigns. The statistical services department created questionnaires through which about 50 key measures could be identified and surveyed on a regular basis. The company therefore had knowledge to hand about customer perceptions of prices, quality, service levels, product availability, cleanliness, speed through the checkouts, freshness, hygiene and other factors that determined the attractiveness of Sainsbury's offer. Because he remained constantly close to the front line through his weekly store visits, a good deal of JD's own decision-making was of course based on his personal observations and what he learnt from talking to the area, district and store managers, and from his regular contact with customers. Nevertheless, this wealth of statistically gathered information was a powerful resource.

JD's degree of vigilance about the presentation and quality of goods offered to customers was perhaps not surprising given that he remained ultimately responsible for the company's trading decisions. The appointment of Roy Griffiths as deputy chairman and managing director had to some extent freed JD to concentrate on long-term retailing and marketing strategy and to delegate certain operational matters. But his attention remained keenly fixed on the daily business too, particularly on the offer in the stores and how this was meeting customer expectations. His reputation for close scrutiny and strong comment on his store visits preceded him. As he puts it, 'How could I walk past a bad display, and not make a comment without giving the impression to the manager that it didn't matter? It most certainly did matter.'

Colin Harvey, former store manager who later became a director of the company, remembers a visit made by JD to his store:

> We had lunch; he had some Sainsbury's bottled beetroot which was soft so he said to me, 'Where does this come from?' I didn't know who the supplier was. He immediately got on the phone and ascertained that there had been a change of supplier. He knew straight away that this product was not as good as the previous one. The upshot was that every product in our entire pickle range had to be looked at again by the pickle-buyer.

Harvey remembers another occasion when he was quizzed by JD on the subject of the appropriate length of the bananas sold in his store. He hazarded an answer which proved to be wrong, betraying the fact that he had not thoroughly read the produce bulletin:

> If I apologised once I apologised 20 times as we went round the store, but I never forgot that lesson about detail. JD only changed the subject when I told him that a new brand of bread called 'Mighty White' was outselling our own brand and why didn't we sell something like it of our own. He turned round and said that

was an excellent idea and immediately got on to the bread-buyers at headquarters to demand why they were not already making a Sainsbury's version of the brand.

In the sphere of buying skills, Tom Vyner's appointment signifi-cantly changed the dynamic within the board. Vyner's expertise was mostly in the negotiation of proprietary brand goods – he had first-hand and thorough knowledge of the manufacturers' side of the business. The discount campaign had reduced margins signifi-cantly on a number of goods, and this had accentuated the need to buy at the keenest possible prices. Some of the improvements he made were simple and immediate. He learnt, for example, that Sainsbury's was paying its suppliers within seven to fourteen days as standard. When he raised a question about this he was told that it had long been a Sainsbury's principle to pay suppliers quickly. Tom Vyner pointed out that management in major manufacturers such as Nestlé or Unilever would only become aware of how quickly companies paid if they ended upon the 'not-paid' list. If Sainsbury's were to pay on the exact due date rather than virtually by return of post they would benefit from a greatly enhanced cash flow. He esti-mated that the extra cash could build 30 stores. The regime was quickly changed, and it became policy to pay on the due date speci-fied in the contract but no sooner.

Other improvements took slightly longer to introduce but had an even greater impact on Sainsbury's bottom line. Tom Vyner started to evaluate exactly what Sainsbury's suppliers were doing. He was determined to understand their marketing spend, their distribution costs, the bonuses they were giving – all in order to be able to chal-lenge them hard on price. He recalls: 'Slowly we began to see that things could be much tighter, so we started to train our buyers to be tougher. Sainsbury's buyers were wonderful people, really know-ledgeable and committed, but they hadn't had enough experience of really serious, tough competitive buying.' From the beginning of the 1980s Sainsbury's buyers were continually exhorted to get better deals, although not all the buyers had quite the same approach to suppliers as Tom Vyner had developed. It was not unusual for the new, more assertive, even aggressive buying style at Sainsbury's sometimes to ruffle suppliers' feathers and so damage their good will.

Tom Vyner's buying experience complemented the other buying

directors. In their own areas of operation, both Cecil Roberts and Bob Ingham were highly gifted buyers with long experience of Sainsbury's trading ethos, particularly the search for quality. Few of Sainsbury's customers would have realised the trouble that was taken to ensure the quality of products that appeared on the shelves. Cecil Roberts recalls how Sainsbury's managed to ensure that they had the very best quality of canned salmon in the business, 'even better than John West' (the acknowledged brand leader in canned salmon worldwide). Sainsbury's buyers would go to Alaska to see the rivers and to work out where the best fish were and who was doing the best canning. 'We would see what John West was doing and what Prince's was doing,' he says. 'They were often buying at about the same time as we were, sometimes from the same factory, so it was our job to make sure we got there first, so they would get what we left behind.'

In a similar vein, Bob Ingham remembers the challenges that he faced to ensure customers were treated as fairly as possible. A practical example of this was the way the yoghurt carton developed within Sainsbury's. Once yoghurt became a generally popular product in the 1970s, its packaging changed from glass to waxed-paper cartons. Initially these had an inverted u-shaped base similar to the punts in some bottles of wine. 'Branded suppliers wanted to have these punts as big as possible to make customers think they were getting more yoghurt,' says Ingham. 'But we just couldn't have that – it wasn't the way things were done at Sainsbury's . . . We stuck to the principles of honesty in everything.'

Working closely with JD, whose uncompromising attitude to detail remained the foundation of Sainsbury's buying style, this became a close-knit buying team which would underpin the success of the company throughout the 1980s and into the 1990s. Tom Vyner remembers:

> Buyers were seen as the lifeblood of the business. The family ethos had always been to treat buyers like gods, because if they didn't get the goods right, there was no hope for those folks out there in the stores. But now we really had to work harder. We were all obsessed with quality and value. With Bob and Cecil, who grew up in the business, it was in their blood. For me it was an obsession because I loved food, I just loved Sainsbury's quality.

Customers appeared to think the same, and Discount 80 maintained the exceptional value they had come to expect. The crisis of the Jubilee strike was history, and even the concept of a price war seemed dated – replaced by an in-built process of constant competitive watchfulness. Sainsbury's and Tesco remained neck-and-neck at the top of the premier league of the nation's supermarkets, but Sainsbury's exuded particular confidence as it emerged from the turbulent years of the 1970s.

Chapter 12

STORE MANAGEMENT
1980–1983

S AINSBURY'S ENTERED THE 1980s in good shape. At last, consumers were becoming a little wealthier and recovering their confidence. National food sales rose in 1979/80. The figures that the company announced in May 1980 showed another substantial rise over the previous financial year, with a 22 per cent growth in sales, and profit growth of more than 40 per cent. Profit margins were almost 4 per cent, having averaged in the low threes during the previous ten years. All the graphs pointed upwards – earnings per share, volume of sales, numbers of customers – and Sainsbury's market share was up another half-point at 9.1 per cent (according to DOI figures). Margaret Thatcher's new Conservative government was far more business-friendly, and appeared to appreciate the contributions made to the economy by the service industry. The 1980s looked open-armed with promise.

Unlike some of its competitors, Sainsbury's had negligible debts. There was the facility to raise cash from shareholders or banks, but the family had always been essentially conservative about raising money, particularly when the store-development programme, the main capital investment, could be paid for by a combination of retained profits, sale and leaseback of property, and the profitable disposal of older high-street sites that no longer met company needs. Financially, Sainsbury's was very secure.

In the late 1970s, during the period of prices and incomes control, JD had made increasing contributions to various trade organisations. And since July 1979 he had been one of five marketing advisers to Peter Walker, Minister of Agriculture, Fisheries and Food, involved in an initiative to make the food industry more alive to marketing needs and to promote government support for British food. In the 1980 New Year's Honours List, when he received a knighthood for his services to the food industry, he commented: 'I believe it is as much a tribute to the company as to me personally and that makes me very happy.'

As a consequence of his personal interests, JD now exercised a growing degree of influence outside the business, particularly in the arts. He had been on the board of the Royal Opera since 1969. After marrying the ballerina Anya Linden in 1963, he and Anya formed the Linbury Trust to support charitable causes, including the arts, and he gave a lot of his Sainsbury's shares to this cause. Like his father, uncle, brothers and cousin, JD was a private benefactor on a large scale, although the breadth of the family's involvement in many trusts and charities would only be brought to light in the media attention surrounding the funding of the Sainsbury Wing of the National Gallery in 1987. At a corporate level, Sainsbury's became a significant sponsor of the arts, dance, music, theatre and community activities during the 1980s.

The board spent no time bathing in the glow of its achievements. The efficiency of the stores remained a high priority, and this task was mostly down to Joe Barnes, as director of retail division. Barnes had already put considerable effort into revising store systems and processes, the better to reflect the increasing size and complexity of the company and its supermarkets. In particular, he focused on the role of the store managers, endeavouring to make them more aware of their accountability for what went on in the stores. Many decisions and activities were carried out at a remove from the supermarkets in the front line of the business, but it was ultimately the manager's job to make sure that customers were served well in the stores.

Barnes was thus determined to create an even more capable group of store managers to drive through the many improvements that needed to be made if the company was going to maintain its competitive edge. He was the right man for this work: he was amiable and approachable but also thoroughly determined to ensure that the stores were run productively and professionally. The *Daily Telegraph* has described him as 'a pleasant man, but with a touch of steel when required'. He worked tirelessly to ensure that discipline, high standards and rigorous attention to detail were the norm in every store. He had a talent for communicating key messages in uncomplicated terms; store managers knew their primary objectives were to keep the store clean and tidy, shelves filled and customers happy. Given the higher average size and the increasing range of the stores, the process of translating these relatively simple instructions into practice actually demanded more skill and administrative ability among store managers than ever before. The board were confident that the programme of opening an average of at least 15 new stores each year would continue. This expansion demanded more store managers and deputies – people with broad skills who could cope with considerable pressure.

Reporting to Barnes, Bert Ellis, as the retail division's personnel manager, stepped up the graduate-training programme which had initially been engineered by Roy Griffiths and remained one of his close interests. Ellis also set out to lure more mid-career store managers and deputies from competitor companies into the Sainsbury's fold; he upgraded existing training programmes, refined appraisal systems and established new career structures in the quest to attract and develop the new breed.

In order that store managers were not distracted from their job of running the stores, strategic decisions were made centrally. It was quite possible for managers to feel isolated in their work, particularly in the largest and busiest of stores where products were selling at what the entire trade considered to be an astonishing rate. One of the strengths of Barnes's approach was his support for the managers; he made it his business to get to know them personally. Either he or Dennis Males, departmental director in charge of retail operations since 1977, would try to visit each store in the chain at least twice a year. This was no mean feat: expansion northwards was finally being achieved, and the schedule involved spending two days each week away from headquarters, sometimes travelling by helicopter to the more distant branches. Males was the key man in Barnes's immediate team. He had spent his entire working life at Sainsbury's and had grown up with the self-service and supermarket revolution. As a result he was highly respected and influential within the stores, and had extensive first-hand knowledge of their operation. Until he retired in 1985, Males was effectively Barnes's 'eyes and ears' in the stores.

This face-to-face style of retail management created a well-motivated and loyal team of store managers who were collectively able to deliver the standards of service the board demanded. It also enabled the board to implement necessary changes, to introduce new technology or refinements and develop best practice in the stores relatively quickly. Almost every Tuesday since 1969, JD had also climbed into his car, or occasionally boarded a chartered helicopter, to make his own visits to about five separate stores in the day. In these he was invariably accompanied by either the area manager or one of the district managers. Sometimes JD and Barnes combined their visits. Whatever the programme, staff were aware that the top brass truly cared about them, their customers, local problems, the grass roots of the business. The visits were more than 'spot-checks' in this respect: from a staff perspective there are few better ways to maintain morale and instil a sense that what one does is important.

Throughout the early 1980s, the process of modification, adaptation and improvement in the stores was constant. New display techniques were introduced, store layouts were refined, checkouts were improved and the allocation of shelf-space changed. In his report to senior management in 1982, JD estimated that improvements such as these made between 1979 and 1981, although seemingly minor, were the equivalent of adding 100,000 square feet of extra selling space. All the while, distribution had become more reliable, and it was at last becoming possible to reduce the amount of store warehousing space, achieving further efficiencies.

For years it had been standard for all Sainsbury's stores to be closed all day on Sunday and Monday and to shut early on Saturday afternoons. This regime had been established in the early 1960s partly in response to the shortage of staff in the sector, and the need to provide staff with two consecutive days off, on Sunday and Monday. With the pressure of competition and changing shopping habits, it was high time that such shopping hours were re-examined. It was believed that extending opening hours even slightly would provide more convenience for customers and thus increase each store's sales. From October 1979 Sainsbury's began opening on Mondays from midday, and then from October 1980 it introduced late Wednesday opening, until 8 pm. In May 1981, stores began opening on Monday from 9.30 am and Saturday hours were extended to 5 pm.

The drive for productivity in the stores was reflected in the steady increase in Sainsbury's sales per square foot per week. In 1980, the company was generating weekly sales of £8.12 per square foot against Tesco's average of £4.74 – or, looked at another way, weekly profits of 29p per square foot of sales area as against Tesco's 11p. By 1983, the company was producing sales of some £12 per square foot against Tesco's £6. This was a measure of sales area only; if the gross store area was taken into account the figure would not be quite so favourable. Nevertheless, during the early 1980s, Sainsbury's was creating the most productive supermarkets in the UK.

In late 1979, a new executive committee, the Chairman's Committee, had been introduced to steer decisions relating to the company's capital-investment programme – primarily this meant decisions about store development. The committee comprised JD as chairman, Griffiths as deputy chairman, Barnes as retail director, Hoyer Millar as development director and David Sainsbury as finance director. In the early 1980s, Ivor Hunt joined as the only non-board member, reflecting the importance of increasingly sophisticated statistics and data used to evaluate the potential of new sites.

At the committee's regular meetings, Hoyer Millar would provide information about proposed sites and those under development. At their most straightforward, new acquisitions might involve the purchase of a single parcel of freehold property; at their most complicated they demanded piecing together a considerable number of freeholds and leaseholds. Hoyer Millar also provided information on planning, the environment, local development activities and the prospect of gaining planning consent. Hunt would add his detailed tactical and strategic site analyses, which enabled greater accuracy in forecasting sales and therefore helped the committee to gauge the amount that the company might sensibly pay for a site. Hunt recalls, 'Altogether, there was a great deal of information brought to bear but inevitably there were occasions when decisions were made to spend much more on a site than the analyses indicated to be appropriate. JD might have a strong feeling about a location and he would be prepared to pay for it. His instincts were often right.'

JD himself reflects that there was sometimes conflict between traders and the financial appraisal department in this process. It is perhaps ironic that over the years Sainsbury's had brought site assessment to a fine art, but in so doing had introduced financial constraints that caused occasional frustration. The financial appraisal department could set the upper limit that Sainsbury's should pay for a new site based on apparently compelling information. By comparison, it seemed that the bids made by Tesco, Asda and other key competitors depended more simply on how much they wanted the site. Sometimes their decisions were also based on strategic factors such as taking sites to block competition in particular areas.

During this period, there was a change in the nature of some of Sainsbury's store developments. At several sites the estates division worked in partnership with local authorities to provide facilities for the local community such as libraries, sports halls and swimming pools; these were built as part of the overall plan centred on a new store. Sainsbury's had in effect become a property developer on these sites, many of which provided space to sub-let to other traders. Gradually, this was bringing in a stream of separate income which, in 1980, exceeded £1 million.

The trade that was being won by Sainsbury's newest stores had changed significantly over the previous ten years. Whereas the new supermarkets had once drawn customers away from myriad local independent grocery stores, Co-ops, butchers, fishmongers and bakers, the market share of these outlets had reduced to such an extent that new trade had to be drawn from other supermarkets; the smallest and least well run of these were the most vulnerable.

All the large multiples, including Sainsbury's, Asda, Tesco and Safeway, and also M&S and Waitrose for their food quality, were competing more directly with each other not only for customers but also for the best edge-of-town sites. When M&S decided that these sites would suit its development purposes, it entered into an agreement to find new sites together with Tesco, far more experienced in this particular activity. Over and above the planning process itself, the increased competition for sites was another challenge to the leading retailers, and one which drove property prices steeply upwards during the 1980s.

As competition intensified, the site proposals attracted vociferous opposition from local traders, who argued that the big supermarket developments threatened the vitality of the town centres. Local planning authorities and central government were often sympathetic to these small traders. It was generally true that small independent food retailers saw their trade collapse or put under significant pressure when large, modern supermarkets arrived on their doorsteps. Hoyer Millar spent considerable time and energy arguing with local planners that the effect on other traders was not a valid reason for refusing planning permission. The public had a right to do their grocery shopping where they chose, and Sainsbury's supermarkets offered more choice, lower prices and more convenience. Planners countered that they did not want to see boarded-up shops in the middle of their towns and villages and often delayed permission, imposed onerous conditions or refused new developments altogether.

The very evident changes that had occurred in the post-war years in the UK's once great manufacturing towns and cities had left many inner-city areas run down and no longer used or fit for manufacturing purposes. The modern trend was for smaller, light industrial units, which were themselves locating on the edge-of-town business and industrial estates. Consequently, inner cities were areas of general deprivation, often with high unemployment. The government had produced a White Paper, *Policy for the Inner Cities*, in 1977, and in his 1978 annual report JD stated a shared concern 'expressed in planning circles and the government about the decay of some inner-city areas'. He believed certain sites might have potential for redevelopment as retail sites because they were close to the centres of population and large enough to offer a good-sized store and ample space for car parks. Later, further suitable inner-city sites became available when utility companies were put under pressure by government to sell redundant or derelict property.

The Nine Elms supermarket on the Wandsworth Road in London, which opened in February 1982, was an apt demonstration of what could be done with otherwise unused inner-city space. The store was built on land surplus to the requirements of the New Covent Garden Market, an area previously occupied by derelict railway sidings. This was Sainsbury's largest Central London store, and the first to be built in the capital for 16 years; while it was bought for an attractive price because of the site's lack of suitability for commercial purposes, it was strategically well placed in one of South London's busiest catchment areas for car-borne shoppers. The rare and precious commodity of car parking for 300 cars was offered alongside a store with a sales area of more than 25,000 square feet. And Nine Elms created 360 new jobs. The store stocked 7,500 lines, the widest range of products of any Sainsbury's branch, including 60 different varieties of bread, 170 delicatessen lines, more than 50 types of fresh fish and a full range of kosher foods. Included in the wet-fish department was an alternative to cod called hokki, imported from New Zealand by the resourceful fish-buyer.

Such was the interest in the new store that there had to be no

Roy Griffiths in the chair as directors take questions at a conference of 200 store managers in January 1977; from left to right: Dennis Males, departmental director; Peter Snow, director; Roy Griffiths, deputy chairman; Joe Barnes, director; and Angus Clark, departmental director

Sainsbury's own-label wines were responsible for the considerable success of the wines and spirits departments

Sainsbury's Discount'78 campaign launched in January 1978 offered long-term price reductions on many products and greatly boosted sales. The campaign was strategically important at a time of increasing competition

First introduced at Telford in 1973, the in-store bakeries in the supermarkets served fresh bread throughout the day

The first SavaCentre hypermarket, at Washington, Tyne and Wear, opened in November 1977 with 78,600 square feet of selling area and 36 checkouts

New own-label lines in early 1980: the breakfast cereals emphasise bran and other natural products, and the range of preserves carry electronic bar codes in preparation for scanning

'Tenderlean' lamb: by developing innovative techniques to improve quality, Sainsbury's maintained substantial sales of fresh meats, even as consumers were turning increasingly to chicken

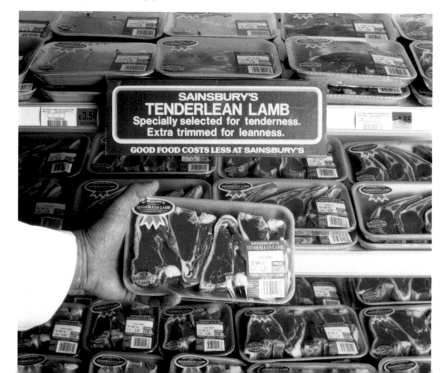

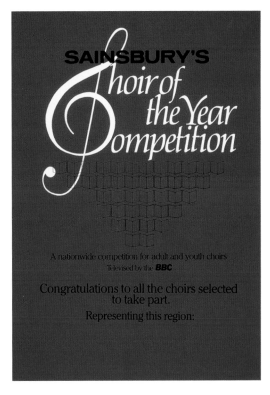

In 1981, Sainsbury's started a programme of extensive arts sponsorship, supporting theatre, ballet, opera and choral work. The Choir of the Year Competition was watched by millions on television

Britain's largest hypermarket, SavaCentre at
London Colney, Hertfordshire, was opened
in 1990 on a 23-acre site alongside Junction
22 of the M25; carrying 39,000 products, it
offered free parking for 1,800 cars

David Sainsbury (right) became chairman
of SavaCentre in 1981. Here he talks to David
Clapham, managing director of London
Colney branch

The wet-fish counter at SavaCentre, a marketing approach successfully adapted from Sainsbury's supermarkets

Sainsbury's took over US supermarket chain Shaw's in 1987. Note the slogan on the customer's shopping bag outside a new store opened in Milford, New Hampshire, in 1991

The inevitable – and successful – Homebase own-label range of products

Gurth Hoyer Millar (left), chairman of Homebase, with Dino Adriano, general manager

fewer than four preview events on the day before the store opened, one for local civic dignitaries, the next for the press and media, the third specifically for suppliers and the last in the evening for senior politicians including Conservative ministers Peter Walker and Geoffrey Howe, and David Steel, leader of the Liberal Party. Later, JD accompanied Margaret Thatcher on a visit to Nine Elms. This drew yet more publicity for the store, but not quite in the way expected. The store was buzzing with photographers and reporters, but none of them had the slightest interest in the prime minister's views on the store. Instead, they quizzed Margaret Thatcher about the resignation that morning of Party Chairman Cecil Parkinson from the Cabinet following disclosure of his extra-marital affair.

Sainsbury's continued to reuse former derelict land or property throughout the 1980s, and by the end of the decade more than half the company's new stores were built on such land. Occasionally, construction involved the thoroughgoing restoration of a historic site as part of the overall store development. In Streatham in South London, the staff restaurant adjoining a new Sainsbury's branch was built within the walls of a listed building which had once been a silk mill. The building next to this was also restored and converted into a day nursery. Edge-of-town stores were also built on unused industrial land.

JD has often referred to the Sainsbury's ethos as 'traditionalist, with a passion to innovate'. Old-fashioned principles of quality, value and service could in fact only be maintained through considerable innovation as the company grew in size and complexity. Innovations that improved productivity or reduced overheads helped to maintain low prices and provide good value; those affecting store layouts or checkouts improved the entire shopping experience.

Ever since JD had announced what appeared to be a far-fetched new concept in 1967, he and the board had closely watched the emergence of 'scanning' in the US, where the technology was developed and increasingly deployed in supermarkets during the 1970s. It involved the use of an electronic 'eye' to record the sale of each item passed before it by the cashier. Not only would customers receive itemised bills with each product named and priced, but the data could be used to improve the efficiency of stocking and ordering. Under the direction of Jeremy Grindle, departmental director in charge of branch services, Sainsbury's started conducting its own trials in June 1979. The company embarked on an intensive programme of research comparing IBM, NCR, Sweda and ICL equipment and thereby gaining substantial expertise in the new technology. These trials were carried out at the Broadfield branch near Crawley, and they attracted plenty of attention from the media and public. The board was increasingly eager to introduce scanning throughout the Sainsbury's chain, but the conversion costs in 1980 appeared extremely high and the technology was still not considered reliable. Only about 3 per cent of products were printed with the new 13-digit European Article Numbering System – better known as bar codes. It was estimated that 85 per cent of products needed to carry these before scanning systems became viable.

The board considered that Sainsbury's had two particular advantages over competitors which underpinned their commitment to scanning technology: Sainsbury's had already developed excellent computerised stocking and ordering systems which it was about to improve further, and a large proportion of the goods it sold were own-label. The company could thus ensure that about 60 per cent of products could be bar coded quickly, and it had in-house technological expertise and a reliable computer system with which to harness and capitalise on scanning technology.

The Broadfield scanning trials continued and were difficult and slow, particularly when American or European equipment broke down without assistance on hand. Bar coding was improvised through the use of specially prepared locally printed labels. But Sainsbury's was learning a lot from the trials: checkouts would need to be completely redesigned; bar-code printers that could be integrated with scales for weighing meat, vegetables and fruit needed to be manufactured; and staff needed special training to operate scanning checkouts efficiently. This technology would not be rushed, and trials continued for several years before the company settled on equipment provided by ICL, the only British candidate, in 1984. ICL was invited to develop a system specifically for Sainsbury's requirements. Only then was the full conversion to scanning technology considered worthwhile. According to JD: 'It is hard to overstate Jeremy Grindle's contribution in the development of scanning, and how much it meant to the success of the stores.'

Just one year later, on 1 October 1985, the Burpham branch opened equipped with the new system, and immediately afterwards the company started rolling it out across the chain. By 1988 almost 75 per cent of all the food scanned in UK supermarkets passed over Sainsbury's checkouts; by 1990, the system was installed in all Sainsbury's stores. JD says, 'It was a huge decision, but one which we got absolutely right. The fact that we worked hard to adopt the right system for us, and then to push ahead very fast was of tremendous benefit.'

Although it had been a cautious development, Sainsbury's was nevertheless about two to three years ahead of its competition in scanning. Tesco had invested very heavily in its own scanning trials at the end of the 1970s but had been forced to abandon the project: its capital resources were needed primarily to upgrade its distribution system, and there were problems with transferring the technology from the US. Sainsbury's now had a customised technology which not only improved customer service but gave the company point-of-sale data that was accurate and timely, and linked directly to the ordering and stocking systems. This enabled Sainsbury's to timetable deliveries more efficiently, to schedule staffing more accurately, to reduce stocking levels where possible and to provide information that allowed manufacturers to schedule their production better. JD had been confident enough about scanning to predict in the annual report of 1979 that this would be 'the greatest change to come in the next decade'. He was proved right.

Sainsbury's appetite for new technology included the adoption of in-store computers. In 1982, the first of these was installed which was able to communicate directly with the mainframe computers at Blackfriars. Over the next few years, dedicated computers were installed in every Sainsbury's supermarket across the country, enabling information about sales and stocks to be relayed to head office far more quickly than before. This meant that slow-moving items could quickly be spotted and weeded out, and faster responses could be made to items that had shelf-lives that depended, for example, on the weather. Store computers were complemented by DISCO, the Distribution Stock Control system which was installed in all Sainsbury's depots between 1982 and 1984. The direct link between stores, head office and depots represented a real logistical advance for the business. The company could be more flexible and immediate in its decisions about stock levels, pricing, distribution and ordering with almost real-time information being provided about the level of sales in the supermarkets. This enabled stock levels to be reduced, and the savings could be passed on to the customer.

By 10 am on a Monday morning the chairman and his board knew the total trade in all the branches of the previous week. A computer print-out showed the percentage change of those sales compared with the week before that, and with the same week in the previous year. The figures were broken down into the different categories and sizes of Sainsbury's branches. JD could not only see the best performances and the worst, but he would notice seasonal variations in sales which he could discuss with the buying directors and then act upon. With the same regularity, he would also expect to know if a competitor had opened near to any of these stores, and could then determine how it affected that store's business.

In another sphere of operations, in 1980 Sainsbury's had begun to experiment with computerised energy-management systems. This innovative programme was led by Peter Ibbotson, manager of the branch-engineering department, who had said at Sainsbury's engineering energy-management conference in January 1980, 'The two most serious problems that will affect the industrial world in the 1980s will be energy and inflation, and we can help to minimise their joint effect on the company's fortunes by continuing to conserve energy by every practical means available to us.' A raft of measures had already been introduced to achieve some energy savings, but the new computerised energy-management system was a radical approach. Tested at the Blackpole branch, it received a 25 per cent grant from the Department of Energy. The initial results were disappointing, so a further trial was launched using equipment designed to Sainsbury's specifications by a group of graduates at Southampton University. The new system appeared to work well, and Peter Ibbotson wrote a report asking the board to do a limited trial at five further stores. When he presented his report to JD he was greeted with, 'If it is as good as you make it out, why do we need another trial? Why shouldn't we just adopt it at every new store?'

The first branch to open with the new system was at Hull in 1984. The system involved recycling heat from refrigeration plants and cold stores, and it was so effective that boilers were no longer needed to provide hot water for staff canteens, washrooms and cleaning. Branches built in the mid-1980s used only 60 per cent of the energy that equivalent-sized branches had used ten years before. By October 1984, Sainsbury's had already reduced its energy costs from 1 per cent to 0.5 per cent of turnover. Not only was this good for the bottom line, but it reinforced an attribute that had been part of the character of the company since it was founded: that of social responsibility. In February 1989, Sainsbury's Burpham branch received the Electricity Council's prestigious Beta award for the most energy-efficient large building in the UK.

Each year the company was turning in results that varied only between the poles of very good and excellent. The *Financial Times* referred to the results in 1981, when sales were up by 30 per cent on the year before and the volume growth of 17.3 per cent represented the highest increase in any year since food rationing ended after the war, as 'flabbergasting figures'. The continuing discount scheme had made the standard Sainsbury's shopping basket among the cheapest on the high street.

In 1982, JD reported to his senior managers that before discount trading, Asda prices had been recorded at an impressive 6 per cent lower than Sainsbury's; currently there was only a 1 per cent difference in Asda's favour. Tesco was still Sainsbury's nearest rival, and its prices were dearer than Sainsbury's by 1.3 per cent. Even Carrefour's competitive position had changed significantly; despite the economies of scale that this hypermarket could bring to bear, its food was now the same price or even a little more expensive than Sainsbury's. SavaCentre by comparison was, as planned, offering consistently lower prices than any food trader in the UK.

Even as Sainsbury's ventured further into the north, where it still had less experience and less confidence about the effects of competition from cheaper outlets such as Asda, some outstanding results were achieved. For instance, when the new store in Leeds was opened in 1981, the first week's trading was a full 33 per cent above the estimate; and when, nearer the Sainsbury's heartland, an edge-of-town store was opened at Rayleigh Weir between Southend and Basildon, it achieved an exceptional level of trade despite competition from the nearby SavaCentre and two other large supermarkets in the region. Living up to its reputation, Sainsbury's formula rarely disappointed either the board or the customers.

Chapter 13

DIVERSIFICATION
1980–1989

SOME DIRECTORS, particularly Roy Griffiths and David Sainsbury, had been concerned during the last years of the 1970s about the long-term sustainability of growth in the retail-food industry in the UK. Was expansion into new territories viable, particularly in the areas where other chains had already intensified their hold? If something approaching saturation were to occur in the UK food market, Sainsbury's – the most heavily dependent of all the supermarket companies on the sale of food – would suffer more than most, and rates of expansion would surely be difficult to maintain.

Nevertheless, JD had great belief in the continued success of Sainsbury's supermarkets, as testified by the popularity of new stores and the continued growth in volumes sold, and his view was vindicated by market research. In 1979, an AGB survey revealed that Sainsbury's was the most popular of all food-retailing supermarkets in the areas in which it traded. But JD had other concerns about the future of mainstream food retailing in the UK – namely, the continued difficulty of achieving planning consent for new food stores and the possibility of further stifling government interventions in the highly politicised food sector. As the commercial potential of edge-of-town sites caught on generally in the late 1970s, other types of retail outlet were also competing for the best sites. The board agreed it was time to think seriously about proper diversification as a means of hedging the company's risks and reducing its vulnerability. SavaCentre was a form of diversification, but with so much of the subsidiary company's turnover derived from food sales, it was reasonably argued that this was essentially a food-retailing operation.

The board considered various diversification strategies. One of the ideas mooted at the time was to launch a fast-food chain. McDonalds had opened its first hamburger bar in the UK in 1974 and had already built a strong business. But the board recognised that this was a very different trade and not an ideal undertaking for Sainsbury's: the technology, tactics and style of fast food were nothing like as close to the company's supermarket expertise as the option of establishing a new home-improvements enterprise. The Do-It-Yourself emporium, providing a substantial range of tools and materials for both professional builders and home improvers, had become a successful style of business – a sector worth almost £1.5 billion in 1979. Within a short time the board decided on not one but two options. The first was to set up a new DIY business in the UK; the second was to acquire an existing food-retailing multiple overseas, where there were fewer constraints on development.

Following experience with SavaCentre, the board decided that forming an alliance with a company that already had expertise in the DIY market would be the best way to establish the first of these new businesses. An ideal partner was soon found in a Belgian company, GB-Inno-BM, which had successfully opened a chain of DIY superstores in Belgium, Holland, Germany and the US under the name of Brico. JD visited Belgium and was impressed by the modern and sleek stores, which seemed to him superior in their presentation and quality to B&Q in the UK, which was the market leader in this sector. In October 1979, Sainsbury's formally announced that they had signed a 75/25 joint venture deal with GB-Inno-BM, with Sainsbury's taking the bigger share. The Sainsbury's/GB stores would be modelled closely on the partner company's successful continental stores. The new business would sell a complete range of builder's materials and garden-centre items as well as the usual DIY products. Each store would have a minimum sales area of 20,000 square feet, and preferably much more than this.

As with SavaCentre, the new company's board of directors represented the two companies in the joint venture. Representing Sainsbury's, Gurth Hoyer Millar and Peter Davis were appointed chairman and deputy chairman of the new business respectively, and were charged with getting the marketing and initial positioning right. Derek Henson, Sainsbury's financial controller, was appointed financial director.

Davis was primarily responsible for creating the new company's brand, including the name, Sainsbury's Homebase, the logo and the distinctive green livery. Hoyer Millar came up with the positioning. He considered that one potential drawback was that DIY did not appeal to women; it was a male concern, and men were responsible for the buying. However, women generally made the decisions. He was determined that from the outset the new company should be styled to attract the attention and interest of women. Part of the solution was to provide far more instruction and explanation concerning the whole product range than competitors offered in their stores. This approach was picked up directly from Brico. Not only was this practical, but it would make women more knowledgeable and engage their empathy with and approval of the product range. Another possibly inspired way of attracting women and promoting the new company was the deal made with Laura Ashley, an extremely popular clothes, fabrics and wallpaper retailer at this time, who agreed to put in units selling their distinctive range at the front of the Homebase stores. It was also decided that far more thought and ingenuity would be put into the development of Homebase's garden products than rivals were then doing.

The plan was to open Homebase stores, where possible, in the same location as new Sainsbury's supermarkets, so that the newer business would benefit from the reputation and the footfall of adjacent supermarkets. They could also share parking and other facilities. The initial plan was, therefore, to establish the first new Homebase alongside Sainsbury's first store in Leeds, which was then beginning construction. But the new Homebase board changed its mind: Leeds was a long way from Blackfriars, and it was felt to be important that the management team could closely monitor the progress of the first store. Instead a site was chosen at Purley Way, near Croydon, in the traditional Sainsbury's heartland, although this store was not adjacent to a supermarket.

A general manager was recruited from outside the company, but the appointment did not last long, and Hoyar Miller drafted in Dino Adriano in 1981 to take over this role. Adriano had been with Sainsbury's since 1964, working on the financial side and gaining broad experience both in distribution and the retail division. Adriano recalls being deeply impressed that, from the outset, this unproven company was going to be identified as 'Sainsbury's Homebase', rather than being launched with an entirely separate identity. He believed this was a brave move, because any failure of the business would inevitably reflect on the reputation of the parent.

But the reputation of the parent was a major driving force behind the company. Hoyer Millar, Davis and Adriano set about building a business that drew as far as possible on Sainsbury's retailing and operational experience. Staff were seconded from Sainsbury's to work on Homebase's merchandising, ranging, customer service, information provision, store design, staff training and other key aspects. Homebase became the first DIY business to adopt a regime of centralised distribution. As a result it soon led the way in the DIY industry in stock-control systems and the use of information technology. Sainsbury's also transferred its strong buying disciplines to Homebase, focusing on quality, as might be expected, and sending buyers into factories to ensure high standards, but also working closely with manufacturers in the development of new products, predictably including a strong own-label range.

Some of the staff who transferred to the new DIY operation initially wondered whether Sainsbury's had chosen the most appropriate industry for diversification. B&Q, then the market leader, was a strong, very well-established rival; the new company's board would have its work cut out promoting the right identity and style to attract customers. But the critical and the concerned should not have worried. When the first Homebase opened in April 1981, it attracted huge interest – so much so that the police demanded that it close temporarily because the crowds flocking to see the novelty were causing severe traffic jams on the surrounding roads. In the first two weeks of trading, more than 60,000 people visited the store. There was general applause. One reporter in the *Daily Express* commented that this was 'a DIY self-service store the size of Trafalgar Square and incorporating the most comprehensive stock of gardening tools and equipment I have ever seen'.

In October 1981, the Leeds store that was originally planned as the show home of the new business was opened. Built next to a brand-new Sainsbury's supermarket, this remained the ideal location, though one it was not always possible to achieve. The strategy for Homebase was to open at least six new stores each year and to apply Sainsbury's ethos and style as a spur to drive the company forward, adding a useful additional profit stream to Sainsbury's main business within a few years.

Whether it was supermarkets, DIY stores or hypermarkets, the board of directors were in favour of a strategy of investing in new sites and expanding these businesses at an ambitious rate. JD's main passion was the development of the supermarkets, which was by far the most dominant of the businesses in the Sainsbury's Group, but he maintained great interest in the progress of the subsidiary companies. As the Sainsbury's Group director of development, Hoyer Millar was now responsible for a programme that saw a steady 15 new stores being opened each year in the supermarket chain, some six or seven Homebases and the occasional new gigantic SavaCentre hypermarket.

David Sainsbury was particularly keen on Sainsbury's programme of diversification, and he became SavaCentre's chairman in 1981, with fellow Sainsbury's directors Joe Barnes, Tom Vyner and Len Payne, plus a general manager and four directors representing the interests of BHS. As the first five hypermarket sites were developed – the last of these opening at Reading in 1981 – the new business started to contribute a small stream of profits following the large initial outlays on its development. But suitable sites for SavaCentre were by far the most difficult to find. They had to be extensive and well located to ensure their full trading potential by drawing customers from as broad a geographical area around them as possible. A fine site was found and developed in Scotland, but by 1984 there were only six hypermarkets in total, and none was opened between 1984 and 1989. These were particularly buoyant years in the British economy, and every commercial enterprise appeared to want a share in the property boom.

Yet the SavaCentres that were opened continued to generate a growing profit for the parent companies throughout the 1980s. Even during the fallow development years between 1984 and 1989, the volumes of goods, sales and profits grew. The SavaCentre in Cameron Toll in Scotland was one of the most successful, and there was the double satisfaction of the healthy trade at this hypermarket and the fact that it was the Sainsbury Group's first involvement in retailing north of the border. The first new SavaCentre to be built in 1989 was a superb store in Merton, South London, offering 108,000 square feet of sales area and ground-level parking for more than 1,000 cars. The overall development included a leisure complex, office buildings, a riverside walk and a museum.

Despite progress, by the middle of the 1980s it became increasingly clear that it was the food-retailing side of SavaCentre's business that drove its success. By the time the Merton hypermarket was opened, the BHS clothing range accounted for only 13 per cent of SavaCentre's overall sales, with home and leisure products contributing only 12 per cent; the remaining 75 per cent comprised food sales. This lack of progress in the non-food range largely reflected gradually failing fortunes within BHS during the 1980s, which prevented the company from contributing as much as it had originally promised to the joint venture.

In 1986, Terence Conran's Storehouse group acquired BHS, but this only served to accelerate the decline in the company's fortunes. Inevitably, BHS paid decreasing attention to SavaCentre, with the result that the clothing and household goods side of the business suffered further. By 1989, BHS was in quite serious financial difficulty, and thus responded happily when Sainsbury's offered to buy its 50 per cent share stake in SavaCentre in March that year.

Having bought the company that had been its first major subsidiary, if not a full-scale diversification, Sainsbury's were able to incorporate SavaCentre more closely into its own mainstream operations, which produced good cost savings for the business. The fascias were changed to 'Sainsbury's SavaCentre', and Blackfriars took over responsibility for most of the store operations, representing a significant change in operation. Sainsbury's signed an agreement with BHS to continue sourcing textiles from its former partner for the next five years, and during this time Sainsbury's buyers also sought to extend the company's supplier relationships and to develop SavaCentre's own 'Lifestyle' range of clothing.

By 1992, there were nine SavaCentres, with an average of 88,000 square feet of selling space and offering a range of 60,000 products. The annual report of that year claimed that customers could buy their food 5 per cent below the average price of the nation's food retailers; other products represented similar if not greater value.

Compared with SavaCentre, Homebase made more consistent progress in the 1980s, particularly in the store-development programme. Stores were built at the rate initially projected of about six a year. And, as predicted, the new company lost money between 1982 and 1985 because of the high initial development costs involved in this programme. But then the DIY market became one of the fastest-growing of all retail sectors. In the five years between 1985 and 1989 the total value of this market almost doubled from some £3.5 billion to £6.4 billion, much of this fuelled by the phenomenal boom in the housing market.

The ICL scanning system used by the Sainsbury's supermarkets was gradually introduced throughout Homebase stores, but with a software system specially developed in America for DIY retailing. By 1985, Homebase was carrying some 18,000 lines, and the new system provided an on-line record of stock movements that gave store managers a detailed breakdown of sales and stock position for every line. In that year, Dennis Males retired from Sainsbury's to take over as general manager from Dino Adriano, who moved back to Sainsbury's as an area general manager.

Homebase had truly become a 'son of Sainsbury's' in its retailing style. The quality of the products and standards of service were probably the highest of any DIY chain in the UK. The products, many of which were now own-label, were well presented in well-stocked shelves; the stores were gleaming and spotless. One of the Belgian directors, representing GB-Inno-BM's 25 per cent, even ventured to complain that the stores were too clean for this market. Perhaps more seriously, the transference of Sainsbury's ethos of exceptionally high standards to the DIY subsidiary may have accounted for a general perception among customers that Homebase was more expensive than its major rivals, although this was by no means the case.

Homebase managers would often use the clout of the parent company in negotiations with difficult suppliers. An example of this was a visit made by Dennis Males to Chicago to negotiate with a director of Stanley Tools who was resisting Homebase's requirement to have supplies delivered directly to a central depot. The director found it more profitable to maintain the delivery of what were called 'minimal drops' direct to the stores – but 'minimal' for the supplier represented expensive in-store stockholding for Homebase. In the discussion, the director said he preferred to keep things the way they were. Males said that he would have to de-list Stanley Tools. The director ventured that Homebase only had some 35 stores and therefore precious little leverage to call the shots. 'Do you think I really care?' he said. Males replied, 'It's not how many stores we've got, it's who we are. We are the most prestigious retail company in the UK. We are going to have central distribution and you will either be part of it or you will not.' He reports that when he returned to the UK, Stanley Tools had somehow solved its 'problems' and was happy to deliver centrally.

During the late 1980s, the primary energy of the Sainsbury's board was being applied to the development of the mainstream supermarket business, with significant success. The Homebase stores that opened during these years were as large as any in the market, and kept pace in terms of sales per square feet with B&Q, the prevailing market leader. Yet although it proved to be a successful business, there were times when JD wondered about Homebase's long-term potential. In May 1989, he called a board meeting to discuss this. He challenged the other directors with a number of points: that the DIY trade was becoming progressively more competitive and would be likely to continue in this way; that the best Homebase could probably expect was a fourth position in the market which meant the company would continue to suffer one particular drawback: a disadvantage in buying power. He was also concerned that every site selected for Homebase should be of out-standing quality, otherwise there seemed to be little point to the venture. For example, he considered the stores in Plymouth and Stockport to be far from ideally located. While he was determined to raise the sights of the board in relation to Homebase, there was an element of devil's advocate in JD's approach. He wanted to find out whether the board really believed in the DIY subsidiary, and at the meeting he even put the prospect of selling Homebase to a vote. The board voted against the motion to sell, with Gurth Hoyer Millar, David Sainsbury and Roy Griffiths most strongly opposed.

Homebase continued as a steady and profitable business, and its retail style, which drew so much on Sainsbury's, brought a new dimension to the DIY market. Dino Adriano returned to Homebase in 1989 as the managing director and succeeded Hoyar Miller as chairman at the end of 1991. 'I am proud of what we had achieved with Homebase,' he says. By 1992, Homebase was contributing £15 million to the Sainsbury's Group's profits from a turnover of £257 million; this was a very reasonable return for a youngish business that had entered a market in the face of well-established competi-tion. But sales represented only 2.8 per cent of Sainsbury's total group sales, and Homebase profits represented less than 2.25 per cent of group profits. As predicted, Homebase was still a signifi-cantly smaller player than its main rivals, with 64 stores in 1992, a quarter of the number of B&Q.

While they were setting up Homebase, Sainsbury's directors started to concentrate on the final element of the company's diversification strategy, which was to buy into supermarkets overseas. 'Overseas' in

JD's mind actually meant the United States, which was the country that he knew best of all and which had been such an innovator in so many aspects of post-war food retailing practices. As early as 1977, the board had made the strategic decision to move into the US market to which it felt that Sainsbury's style was better suited than to food retailing in continental Europe. JD had visited the US on many occasions since the 1950s, and had established a network of business friends and contacts in the retail industry.

The board now commissioned Boston Consulting Group to research the leading food-retailing chains in the US and to advise the Sainsbury's board in its objective of buying a US company. The most suitable candidate turned out to be Shaw's, a supermarket chain based in New England, and one that was already quite well known to Sainsbury's. In 1978, Jeremy Grindle, then departmental director of branch services, had visited Shaw's to report to the board on developments in scanning in the American food-retailing sector. Grindle reported back that Shaw's adoption of the new technology was by far the most impressive he had seen. In November 1983, Sainsbury's secured its interest in Shaw's by acquiring a 21.2 per cent share for £21 million.

Shaw's was an apt choice in many ways, for there were distinct similarities to Sainsbury's in its style and approach. It had developed as a business that was initially run by successive family members after its foundation at the end of the nineteenth century, and it had a reputation for being well managed. Like Sainsbury's, it was essentially food-oriented and had a good reputation for perishables. It was small to medium-sized, with only 41 stores in its chain, but its operating margins were well above the industry average. Like Sainsbury's, the new, larger stores had in-store bakeries, delicatessens and a supporting range of non-food items including household goods; it also sold newspapers and magazines, which Sainsbury's would shortly add to its own range. Not least, the American company shared Sainsbury's most fundamental trading principles, seeking high quality and consistently low prices; it also had high sales per square foot.

The company had grown strongly over the previous decade, and had a 4 per cent share of the New England market, with a significantly stronger share in Maine and New Hampshire of about 10 per cent. There appeared to be plenty of potential for Shaw's to expand around Boston and other parts of New England.

Although the Davis family who owned Shaw's got on well with JD and the Sainsbury's board, they wanted to take the relationship step by step. Sainsbury's waited until 1986 before acquiring a further 7.3 per cent, a move prompted by Shaw's obtaining a NASDAQ National Market Listing following a successful public sale of 10 per cent of its shares. Then, in 1987, Sainsbury's obtained another 20.9 per cent. Finally, in July 1987, Shaw's accepted Sainsbury's offer of £184.4 million for the remaining equity.

The gradual nature of the acquisition allowed a useful if protracted courtship period in which both companies could learn more about each other's methods. Although JD and others in Sainsbury's board had significant knowledge of the American food-retailing sector, the actual process of running an American supermarket chain was markedly different from counterpart businesses in the UK. Buying practices were particularly frustrating in the US, where legislation greatly constrained retailers in the negotiation of volume discounts. This meant that increasing the size of the operation would not readily improve a company's purchasing leverage, and there were few opportunities for buyers to negotiate special deals. The geography of the US meant that supply chains were usually regional rather than national, which tended to reduce competitiveness between suppliers. Because of the sheer size of the US, the most successful companies tended to be large regional companies, located in two or three adjacent states, rather than 'national' in the UK sense. Importantly, retailers were generally more passive in US supply relationships; for example, they were not usually involved in product development, which was, of course, one of Sainsbury's stronger points. In the US it was the suppliers who took responsibility for developing new products; they promoted these heavily to food retailers, and it was the suppliers' rather than the retailers' decision to stock them, depending on sales.

Another notable difference between Shaw's and Sainsbury's was the former's almost total lack of own-label products. The relatively few own-label goods sold in Shaw's did not even carry the company name; they were developed through an agency in Chicago who also sold them to other non-competing chains in the US. There was no possibility of monitoring the quality or determining the price of these products. In Shaw's, as in the US generally, own-label goods, known in the trade there as 'generic goods', were widely regarded as second-class citizens.

JD was particularly keen to change this, and, following the company's acquisition, he despatched staff from Sainsbury's to go to Shaw's and make significant changes to the company's buying and merchandising culture. Yet making experienced people understand and accept a different way of doing things was not easy. It wasn't until Sainsbury's actually transferred its own representatives into Shaw's top management – notably Ross McClaren, a departmental director of dairy and frozen foods at Sainsbury's – that the kind of changes that the parent board sought were made. With hindsight, JD believes this transfer of top staff should have happened sooner.

Nevertheless, in September 1990 Shaw's first 'Sainsbury's-style' own-label products were launched. The brand was built on Shaw's reputation and carried a special red seal as the company's own signature of own-label quality. This development was firmly based on Sainsbury's quality control and buying methods. Shaw's own-label products, like Sainsbury's, were as good or better quality than the leading brands, but at a lower price. Shaw's also adopted the Sainsbury's slogan, 'Good food costs less', and its marketing policies increasingly matched Sainsbury's own. The subsidiary's own-label products became successful and grew steadily, numbering some 1,400 lines by 1994. They were an unusual example of a British food-retailing stratagem being successfully imported into the US when for so many years the UK had been on the receiving end of the flow of ideas and new technologies.

Shaw's profits were variable during the late 1980s and early 1990s; between 1988 and 1990 they rose from £12 million, to £23 million, to £34 million and, as recession took hold in the US in 1991 and 1992, declined to £30 million and £21 million. By 1992, the number of Shaw's outlets had increased to 73 and the company's sales area was up from 1 million to 2.2 million square feet. The operating margins of the US business were much lower than was generally in the case in the UK, but the total return on investment was similar to that achieved by Sainsbury's mainstream business. This was mainly because the cost of opening a new store in the US could be as much as 75 per cent cheaper than in the UK.

Sainsbury's was proud of the progress of the US operation, and much was made of Shaw's relatively strong performance compared with other US retailers. As a UK retailer determined to set its own imprint in the US, Sainsbury's had made headway where other major British retailers were failing, including WHSmith, Boots and Marks & Spencer. But behind closed doors there was some disappointment that the company's growth was not as rapid as had been hoped, and that the introduction of Sainsbury's more efficient retail practices had turned out to be much more difficult than anticipated.

To some extent this was a common theme in the standing of all Sainsbury's subsidiaries. The difficult trading conditions in the UK which had prompted their emergence – or acquisition in the case of Shaw's – improved significantly during the second half of the 1980s. As a result, although they became profitable and successful companies in their own trading contexts, the subsidiaries amounted to little more than a sideshow compared to the main parent. By the mid-to-late 1980s, the performance of Sainsbury's UK supermarkets was starting to dazzle.

Chapter 14

LEADING THE FIELD
1983–1988

A FTER THE PERIOD of planning difficulties at the end of the 1970s, the store-development programme had stepped up a pace in the 1980s; in the first seven years an average of 15 or 16 stores opened annually. The estates division also continued to upgrade the premises and equipment of the smaller, older stores, reducing their vulnerability to competition. As competition intensified the pace quickened further. These developments sustained the increases in volumes sold in the supermarkets and drove further productivity gains; in both areas Sainsbury's was steadily outstripping its closest competitors.

From 1983, Sainsbury's started to pull away from Tesco, and became the UK's most profitable and effective supermarket chain. As front-runner, it was under pressure to continue to set both the style and the pace of food retailing. Alongside store development, a key to this was the energy and originality of buyers in developing the own-label range.

Customers could save considerable money by buying own-label goods, and in these the attention to quality remained absolute. Under Vyner, Ingham and Roberts, buyers were not only improving their negotiating skills but they were being more inventive, spotting gaps in the market or trying out every permutation of style or flavour. Every department benefited from this process. Week after week, a steady stream of new products was introduced following the departmental directors' meetings with JD, where the chairman personally approved every new item. Customers were treated to a prolific range of ready-to-cook pizzas and seafood meals, pitta bread, new pastas, seafood sauces, soft drinks, cake mixes, chocolates, toffees, marmalade, decaffeinated coffee, fruit juices, luxury mincemeat and further new styles of breakfast cereal.

In 1983, Sainsbury's was selling far more wines than any other British retailer. It was estimated that the company sold one in every seven bottles of wine bought in Britain. The range now included varieties in three-litre boxes, and the off-licence department added further own-label whisky, gin and vodka and Sainsbury's own-brand Armagnac. Under the direction of Allan Cheesman, the wine buyers gained a formidable reputation and were often headhunted by other companies. As the ultimate accolade, in 1986 Cheesman won the prestigious *Ordre du Mérite Agricole* awarded by the French government, for his and the department's role in encouraging British customers to appreciate French wines.

Often Sainsbury's own-label products were printed with recipes that were researched and tested by the home-economics department; since 1972 this small department had compiled more than 1,000 such recipes either printed on labels or produced in leaflet form. Even Sainsbury's gravy granules had a recipe printed on the label.

Over the previous decade, Sainsbury's had also established its own highly successful imprint as a publisher of cookery books. To satisfy increasingly esoteric tastes, Sainsbury's produced scores of illustrated cookery books covering all culinary styles and subjects: Thai cooking, Mexican cooking, cooking with a microwave, home baking, party cooking, fish recipes, meat recipes, vegetarian dishes – even books on slimming to point customers towards the health foods and low-calorie product range. These publications were commissioned from well-established writers, and they made an attractive 'impulse buy' for customers as they moved through the checkouts. They were cheap but not cheaply made. There was a range of hardbacks with full-colour illustrations, such as those in the 'Sainsbury's Book of' series, with such titles as *Wholefood Cooking* by Carole Handslip or *Preserves & Pickles* by Norma MacMillan. These sold for only 99p in the early 1980s. There was also a series of small booklets, Sainsbury's Food Guides – for example, Hugh Johnson's *Understanding Wines* – priced at just 30p.

Sainsbury's also published a number of larger, specialist cookery books by top-selling authors. Josceline Dimbleby, the first to become involved in this programme, was an award-winning writer of cookery books who produced popular Sainsbury's titles in the 1980s, including *Cooking for Christmas, Curries and Oriental Cooking* and *Sweet Dreams*. Dimbleby sold more than one million of these titles through Sainsbury's branches. By 1985, the company recorded that 13 million books had been sold through the chain;

they were a profitable line, though purely because of the quantity sold on the slimmest of margins. The reasons behind this in-house publishing venture were to reinforce Sainsbury's position as an authority on food and wine, to provide extensive information matching the offer in the stores, and to encourage customers in the exploration of new foods. Sainsbury's only broadened the subject range by developing children's books, which branches sold in close proximity to baby and toddler food and disposable nappies. Sebastian Walker proved to be an excellent choice as an affiliated publisher of these books. He took pains to find the best possible illustrators for his authors' books, with the result that customers could buy children's books of a critically high standard while the volume sold ensured that they paid prices that other publishers could ill afford to match.

In such ways, the company developed a reputation for its response to new consumer trends, one of the most important in the 1980s being a demand for healthier food. The consumption of milk fell by some 56 per cent between 1982 and 1992 when it was realised that the fats in milk might be implicated in heart disease and that milk intolerance was one of many allergies that could affect children. Yet Sainsbury's own milk sales remained remarkably stable during the period, because the buyers developed ingenious alternatives. In 1981, Sainsbury's introduced Vitapint, a reduced-fat, vitamin-enriched milk as one of its unique brands; no proprietary brand offered anything like this, and it was a significant improvement on the UHT milks that were being presented as an alternative to the standard. Sainsbury's introduced various other types of healthy milk, and extended its offer of fat-reduced products by introducing lean mince, virtually fat-free yoghurts and fruit canned in juice rather than syrup. Some new products fell by the wayside as experiments do: low-fat coffee yoghurt was not among the longer-lasting flavours of an otherwise popular range.

There were also changing fashions in the nation's attitude to meat, with a fall of about 15 per cent in the consumption of beef and veal between 1975 and 1985 and a fall in lamb and mutton consumption of nearly 20 per cent. This was largely due to health concerns, more varied diets, fewer family meals and a growing interest in animal welfare. It was also a reflection of the enormous growth of poultry, particularly chicken, which had become the major type of meat consumed in the UK and was far cheaper than any other fresh meat. Sainsbury's response was to launch traditional joints of beef and 'Tenderlean' lamb and pork. The meat was hung in the traditional manner to improve its flavour. In 1984, Sainsbury's meat buyers and Quantock Veal of Dorset developed a new packaging technique known as Controlled Atmosphere Packing (CAP). This trapped harmless gases which prevented the discolouration of the meat and delayed the formation of bacteria, so that the meat had a longer in-store shelf-life and would also last longer in customers' homes.

But these developments were only a part of the national drive for healthier food. Both retailers and manufacturers found themselves under increasing pressure to remove additives from food, as reports proliferated in the media about the use of too many colourings, preservatives and flavour enhancers. There were claims that people developed allergic reactions to additives such as monosodium glutamate and the yellow colouring, tartrazine. From 1983, Sainsbury's buyers were instructed to remove additives where possible from the company's own-label products; it was generally noted that the supermarkets were more responsive to the anti-additive campaign than manufacturers. Initially, Sainsbury's focused on children's food, introducing colour-free ice-cream, additive-free 'Mr Men' yoghurt and 'High Juice' fruit squashes. Gradually, the removal of additives extended to other lines.

An unfortunate side-effect of this programme, which was adopted by more and more retailers and manufacturers, was a significantly higher incidence of food poisoning in the population. Research indicated that the removal of preservatives led to the build-up of bacteria in certain products, and new strains of listeria were found that could breed on food even when refrigerated. But nothing bred as quickly as reports in the media, and soon the country was in the grip of 'listeria hysteria', a scare that only abated when there was an even more sensational alarm about salmonella in poultry products, particularly eggs. The media steered the public's gaze and lurched from one scare to another, often in a fog of exaggeration and misinformation.

Sainsbury's was in a good position to reassure its customers and the general public because of its reputation for hygiene and high standards. Sainsbury's hygiene officers checked all the refrigerated cabinets in every store to ensure that they were being kept at the right temperature. The company had already invested substantially in an efficient cold chain, which included a fleet of lorries that could transport food at various temperatures to ensure optimum conditions. It now introduced new automatic technology which could constantly monitor temperatures in the refrigeration equipment. Virtually all store employees undertook a demanding training course to ensure best practice in handling food safely. This course was the first to be accredited by the Institution of Environmental Health Officers; later the 1990 Food Safety Act required that all retailers' standards for handling food were similar to those established by Sainsbury's.

In January 1985, Sainsbury's was the first food retailer to introduce nutritional labelling in response to research indicating that customers wanted to be able to make more informed choices about the nutritional value of the food they purchased. The energy, protein, carbohydrate and total fat content of all items were listed as core items, while dietary fibre and vitamin contents were added if they were present in a material quantity.

In all its buying policies, Sainsbury's became committed to championing British food. One of the company's small subsidiaries, Breckland Farms, was already contributing a significant amount of the pork used by its other meat-processing subsidiary, Haverhill Meat Products. Each September between 1980 and 1983, Sainsbury's ran an annual 'Best of British' promotion and supported the marketing organisation, Food from Britain, set up by the Ministry of Agriculture, Fisheries and Food in 1982. In that year, 75 per cent of the bacon sold in Sainsbury's stores was British, compared with the national average of only 40 per cent.

Nevertheless, as the number of foreign holidays increased steadily, Sainsbury's continued to respond to the developing tastes among consumers for continental and American foods that inevitably followed – pizzas, pastas, German bio-yoghurt, American ice cream and hundreds of other products, including French bread part-baked in France and cooked in the company's in-store bakeries. The pizza range was the fastest growth area in Sainsbury's prepared-food sales in the early 1980s, reflecting the growing popularity of fast food.

Customers had long associated Sainsbury's with the quality of its perishables, traditionally dairy products and fresh meat. Now, fresh fruit and vegetables were often at the top of the department league table with the largest year-on-year volume increase in sales. Sainsbury's had effectively become the UK's biggest greengrocer. Almost every supermarket greeted its customers with a wide range of loose vegetables and fruit, piled high on the new Y-shaped tables and all religiously kept brim-full during opening hours. Alongside the standard offerings, the occasional new type of fruit or vegetable was launched on bemused customers. When buyers first introduced the kiwi fruit to customers in several stores during September 1979, many people had no idea what they were supposed to do with what one interested observer referred to as 'this small green furry egg'. In time, other exotic fruits beckoned to the curious at the entrances of Sainsbury's stores: carambolas from Malaysia, pawpaws from Brazil and horned melons from Kenya.

New foods, new tastes and Sainsbury's reputation for freshness, quality and price were constantly promoted to customers through a series of witty poster campaigns devised by the company's advertising agents, Abbot Mead Vickers. The buyers' invention extended to all departments, including non-food, so that customers were offered tableware, classic-shaped wine glasses, decorated toilet tissue, roasting bags and sandwich bags, bakeware, safety plugs, countless beauty accessories, new lines of ribbed tights. And improvements were constantly introduced to the packaging and presentation of goods. For example, Sainsbury's olive and vegetable oils were packaged in a new material called PET – polyethylene terephthalate – which was as clear as glass but unbreakable, safe to handle and leakproof, and, unlike conventional plastic bottles, it contained no additives.

In his annual address to shareholders in July 1984, JD offered some insight into the complexity of the logistical operation involved in supplying the supermarkets. He said that in a typical day the 250 branches would order up to 10,000 different products, producing orders totalling nearly one million cartons. These would mostly be delivered to the stores within 24 hours, with every shop receiving its delivery of perishable food and produce before opening time. Between 5 pm in the afternoon and 3 am in the morning, the central-office computer received and analysed some 350,000 separate orders from the stores, processing and transmitting them to the distribution depots, which included several contractor depots, while maintaining a complete warehouse inventory and accounting controls.

Despite the fears of many in food retailing, including members

of Sainsbury's board, there was no sign of the market becoming saturated; no ceiling was hit; sales volume, turnover and profits in
Sainsbury's core supermarket business went from strength to
strength. By 1984, Sainsbury's was selling more than twice the volume of products it had sold ten years before, and its weekly
customers numbered in the region of six million. In ten years,
Sainsbury's had opened 126 new supermarkets and closed 81
smaller and older branches, with the result that the company's sales
area had doubled and the average store size was about 50 per cent
larger. Net margin had now crept up above the 5 per cent mark for
the first time. More than 24,000 jobs had been created in this
period, and there were now some 10,000 employees who were also
shareholders.

Not only was the City impressed as the shares rose steadily, but
Sainsbury's performance was hailed across the world. In 1984, JD
visited Dallas to receive a new international award given by the
Food Marketing Institute of America for 'The Outstanding Supermarket Chain'. The award was the equivalent of an Olympic Gold.

The main thrust of investment was now on the new, larger stores.
The 15 new stores built in 1983/4 included an ingenious development at Cromwell Road which involved converting the former West
London Air Terminal into a modern and spacious supermarket with
an adjoining car park. Developments also included Sainsbury's new
largest supermarket at Crystal Palace, with more than 37,000 square
feet of sales area. The store offered some 8,000 lines and had 600
full- and part-time staff. Yet Crystal Palace made up a little under a
tenth of the total new sales built in 1983/4, which at 383,000
square feet was the largest the company had ever opened in one
year. Store investment of £181 million also exceeded that of any
other retailer in the country.

Somewhat controversially, the Crystal Palace 'superstore' was
built on the site of Selhurst Park, the Crystal Palace football ground,
and the development included the construction of a social club for
football supporters and the rebuilding of a spectator's terrace. Crystal Palace was not without its problems; the development division
had underestimated the effect of the disruption caused by the football club. On the days of the home matches the 450-space car park
had to be available for football fans while Sainsbury's shoppers had
to fend for themselves.

In the first half of the 1980s, planning obstacles remained an area of friction. Delays were sometimes inordinate. For example, Sainsbury's had applied for planning permission to build a spacious modern store in Ipswich on 23 December 1980; planning permission was finally obtained on 27 January 1983 through an appeal to the Department of the Environment; eventually the store was opened in 1985. Reporting an unprecedented number of planning appeal rejections in 1983, JD could not restrain from comment: 'The function of the planning system is the limited one of regulating the use of land in the public interest, not deciding who should compete with whom or whether the public "need" another supermarket.'

Then, in 1985, Peter Walker, Secretary of State for the Environment, introduced a new policy which looked, for once, favourable for supermarket development. In line with JD's and Hoyer Millar's own argument, he stated that 'commercial competition as such is not a planning consideration'. He therefore ruled that decisions about planning applications and on appeals should not concern the effect that a proposed major retail scheme might have on other retailers. The intention was to remove some of the pain out of the planning application and appeal system. The government were also continuing to encourage utilities and local authorities to make unneeded land or derelict land available for appropriate commercial purposes, and this was having a more beneficial effect. Sainsbury's did find more appropriate sites for future expansion, the only problem being that the competition was interested in them too.

Even before this unusually helpful government intervention, Sainsbury's had been able to develop several more stores that more closely matched the ideal. A new store at Burpham, opened in 1985, was one of the company's largest, with more than 32,000 square feet of sales area and surface parking for some 600 cars. Ideally situated in a Sainsbury's heartland area, near Guildford where the company had traded since 1906, the store was an instant success. Among other stores opened in this year that approached the ideal were those at Chichester, Ipswich and Swansea. Each supermarket traded well above its forecast levels. Chichester was trading at more than 100 per cent above the estimated figure. This discrepancy in forecasting was partly because of the long delays between the time that the Chairman's Committee evaluated trade levels and the actual opening of the stores. In Chichester's case this amounted to six years, from 1979 to 1985. Such an enormous underestimation of sales potential of sites did not assist the mechanics of site acquisition. In 1986, the whole process of sales forecasting was closely reviewed in order to achieve more accuracy.

Although Sainsbury's had established a foothold in Yorkshire and the north-west, with a small number of successful stores by the end of the 1970s, it was during the 1980s that the company truly established an identity as a national supermarket chain. The numbers of new stores on good sites in the north-west grew steadily, with branches at Birkenhead (1982), Liverpool (1982 and 1983), Blackpool (1984) and Lancaster (1985). In Yorkshire, ten stores would open during the decade and a large store was opened in the north-east at Middlesbrough in 1989. In Wales, further stores were opened in Cardiff, Newport and Swansea. With generally high and rising unemployment, the announcement of a Sainsbury's supermarket in these regions was newsworthy, particularly in the recently decapitated industrial and mining regions. In South Wales, for example, Sainsbury's £20 million investment in three stores represented 1,200 new jobs and attracted significant media attention.

By 1986, Sainsbury's could lay claim to being the largest food retailer in each of its main food sectors: produce, frozen foods, provisions, groceries, off licence, and fresh meat and poultry. The good will attached to Sainsbury's own-label – which continued to contribute no less than two-thirds of the company's sales – was unmatched in the entire food trade, with the exception of food produced by M&S. This was 100 per cent own-label – although the range was far smaller than Sainsbury's. However, the Sainsbury's board was aware from its frequent surveys that about 50 per cent of the company's customers also bought some of their food at M&S, and that food now represented about 40 per cent of this well-respected rival's turnover. In his senior management meeting in 1986, JD had commented: 'Their range has interest and excitement because of the degree of novelty that is always there. I believe we have learnt from them, but still have more to learn in particular areas of their trade.'

While Sainsbury's market share had grown substantially over the previous five years, only the Dee Group, which acquired Gateway and Carrefour, and the Argyll Group were making reasonable progress among the other multiples. The major losers in market share were the independent shops and the Co-op. Asda's growth, which once seemed such a threat, was now tailing off; they had suffered management problems, with two changes of managing director in the space of four years, and the link between Asda and its MFI furniture subsidiary did not appear to be prospering.

By comparison, the make-up of Sainsbury's top management was remarkably consistent. In the mid-1980s, a good proportion of the directors – not including family members – had been in office for up to 20 years. Two non-executive directors, Sir James Spooner and Dame Jennifer Jenkins – the first woman on the board – had joined the company in 1981 and 1982 respectively; they were the first ever non-executive directors at Sainsbury's who were not family members. In 1984, David Quarmby was the first full executive appointment on the board for some time. Coming from the board of London Transport, he was to take responsibility for distribution from Len Payne in the latter's run-up to retirement. In 1985, Jim Prior, a former Minister of Agriculture and a very successful farmer, was appointed as a further non-executive director.

The only upset in a united management team occurred when Peter Davis announced his decision to leave the company in early 1986. He soon afterwards joined Reed International. Davis had wanted an assurance that he would be JD's successor as chief executive. But in 1985, when the matter had arisen, JD was in no position to consider succession to chief executive, or to offer the crown to Davis or any other heir. With seven years to go to retirement, he felt it was far too early to make such decisions. Moreover, his cousin, David Sainsbury, finance director since 1973 and popular among senior management, was likely to succeed him as chairman. He was also Sainsbury's largest shareholder. As JD saw it, decisions about future senior appointments should be made together with David when the time came. Nevertheless, some industry observers were, at this stage, interested in what might happen when JD retired. In 1986, one new magazine, *Business*, carried the comment: 'John Sainsbury knows more about his business than anyone else and has succeeded in making himself irreplaceable.'

Following Davis's departure, Barnes and Vyner were appointed assistant managing directors of retail and of buying and marketing respectively. Diana Eccles succeeded Dame Jennifer Jenkins as a non-executive director when she left the board in 1986. The board remained welded to JD's leadership both in composition and purpose, and this solidarity remained one of Sainsbury's competitive strengths.

Tesco's share of the market had not significantly improved since the beginning of the decade, when the company had suffered a cash crisis and its formerly impressive store-expansion programme had slowed. Nevertheless, it was still a keen rival, and, early in the second half of the decade, it started to build a respectable number of new stores, all of a significantly larger size than Sainsbury's and with probably more ideal store sites in the mix than Sainsbury's was achieving. Tesco disposed of many of its smaller properties and sold the Victor Value chain.

For the first time ever, the average size of a Tesco store in 1986, at about 19,000 square feet, was marginally larger than the average size of a Sainsbury's store, at 18,000 square feet. Ian MacLaurin and his board continued to approach the benchmark set by Sainsbury's. Tesco was allocating more space to food than it had before, its new stores appeared to be cleaner and tidier, and there was some distinct improvement in the quality of Tesco products, including their own-label offer. Virtually all new Tesco stores were opening with coffee shops included on the premises as a customer amenity, an idea that Sainsbury's decided to trial for itself, particularly in the edge-of-town and out-of-town sites.

Safeway, too, was becoming another chain to watch. In the second half of the 1980s, it opened a steady stream of stores, and, despite having prices that were as much as 5 per cent higher than Sainsbury's, this up-and-coming rival was starting to offer real competition, particularly in the areas where Sainsbury's did not have good modern stores.

Sainsbury's had been engaged since the early 1970s in a more intensive programme of store-opening and refurbishment than any other food retailer in the UK. It has been considered that it had an advantage over competitors in being able to bid more for key sites simply because of the return it could make in terms of sales per square foot of selling area. It is understandable how commentators have reached this conclusion: Sainsbury's continued through the 1980s to have the highest sales per square foot of any supermarket business. By 1988, the business was generating sales per square foot of £14.40 against Asda's £10.60 and Tesco's £9.50. But the advantage in terms of return per square foot has to be set against the fact that construction costs for Sainsbury's stores were usually higher than rivals' per square foot because of the higher costs of finishes and building. The typical Sainsbury's store still contained more area that was not used for sales but for warehouse storage areas and expensive plant supporting the stores. And site acquisition was becoming steadily tougher and more competitive. Despite the expertise the estates division and the Chairman's Committee had accumulated, mistakes were inevitable; each location had its own potentials and drawbacks, and, even though the performance forecasts improved, no amount of statistical data was likely to provide an exact picture of how well a particular new store might perform.

Thus, the supermarket trade was embarked on a new dynamic in the later 1980s; the pace of competition was stepping up and the gap in quality was closing. Sainsbury's had won itself a significant lead, but the board watched their nearest competitors with ever closer care. In 1987, JD announced that Sainsbury's was raising the stakes and would henceforth be opening no fewer than 20 new stores each year, including replacements. On top of this would be more capital invested in upgrading existing stores. A significant factor in this decision was the increased number of experienced staff that were, through the company's training programme, becoming available to take on the vital position of store manager.

In addition to the offer in the stores, during the 1980s people started to take notice of another distinctive element to Sainsbury's, namely the exotic nature of some stores' architecture. The Canterbury store, for example, which opened in September 1984, was designed by the architects Ahrend, Burton & Koralek, and was the winning entry in a competition organised by Sainsbury's. The design incorporated exposed structural beams and masts as decorative features, and was compared by one commentator to an insect's exoskeleton. The building was viewed with mixed feelings by the public, although widely acclaimed in the architectural profession. Another remarkable store in the 1980s was designed by architect Nicholas Grimshaw in Camden, where the local authority demanded a high-tech replacement to an old bakery building. The resulting design included a series of webbed-steel cantilevers and steel hawsers to support the entire expanse of the roof with no interior columns. The 30,000 square-foot store, opened in 1988, was described in the *Guardian* as 'the most extraordinary piece of take-no-prisoners architecture since the Lloyds building'. JD comments, 'I think this was the ugliest store exterior that we'd ever built.' Other dissenting voices were heard. When Sainsbury's opened a store in Warrington, Cheshire, in 1985, one architectural critic referred to it as 'a horrible brick and metal lump, which stands right opposite one of the finest parish churches in England. For sheer ineptitude this has to be seen to be believed.'

In the mid-1980s, JD asked Colin Amery, then architectural correspondent for the *Financial Times,* to assist him in assessing the designs put forward by the development division. Amery comments: 'A group of us met regularly. John was particularly keen to get the right combination of excellent function and aesthetic appeal.' Amery recalls that some of the more adventurous buildings were a result of the demand from local planners to produce dynamic, modern constructions as centrepieces of new local developments. Camden had been a case in point, where the new Sainsbury's store was required as a kind of flagship in a complex that included housing, workshops and other community amenities. 'It was often the case that these stores were applauded more by the profession than the public,' he adds.

Reactions were by no means all bad. The development division received significant approval within the industry, gaining no fewer than 24 awards for either architectural or environmental excellence between 1983 and 1989. The Burpham store at Guildford seemed to have achieved the right balance between function and aesthetics. One customer wrote to Sainsbury's to say that shopping in this store was like visiting a cathedral. Occasionally, the architects were highly innovative in the way they adapted historic buildings. In 1988, a spectacular branch opened in Wolverhampton in which architects had created a sales area of more than 26,000 square feet by converting and extending the former St George's Church. The front entrance was directly under the steeple, and most of the original surrounding façade remained in place. Customers were greeted inside with decks of flowers in the new Sainsbury's florist department, as well as magazines and newspapers which were also part of the new range.

Although of reasonable size, this was actually one of the smaller new stores opened during 1988; the average store size had grown significantly, to 30,000 square feet, and the locations were of a high standard and sometimes notable for their positioning. At Ladbroke Grove in London, for example, a new store with 33,000 square feet of sales area was built on former utility land directly alongside the Grand Union Canal, the towpath of which was renovated as part of the development programme. Customers could arrive by boat and moor right next to the supermarket. One local paper carried a story about 'the store that was convenient to barge into'.

Occasional criticism in trade journals threw no shadows. For the most part Sainsbury's was the darling of the financial and business media. In October 1986, *Marketing Week* printed the result of a survey in which 650 leading marketing executives in seven sectors of industry were asked to assess the marketing performance of leading companies in their sector. Sainsbury's was rated the top performing company overall. It drew first place for the quality of products or services, the profitable pricing of products or services, the overall financial performance of its sector, and the ability to attract, develop and keep talented people. It drew second place for the design of products or services, and third place for the successful development of existing products and services, and the development of successful new products or services.

In April 1987, *Business* asked 30 analysts from leading stock-broking firms and large investment institutions to assess the 160 largest British public companies against five criteria: management dynamism, marketing skills, financial management, quality of products or services, and personnel management. Again, Sainsbury's was rated the top company overall.

When the company announced its 1987/8 results, the tempo of the headlines was raised another notch because Sainsbury's had broken through the magical £5 billion turnover figure – just one year after it had passed the £4 billion mark; moreover, its turnover now exceeded M&S for the first time. The headlines were more than usually enthusiastic: 'Housewives' choice – Sainsbury's hit the jackpot'; 'Sainsbury's topples M&S with peak £5bn sales'; 'Sainsbury's getting bigger and better'; 'Sainsbury's soars on £5 billion sales'. Perhaps the most observant headline came from the *Daily Mail* with 'Sainsbury's secret: retail detail down to its socks'. The Lex column in the *Financial Times* commented: 'With every flawless set of results produced by Sainsbury, its rating is surely justified, and while Tesco has yet to make its move into the US, Sainsbury has already done so to great effect.' This was true enough; Shaw's had contributed £30 million, or 9.1 per cent towards the group's profits of £308 million, and the subsidiary's profitability had grown tenfold since 1983. Sava-Centre and Homebase were turning in good results too, less than Shaw's but showing a steady and comfortable increase on previous years – all of which assisted the group's achievement of a net margin of 6.62 per cent, which was another all-time record.

Sainsbury's became Britain's leading greengrocer during the 1980s, selling an increasingly wide range of fresh fruit and vegetables

Wines and spirits at Crystal Palace in 1984, by which time Sainsbury's had become the UK's largest off licence

Top left: joint managing director Joe Barnes (right) and assistant managing director Tom Vyner discuss new products in the ready-meal range. *Top right*: Malcolm Kane, head of food technology in Sainsbury's Scientific Services Division, visiting a supplier factory in Chard, Somerset, to check chilli con carne in production. *Below*: JD addresses the world ozone conference in March 1989, and departmental director Peter Ibbotsen with Prime Minister Margaret Thatcher at the company's energy-saving exhibition

The Burpham branch, near Guildford, was highly acclaimed for its environmentally sympathetic design

Sainsbury's at Tunbridge Wells – one of the more harmonious store designs of the 1980s

Sainsbury's at Bath, where a disused railway station was converted to a covered car park serving the store that can be seen in the background

In the plant room of the supermarkets, the waste heat from the refrigeration system was used to provide heating for the store – this led to huge energy savings in the 1980s

An award-winning advertisement, one of a series devised for Sainsbury's by Abbot Mead Vickers in 1989

An oil change will make your salads go even faster.

To improve your performance in the kitchen, Sainsbury's present their range of speciality oils.

Walnut, hazelnut, sesame and grapeseed.

(The days of the bland salad are definitely over.)

Our walnut oil comes from the Dordogne region of France, where it is made from the first pressing of specially selected walnuts.

Try it in a dressing for Waldorf salad, or in a vegetarian nut roast, or walnut cookies.

Our hazelnut oil, also from France, has a more delicate flavour.

As well as being ideal for sauces and vinaigrettes, it also enhances the flavour of cakes and desserts.

The sesame oil comes from the Far East and you can stir it into salad dressings but it is equally at home in stir-frys. (Don't use too much, its flavour is full and heady.)

Grapeseed oil is just the opposite. A light, gentle oil made from the seeds of selected Italian grapes.

It is wonderful for salad dressings, baking and shallow-frying.

Sainsbury's speciality oils, although special, are very keenly priced.

Your salads may go faster, but they won't be super-charged.

Good food costs less at Sainsbury's.

Cucumbers have a 'season' lasting some ten months of the year if they are grown under glass. Here, produce-buyer Richard Bickerton and food technologist Mike Corbett carry out a quality-assurance visit to a supplier in Hull, 1992

Fish-buyer Andrea Chambers with a supplier checking the quality of the newly arrived catch at Peterhead Fish Market, on the north-east coast of Scotland, where Sainsbury's bought a large proportion of its fish

Accompanied by his wife, Anya, and John O'Sullivan the store manager, JD escorts the Queen Mother on a visit to Sainsbury's Cromwell Road branch in London

Lord and Lady Sainsbury with managers from the north-west region at one of several retirement functions in 1992

Passing the baton in November 1992: JD and David Sainsbury, his imminent successor

Chapter 15

SUMMIT
1988–1992

AT THE CLOSE OF THE DECADE, Sainsbury's growth appeared to be almost self-propelling, although this was far from being the case. Progress was sustained by the board, driven by JD and made possible by what others in the trade recognised as the most committed workforce in the food-retailing industry.

A phenomenal degree of commitment and energy emanated from the apex of the company down. While the stores were managed to a generally high standard, there can be no doubt that much of the company's drive since the mid-1970s was owing to the way the board operated. According to Joe Barnes: 'Everyone trusted and respected the roles played by other board members; there was no sense of looking over your shoulder; there was very little in the way of distracting office politics. We each knew what we had to do.'

As the 1980s drew to a close, some board changes were necessary because of retirements. In July 1988, Roy Griffiths retired in an executive capacity but remained a non-executive director. He was now Sir Roy Griffiths, having received a knighthood for his services since 1983 as the architect behind the reform of the NHS; his contribution led to the greatest overhaul of the NHS's structure and operations since it came into being.

Gurth Hoyer Millar, a board member since 1967, retired from the position of development director in 1988 but remained on the board as chairman of Homebase and J. Sainsbury Properties. He had been responsible for finding, acquiring or leasing more than five million square feet of sales space since his appointment as development director in 1974, including premises for Sainsbury's supermarkets, SavaCentre hypermarkets and Homebase stores. Bob Ingham, who had been with the company since 1952 and on the board since 1977, also retired at the end of October 1988. He had made a substantial contribution to the company's trading in the dairy, produce, frozen food, and beer, wines and spirits departments. Cecil Roberts took over these responsibilities, while Bob Cooper was promoted from departmental director to take over Roberts's buying areas, including meat, pork products and bakery departments.

David Sainsbury assumed Roy Griffiths's role as deputy chairman, and Joe Barnes and David Quarmby now became joint managing directors. In all these changes, there was an element of gradual transition, so that key executives did not disappear from the board but moved aside as others took control of their responsibilities. This secured the continuity of operations that had been built and refined over so many years.

For the key position of development director, replacing Hoyer Millar, the board employed headhunters to find a top property professional. Ian Coull was duly approached when he was a director of Ladbrokes, and was persuaded to join Sainsbury's in January 1988. Coull had plenty of experience of the retailing sector, having worked previously for both Texas and Argyll, and, like Payne and Vyner when they had joined Sainsbury's from different backgrounds, he brought new ideas and disciplines to the job, which he quickly made his own. Coull remembers his surprise at how large the development division was when he joined. For every development project Sainsbury's fielded its own planning team, construction engineers, electricians, refrigeration engineers, and most other professional disciplines involved in site acquisition and construction. Some of the department's supplier relationships had lasted many decades, even going back as far as the First World War. According to Coull, 'This was great in terms of being the trademark of a loyal and committed organisation, but so many of them had stagnated. When I first came in and had looked at the business, I recommended that we should dramatically prune the activities we carried out internally. In-house architecture and engineering became things of the past and we set about "refreshing" some of our external suppliers.'

The month-by-month advance of sales and profits demonstrated that these board changes did not upset the company's progress. But, above all, it was JD's presence and leadership style that bound the team together. This view is well illustrated by Jim Prior, one of the board's few non-executive directors. He vividly remembers how JD conducted the monthly meetings. They were extremely businesslike; small talk was noticeable by its absence.

Nor was there much wide-ranging discussion among the directors; rather, each meeting involved close scrutiny of carefully prepared paperwork. First, everyone would look at the latest sales figures and the gross margin, sales per square feet, productivity in terms of items handled per man-hour in the depots and sales per employee in the stores, and other such performance indicators. One indicator that the board was increasingly able to take for granted by the late 1980s was the significant reduction in stock days – this was a useful measure of working capital, representing the number of days the company had stock in store before it was sold. In the early 1980s this had been 31 days; by the end of the decade the figure was only 18 days, showing remarkable control of working capital. When all such figures had been pored over, JD would ask each director about any problems he might be experiencing in his sector of business. According to Prior, 'This was really an operational board and it was dominated by John in a way that I had not experienced in other boardrooms.'

Each month the board would look at a basket of 150 frequently bought items indicating Sainsbury's current price competitiveness. This assessment had started in 1972 and had been followed religiously; all the information was carefully collected from rival stores by Sainsbury's own research team. Prior comments: 'John watched his competition more closely than anyone I've ever known, particularly Tesco, but also Asda and Waitrose and perhaps M&S for their quality at the top end of the market.' Prior describes JD's attention to detail in the board meetings: 'There must have been literally mountains of board minutes relating to deliberations over the acceptance of bank cards. John would take his time and was exceptionally thorough over these kinds of arrangement. This was for the board to discuss and John to decide.' Whether or when to adopt credit cards is a good example of the decisions that caused some bother across the whole of the retail sector in the 1980s. From JD's point of view, such a move could only be justified by how much customers wanted it.

JD clearly had an iron grip over the conduct of the business. And the larger and more complex the business grew, the greater his determination that the traditional quality and value would be maintained. This actually represented an enormous demand; somehow there had to be a means by which the importance of sustaining high quality could be communicated on a daily basis through every fibre of the business. This means was John Sainsbury. JD insisted constantly that his executives, the senior and middle managers and the trainees in the hierarchy below him, attended to detail. 'Retail is detail', as the *Daily Mail* had mimicked, was a favourite and very well-used phrase, and for JD it meant observing closely and acting quickly on what you see – it also meant talking frequently and personally to customers in the stores. Everyone on the board, and many people throughout the company, were acutely aware that JD could react explosively if he felt that complacency or lack of attention to detail had led to a situation in which customers were not being served as they should.

In this respect, JD's store visits were legendary, and store managers would await the chairman's verdict on how well he thought their store was doing with a degree of trepidation akin to that of a schoolboy in the headmaster's study. If JD was not happy, he would be extremely forthright and take the manager to task; or if he found a problem that he knew related to supply or some lack of diligence at head office he would be on the telephone straight away, demanding to know how this had come about. When he was content with what he saw he would be full of praise. Some store managers were subject to both the anger and the charm of JD; following the outburst the chairman would give friendly words of encouragement before he left the store so that the manager was not left with his dignity ruffled or his hopes dashed.

JD's own attitude to his approach is simply that he visited the store with a customer's eyes, and if he found the service poor, the shelves empty, or noticed heavy queues at the checkout, he wanted to know why. 'The other point', he says, 'is that by picking up a problem, even if it was a relatively small matter of detail, I was providing an example. It was of course impossible to check and comment on everything, but the managers and the buyers learnt from the examples.' An essential aspect of the store visits was to check on how well head office was performing. Missing products, late deliveries or imbalances in the product range in the stores inevitably reflected on the central departments.

On his return from the store visits, JD would busy himself producing a stream of memos concerning his observations and instructing checks or improvements. Memos would also fly if JD picked up the smallest scent of criticism of Sainsbury's products or stores. A typical example is a note copied to Barnes, Vyner and Roberts: 'As no doubt you were, I was shocked to read that *The Sunday Times* thinks Tesco sausages are better than ours. This is so important that I would be grateful if all three of you would do a blind sampling and see if there are any grounds for such an absurd idea.'

Another example, from a memo to Vyner and Roberts, concerns the thickness of granary bread: 'It is astonishing how the thickness varies. I myself saw this morning out of one loaf a slice that was almost half an inch thick and another that was barely an eighth of an inch thick. Why cannot we control the regularity of the thickness of the slice?' In the same month, another memo demanded to know why the smartest of Sainsbury's kitchen paper was available at the Nine Elms store but not at Cromwell Road: 'Please report facts and figures to me.' Nor was Homebase allowed to escape the watchful eye of the chairman. On the same day as the kitchen-paper memo, JD sent a note to Hoyer Millar, chairman of Homebase, suggesting that the quality of the basin plugs should be improved and there should be more than just vinyl plugs available. He also thought there should be black-rubber strip matting or plastic used for walk-ways to save wear and tear, and suggested a better selection of Contact or Fablon with a variety of widths to choose from.

Such examples may appear extraordinarily pernickety given that JD was the chairman and chief executive of one of the ten largest companies in the UK, with a fast-growing, multi-billion pound turnover. But they illustrate the genius behind the company. Like his father, grandfather and great-grandfather before him, JD wanted the Sainsbury's shopping experience to be the very best, and, despite the size of the company and its stores, he wanted to preserve the sense of personal service, accountability and attention to detail that customers would have expected in old-fashioned service shops. In an interview in *Marketing Week* he said: 'We never allow ourselves to forget the virtues of the small business. It is very hard to be a successful large-scale retailer – you perhaps become less enterprising, more committee-bound, more bureaucratic.' As we have learnt from Jim Prior, under JD's direction Sainsbury's suffered no such drawbacks. He was a decision-maker who cut to the thrust. And although he used every tool available to him to monitor growth, productivity, quality and value so as to ensure the supremacy of Sainsbury's among all the food retailing giants, he was never a corporate man, always a retailer.

*

Another sustaining factor behind the company's success was staff loyalty, morale and commitment. Ivor Hunt has said, '110 per cent was demanded of us and we gave 120 per cent,' and this comment seems to have held true throughout the company. Staff felt secure in their career and generally well rewarded. When the excellent 1988 company results had been announced, the press trumpeted the record sums that were divided between the staff under Sainsbury's profit-sharing scheme. That year, nearly £24 million was shared between 37,800 qualifying employees – those who had worked for two years or more in the company, including part-time staff. This amounted to an average of almost 10 per cent of an employee's annual salary. There were also 22,000 employee shareholders with shares worth some £37 million. Without doubt, shareholding and profit-sharing were contributing to the good morale and commitment of employees. Since the introduction of profit-sharing in 1979/80, until the end of the 1980s, more than £160 million had been divided between the staff. During the same 11-year period staff turnover, which has traditionally been high in the industry, noticeably reduced.

Money was a great incentive, but it was only part of the reason for the unusual degree of commitment and loyalty given by Sainsbury's staff. A large proportion of employees believed in the company's values, vigorously and continuously reinforced by JD, most of which had permeated the company since its early days. Dave Smith, who worked for many years in the company, and who became an area manager in 1991, said at a reunion meeting in 2005: 'We first published a set of Group Objectives in 1985, although we had been living them and building a hugely successful business upon them, for many years . . . They were simple, clear and probably the most honest set of objectives we have ever published.' Every store had a copy of these objectives on the wall. They bear repeating:

1. To discharge the responsibility as leaders in our trade by acting with complete integrity, by carrying out our work to the highest standards, and by contributing to the public good and to the quality of life in the community.
2. To provide unrivalled value to our customers in the quality of the goods we sell, in the competitiveness of our prices and in the range of choice we offer.
3. To achieve the highest standards in efficiency of operation, con-

venience and customer service in our stores, thereby creating as
attractive and friendly a shopping environment as possible.
4. To offer our staff outstanding opportunities in terms of personal
   career development and in the remuneration relative to other
   companies in the same market, practising always a concern for
   the welfare of the individual.
5. To generate sufficient profit to finance continual improvement
   and growth of the business whilst providing our shareholders
   with an excellent return on their investment.

   Through the turbulent 1970s and buoyant 1980s, Sainsbury's Staff
Association had continued to bring employees together in the pursuit of social, recreational and sporting activities. This maintained
and promoted the sense of pride and belonging that staff felt. The
Veterans' Association for retired employees was equally active, and
both organisations were subsidised by management. Many years
before, Roy Griffiths had started the 25 Club, through which, as the
name suggests, the company wined and dined all those who had
worked for the company for 25 years. There were 40th anniversaries
too, and JD and other directors, often accompanied by their wives,
would present gifts and give heartfelt thanks to these long-serving
personnel.
   Employees were also rewarded with careers that offered real
prospects and security. At the branch managers' conference in 1988,
Joe Barnes opened proceedings by reading out a roll-call of senior
management promotions; this was the longest ever such list
recorded at these conferences. Later JD told delegates, as 'a measure of what JS expansion can mean for JS people, no fewer than
2,100 men and women in branch management were promoted to a
higher grade – that is 48 per cent of those in retail management'.
Along with good prospects, Sainsbury's offered increasingly comfortable working conditions to its senior branch staff and store
managers, who were the most vulnerable to poaching by competitors. A new promotion structure was introduced in 1988 to simplify
the previous, rather complicated five-tiered progression between
assistant deputy manager and store manager. The working week
was also reduced from 44 to 39 hours.
   Considering that wages and salaries represented by far the
largest part of Sainsbury's operational expenses, the substantial
amounts that the company was now spending on training also

proved to be a good investment. This improved staff morale and confidence, and contributed to improved productivity. The squeeze to sell more products per employee had been constant since the early 1970s, yet between 1988 and 1992, this measure of productivity continued to improve by between 4 and 5 per cent each year. Such improvements were owed to some extent to Sainsbury's creativity during the 1980s in the development of new programmes to foster the capabilities of the company's staff and to recruit capable people. Year on year a higher proportion of A-Level students and graduates were recruited to be groomed into management positions.

A report prepared for the Department of Education and Science in 1987 illustrates the sophistication and depth of Sainsbury's training, which at the time was costing the company about £18 million a year – by 1992, the programme would cost £30 million. Dr Paul Johnson, the author of the report, spent six months in Sainsbury's training department gathering information. He reported that Sainsbury's had an exemplary range of training for staff at every level of the company. He noted that more than 1,000 staff were involved as trainers or mentors; that in the previous year more than 13,000 employees had received off-the-job training; that Sainsbury's provided 120 in-company training courses at five area training centres, head office and two business centres – at Fanhams Hall and Dulwich. Every level of the company was covered by these courses. No fewer than 150 senior managers had received training to extend their business skills and knowledge; and 2,000 middle and junior managers had been involved in 40 separate courses. Johnson gave an account of the company's Youth Training Scheme (YTS). In the previous year there had been an intake of 411 YTS trainees, 332 of whom completed their training, and 95 per cent of these were offered permanent employment. In fact, since the scheme had started in 1983, Sainsbury's had offered full-time jobs to every trainee who satisfactorily completed the course. Johnson also reported that 800 graduates and A-Level school-leavers were recruited in one year, with graduates accounting for about 170 of these.

The report also covered Sainsbury's training methods. Johnson particularly approved of the focus on practical work, discussions, role-play and question-and-answer tutorials. He recommended that further-education establishments adopt some of these. In the next few years Sainsbury's built on these achievements, introducing Sainsbury's-sponsored degrees and developing a new Retail Marketing degree in conjunction with Manchester Polytechnic; this was a part-distance-learning course aimed at Sainsbury's A-Level trainees.

Sainsbury's training was high-profile and it was part of the company's attraction, particularly in the graduate recruiting market of the early 1990s. Although the recession which occurred then served to reduce overall demand for good graduates coming into business, industry and commerce, there was still a relative shortfall because of the coming of age of the post-baby-boom generation, which produced fewer children. In the generally buoyant mid-1980s, major companies were very aware of the shortfall that was about to occur and were all focusing on the best ways to offer an attractive proposition to graduates and A-Level students. It was all the more gratifying in such a competitive recruitment environment for Sainsbury's to win the prestigious *Sunday Times* Hemington Scott Award in 1988. This was made following a survey of over 1,000 company directors and city analysts to find the most respected companies in the UK. Sainsbury's was ranked third place overall, but received first place as 'Most Respected Company' in the food retailing sector, first place for 'Ability to Recruit and Retain High-Calibre Employees', and also first place for 'Management Calibre'.

The whole business of recruiting, nurturing and training staff fed into the main objective of sustaining the virtuous circle of Sainsbury's growth: more and bigger stores, more choice, more customers, larger volumes sold, increased turnover, profits and productivity, more stores and so on.

In this front-line process, Sainsbury's had not only matched the consumer trend towards healthy eating in its product range, but stamped its authority on this programme by producing regular information on the subject. It launched a series of award-winning 'Living Today' leaflets, and distributed millions of these through the stores. The company's marketing was constantly tuned to the health theme. By 1990, consumers were generally aware that fresh fish was both a nutritious and a healthy food. Sainsbury's had already developed more than 50 wet-fish counters, and there were plans to have more in every new store and, wherever possible, in existing stores. Buyers also developed a range of ready meals based on fish recipes.

In the same period, Sainsbury's continued to develop its fresh foods generally, and were now selling free-range poultry. Buyers set up close working relationships with the British suppliers of fruit and vegetables to ensure a supply of good-quality organic produce to meet a slowly emerging but evident demand. In 1990, Sainsbury's was offering other organic products, including bread, flour, wine, cheese, tea and milk. Sainsbury's was also making its mark as a leading supermarket espousing the 'green' revolution that was well under way by the late 1980s. It stocked a growing variety of natural detergent products which were 100 per cent biodegradable and no longer contained phosphates or optical brighteners. Own-label and proprietary lines included toilet tissues, facial tissues and kitchen towels made from recycled pulp, and stationery items from recycled paper. None of Sainsbury's own-label toiletries or cosmetics had been tested on animals, nor, in the previous five years, had any of the ingredients been so tested. Sainsbury's even introduced an own-label nappy made from non-chlorine-bleached pulp, as a means of reducing the toxic waste resulting from the chlorine-bleaching process. To prevent damage to the ozone layer, the company also advocated the removal of chlorofluorocarbons (CFCs). In March 1989, JD addressed a world ozone conference describing the measures that had taken place within Sainsbury's to replace CFCs in all refrigeration plant and in building and packaging material.

Environmentally friendly, organic, healthy – these evolving themes in consumer demand suited the Sainsbury's ethos and the company's buying and product-development disciplines. They offered a rich vein for the development of new lines. As a food retailer that had remained committed to quality and freshness, Sainsbury's offer of such products had strong credibility within a consumer population that was far better educated – choosier, more critical and concerned – about food than was the case even five years before.

The rate of increase in own-label goods accelerated, so that no fewer than 1,000 lines were launched in 1989/90, 1,300 in 1990/1 and 1,500 in 1991/2. By mid-1992, 8,000 own-label lines were sold in the largest of the supermarkets. Along with the buyers, the company's scientific services division, still known as the laboratories, remained central to this operation. This division dominated the industry in its work of sampling, testing, research and food safety. In

1990, a share analyst's report, which recommended Sainsbury's as a 'strong buy', noted that there were 167 personnel in Sainsbury's scientific services division, which had an annual budget of £5 million. He particularly approved the close link between the buying teams and suppliers in product development and quality control: 'So closely have the relationships developed with key suppliers that Sainsbury's, more than any other retailer, has been responsible for pioneering the introduction of certain new product categories into the UK market, fromage frais being an example. These had been subsequently copied by both branded manufacturers and other own-label operators.'

JD paid tribute to the company's scientific services division in his address to shareholders in 1990. He was not given to exaggeration, so his commendation is impressive: 'I am confident that today we have the most respected team of food scientists and technologists of any supermarket company either in this country or in the United States.' Recognition of the reputation of Sainsbury's work in this field came in 1988 when Dr Roy Spencer, director of scientific services, was appointed to the Richmond Committee, set up by the government to consider the microbiological safety of food.

Sainsbury's advance now appeared irresistible. The intention had never been to be the biggest food-retailing supermarket in the UK, but to be the best. Yet scale was being added to quality at an extraordinary rate, and Sainsbury's development programme was more impressive than any other food-retailing multiple. In 1991, the Sainsbury's Group reported opening a total of 150 outlets in the previous three-year period, including new stores for Homebase, SavaCentre and Shaw's. Meanwhile, customer transaction figures, group sales and profits climbed inexorably. Earnings per share rose by more than 20 per cent, as they had done in each of the previous 12 years.

Apart from store development, training and recruitment, significant new investment in the company's distribution system was made to maintain this advance. Twenty-five million pounds alone had been invested in the company's highly sophisticated cold chain over three years, since 1988. A new high-bay storage warehouse was opened in Buntingford. This was completely automated, with the 100-foot high storage racks taking up to 320,000 cases of non-perishable products.

Marketing initiatives in the stores helped to sustain increases in the volume of sales. For example, in 1990, multibuy offers were launched to tempt customers with significant reductions when they bought a number of items of the same product. By such means, the company was able to continue to offer the keenest prices and watch a very satisfying rise in the volume of sales. We might remember that at the beginning of the 1980s, there was some satisfaction that the company's net profit margin was up from its previous ten-year average of about 3.3 per cent to a healthy 3.7 per cent. Net margin for 1990/1 was 7.9 per cent. This was larger than any other supermarket chain in the UK or overseas.

As JD approached his own retirement, two of his closest allies on the board preceded him. In 1990, both Sir Roy Griffiths and Joe Barnes retired, the former from his position as a non-executive board member, the latter moving from an executive to a non-executive position. Added to the accolades received by the company, JD had himself been elevated to the peerage as Lord Sainsbury of Preston Candover in 1989. In the same year, he was also awarded the Albert Medal of the Royal Society of Arts, Manufactures and Commerce, in recognition of his 'outstanding contribution in the fields of business and the arts'. In 1992, he joined the inner sanctum of the highly honoured by being created a Knight of the Garter.

Quite apart from the donation made by John, Simon and Timothy Sainsbury to create the new Sainsbury Wing of the National Gallery, which opened in 1991, all the main family shareholders in the company were substantial private benefactors within the community. At a corporate level, Sainsbury's Arts Sponsorship Programme was a particular success. This was launched in 1981, and under the initiative Sainsbury's Choir of the Year competition had achieved international status. The annual televised competition attracted millions of viewers. Sainsbury's also contributed to numerous other community, education, business set-up and environmental initiatives. Across the country, Sainsbury's Staff Association members in each supermarket devised branch-level schemes and events which raised hundreds of thousands of pounds on behalf of locally based charities.

During JD's last year as chairman and chief executive, trading conditions became tighter with the effects of the recession and with competitors opening on Sunday. Within the board there had been some debate about Sunday opening – in principle JD was not particularly happy with the idea, but Sainsbury's decision had to depend on what his customers wanted. The board decided to test shoppers' wishes by opening about a third of its supermarket branches on Sundays, as well as Homebase stores and SavaCentre hypermarkets. The result was conclusive, with customers clearly finding Sunday opening an added convenience.

JD wrote his last chairman's statement in the annual report of 1991/2. The company's performance was a fitting tribute to his own achievements as chairman of Sainsbury's for the previous 23 years. A Consumer Association survey of January 1992 had recorded that Sainsbury's was by far the most popular supermarket in the UK. Group sales had reached £9,202 million, while profit before tax was £628 million. This represented almost 24 per cent compound growth in profit per year over the last 23 years. There were now 313 supermarkets, 64 Homebase stores, 9 SavaCentres and 73 Shaw's supermarkets in the group. In 1969, there had been just 82 supermarkets and 162 service shops. Some 9.5 million customers shopped at these outlets each week, whereas the 1969 figure was in the region of two million. There were nearly 73,000 full-time-equivalent employees in Sainsbury's supermarkets, and approaching 110,000 in the whole group, 95,000 based in the UK; in 1969, the figure was 23,500. Each employee generated £214 of profit each week. The nearest competitor, Tesco, could generate only £159 per week per person. In 1969, Sainsbury's profits had been less than half of Tesco's.

No fewer than 1,500 new own-label lines had been added during 1991/2 and the exploration of new styles and tastes had continued. New lines included Boboli pizza, ciabatta bread, Condiverde pasta sauces and almost 50 new ready meals; alternative fruit and vegetables included *fraises de bois*, pink currants and baby coconuts. And the Sainsbury's off-licence department had introduced more than 100 new wines during that year. Own-label products now comprised more than half of the total offer of some 16,000 lines.

In 1992, Sainsbury's also became the most profitable retail company in the UK, overtaking M&S. British food retailing was now so concentrated in the UK that just seven chains accounted for more than 50 per cent of the entire British grocery market. Tesco was in second place and had made great strides in recent years to shed its former downmarket image under the determined management of

Ian MacLaurin and David Malpas. After more than a decade of
struggle to change Tesco's image and enhance the quality of its
products, Tesco's stores were beginning to be seen in a new light.
The food quality was generally improved, and the overhaul of the
company's distribution structure was paying off. In the four years
between 1988 and 1992 Tesco had increased its market share from 9
per cent to 10.1 per cent, but it was still some way behind Sainsbury's
both in sales, which totalled £7 billion, and profits, totalling £509
million.

Another keen competitor in this year was Safeway, which had
only started to show its potential after the company had been
acquired by the Argyll Group in 1987. After that, Safeway became a
serious and innovative player in the food-retailing industry. By 1992,
it was beginning to reap significant rewards after having integrated,
under the Safeway and Presto names, the numerous smaller grocery chains that had been acquired in the previous two decades.
Safeway was now a distant third behind Tesco and Sainsbury, but its
market share had grown impressively, from 6.9 per cent to 7.5 per
cent between 1988 and 1992, and it was working hard to make best
use of a mixed portfolio of stores.

M&S, the Co-op and Somerfield were also important competitors with significant shares of the grocery market, but in each case
their share of national food sales had been declining for a number
of years. M&S had remained a niche player, focusing on the sale of
convenience foods and prepared meals rather than challenging
Sainsbury's far broader offer. The Co-op now operated a number
of large out-of-town supermarkets alongside numerous high-
street stores, but it had never overcome the problem of having
a disparate structure which had led to an incoherent strategy
and mixed trading results across the UK. Sales per square foot in
the Co-ops were on average less than half those of Sainsbury's.
Somerfield, which also traded under the Gateway fascia, was a well-
known name on many high streets, but its smaller stores could not
really compete with the larger, more efficient, out-of-town supermarkets.

And where was Asda placed in this field? By the mid-1980s the
success of Asda's strategy had been recognised across the industry.
Asda's operating margins reached 6.3 per cent in 1985 compared
with Sainsbury's then impressive 5.2 per cent. But only five or six
years later Asda had come seriously unstuck. It had borrowed heav-

ily in order to fund an aggressive expansion plan: between 1985 and
1991 it had doubled its store portfolio from 101 to 204 stores, extending its area into the much costlier south of England, introducing
new distribution systems and launching a range of own-label
products, clearly influenced by the Sainsbury's model. Asda had
struggled to manage MFI, the furniture retailer the company
bought in 1985 – an acquisition that had never seemed to offer any
obvious advantage to a successful food retailer. By the beginning of
the 1990s, the country was in recession, Asda's finances were
stretched to the limit, and the City began to lose faith in the ability
of the senior management team. In 1991, the shareholders had
finally ousted them in favour of Archie Norman, a 37-year-old former partner of McKinsey and group finance director at Kingfisher.
But the action taken by the City had not come soon enough. In 1992,
Asda posted a loss of £365 million and the share price plummeted to
20p from its high of £1.70 just three years earlier. Under Norman's
astute guidance Asda would make a spectacular recovery, but, at the
time, the company's fortunes were at an all-time low.

When JD announced the year's results at the July 1992 annual
general meeting, he took time to reflect on the company's achievements since 1969 and explained what he felt were the main reasons
for the company's success:

> The first point is that it is not because we sought to be the largest
> or the most profitable. Our objective was, as it always had been
> and is to this day, the very basic one of seeking to provide our
> customers with better quality, better prices and better service
> than any competitor.
>
> Our success is more than anything else due to sticking to that
> very clear, very simple, but very difficult objective. In doing so we
> were following the principles and priorities established by the
> founders of our business in 1869 and held to by each generation
> since.
>
> That tradition, one that might be described as the 'primacy of
> the customer', is part of our inheritance. Together with it goes
> another quality that successive generations of the company have
> followed. That is the desire to constantly improve; what I have
> called 'the passion to innovate', the recognition that however
> well we are doing today, we can always do better tomorrow. That
> goes with relishing competition, which is the best spur to have,

in that commercial race called 'the pursuit of excellence', in which we are engaged.

The explanation is both fluent and compelling, but it omits a key factor, which is leadership of an apparently inimitable kind. Perhaps it is fitting to reiterate the words spoken by Sir Roy Griffiths at a dinner in 1991 to mark JD's forty years in the company:

He has taken the view that the prerequisite of any corporate greatness is quality – quality of product, quality of service. Nothing, but nothing must get in the way . . . No senior member of a family ever cherished the family traditions more closely. No Roman ever guarded the household gods more zealously, no chairman has ever looked after the corporate values so committedly, and nothing has been too much, no generosity too great for people who serve the customer, and by definition the company, well.

Appendix 1: Performance Statistics 1950–1992

The data in this appendix was prepared by Dr Simon Learmount of Judge Business School, University of Cambridge

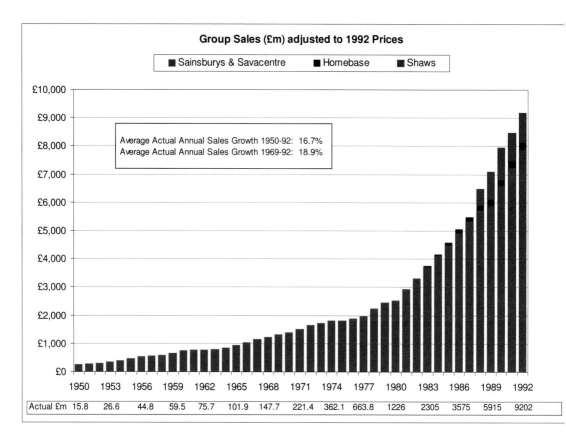

Group Sales (£m) adjusted to 1992 Prices

Legend: ■ Sainsburys & Savacentre ■ Homebase ■ Shaws

Average Actual Annual Sales Growth 1950-92: 16.7%
Average Actual Annual Sales Growth 1969-92: 18.9%

	1950	1953	1956	1959	1962	1965	1968	1971	1974	1977	1980	1983	1986	1989	1992
Actual £m	15.8	26.6	44.8	59.5	75.7	101.9	147.7	221.4	362.1	663.8	1226	2305	3575	5915	9202

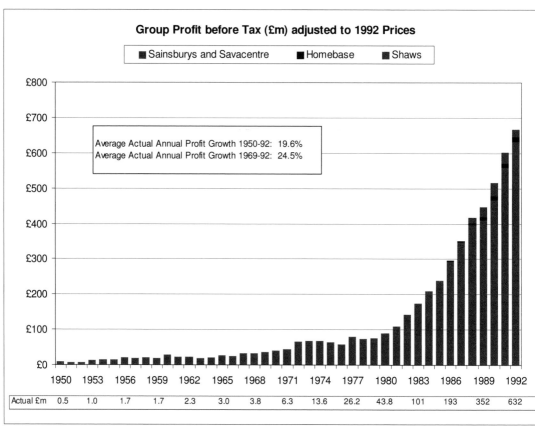

Group Profit before Tax (£m) adjusted to 1992 Prices

Legend: ■ Sainsburys and Savacentre ■ Homebase ■ Shaws

Average Actual Annual Profit Growth 1950-92: 19.6%
Average Actual Annual Profit Growth 1969-92: 24.5%

	1950	1953	1956	1959	1962	1965	1968	1971	1974	1977	1980	1983	1986	1989	1992
Actual £m	0.5	1.0	1.7	1.7	2.3	3.0	3.8	6.3	13.6	26.2	43.8	101	193	352	632

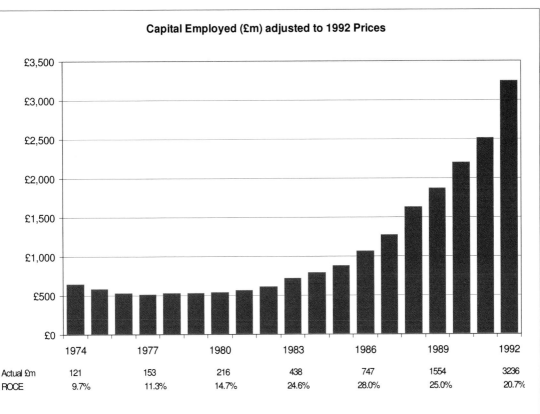

Capital Employed (£m) adjusted to 1992 Prices

	1974	1977	1980	1983	1986	1989	1992
Actual £m	121	153	216	438	747	1554	3236
ROCE	9.7%	11.3%	14.7%	24.6%	28.0%	25.0%	20.7%

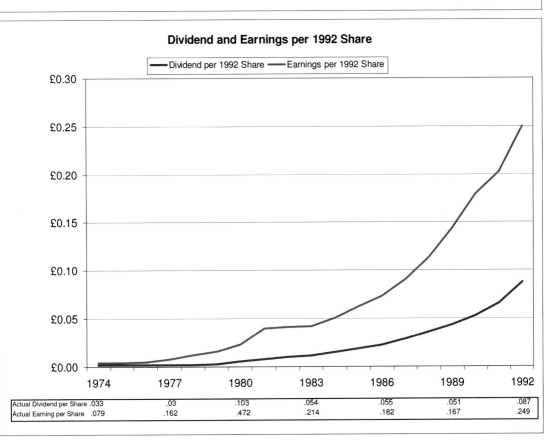

Dividend and Earnings per 1992 Share

— Dividend per 1992 Share — Earnings per 1992 Share

	1974	1977	1980	1983	1986	1989	1992
Actual Dividend per Share	.033	.03	.103	.054	.055	.051	.087
Actual Earning per Share	.079	.162	.472	.214	.182	.167	.249

Comparative Share Price Growth (1973 = 1)

Sainsbury — Asda — Tesco — FTSE All-Share

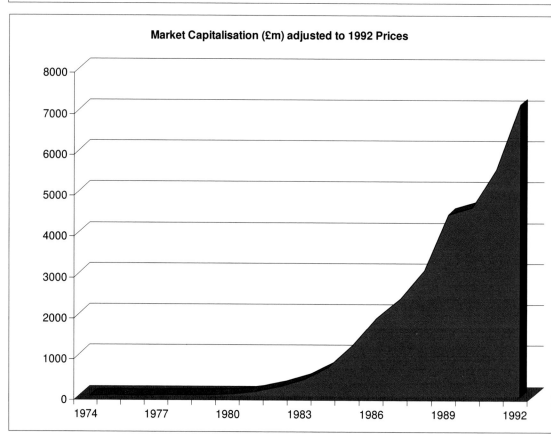

Market Capitalisation (£m) adjusted to 1992 Prices

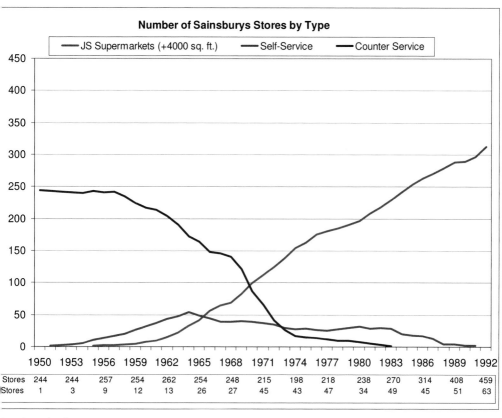

Number of Sainsburys Stores by Type

Legend: JS Supermarkets (+4000 sq. ft.) — Self-Service — Counter Service

	1950	1953	1956	1959	1962	1965	1968	1971	1974	1977	1980	1983	1986	1989	1992
Stores	244	244	257	254	262	254	248	215	198	218	238	270	314	408	459
Stores	1	3	9	12	13	26	27	45	43	47	34	49	45	51	63

tores in previous 3 years
s Homebase & Savacentre

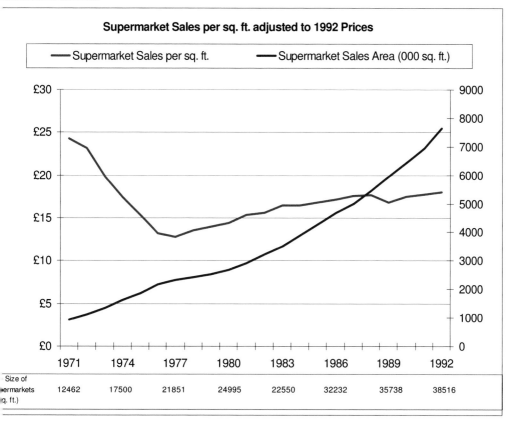

Supermarket Sales per sq. ft. adjusted to 1992 Prices

Legend: Supermarket Sales per sq. ft. — Supermarket Sales Area (000 sq. ft.)

	1971	1974	1977	1980	1983	1986	1989	1992
Size of ermarkets q. ft.)	12462	17500	21851	24995	22550	32232	35738	38516

Comparative Total Supermarket Sales Area (000 sq. ft.)

— J Sainsbury & Savacentre   — Tesco   — Asda

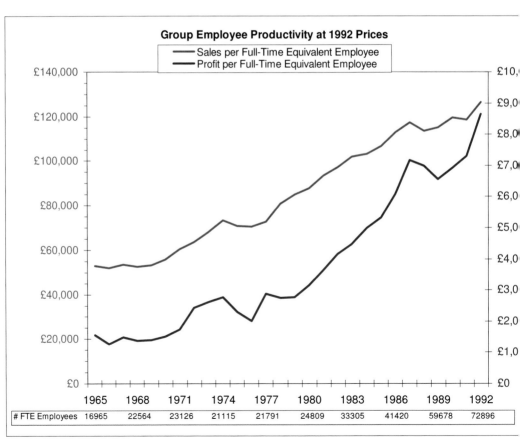

Group Employee Productivity at 1992 Prices

— Sales per Full-Time Equivalent Employee
— Profit per Full-Time Equivalent Employee

	1965	1968	1971	1974	1977	1980	1983	1986	1989	1992
# FTE Employees	16965	22564	23126	21115	21791	24809	33305	41420	59678	72896

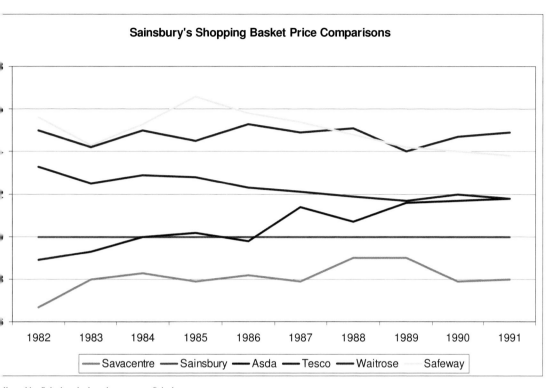

Sainsbury's Shopping Basket Price Comparisons

Savacentre ── Sainsbury ── Asda ── Tesco ── Waitrose ── Safeway

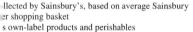

llected by Sainsbury's, based on average Sainsbury
er shopping basket
s own-label products and perishables

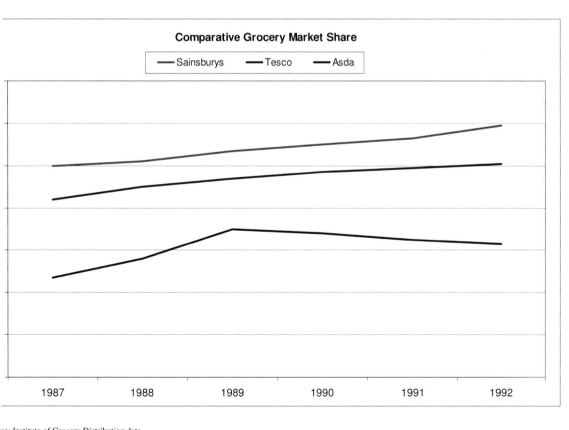

Comparative Grocery Market Share

── Sainsburys ── Tesco ── Asda

e: Institute of Grocery Distribution data
ta for earlier years is not presented because of
ges in data collection methodologies

Appendix 2: Executive and Non-Executive Directors of J. Sainsbury plc 1950–1992

Executive Directors

A. J. Sainsbury (Lord Sainsbury)	1933–67	Chairman: 1956–67	President: 1967–98
R. J. Sainsbury (Sir Robert)	1934–69	Chairman: 1967–69	President: 1969–2000
F. W. Salisbury	1941–62		
J. A. Sainsbury	1941–74		
N. C. Turner	1945–67		
J. D. Sainsbury (Lord Sainsbury)	1958–92	Chairman: 1969–92	President: 1992
S. D. D. Sainsbury	1959–79		
W. M. Justice	1959–72		
T. A. D. Sainsbury (Sir Timothy)	1962–74	Non-exec.: 1974–83 & 1995–99	
B. T. Ramm	1962–79		
A. S. Trask	1965–72		
D. J. Sainsbury (Lord Sainsbury)	1966–98	Chairman: 1992–98	
G. C. Hoyer Millar	1967–89	Non-exec.: 1989–91	
P. A. C. Snow	1969–76		
J. H. G. Barnes	1969–90	Non-exec.: 1990–93	
E. R. Griffiths (Sir Roy)	1969–88	Non-exec.: 1988–90	
L. S. Payne	1975–86		
C. Roberts	1975–92		
R. A. Ingham	1977–88		
P. J. Davis (Sir Peter)	1977–86		
R. T. Vyner	1978–97		
R. A. Clark	1979–96		
D. E. Henson	1980–92		
D. A. Quarmby	1984–97		
K. O. Worrall	1986–95		
I. D. Coull	1988–2002		

R. Cooper	1988–98
J. E. Adshead	1989–2004
C. I. Harvey	1989–97
D. B. Adriano	1990–2000
R. P. Whitbread	1990–2002
R. P. Thorne	1992–99

Non-Executive Directors (*not Formerly Executive Directors*)

Sir James Spooner	1981–94
Dame Jennifer Jenkins	1982–85
Lord Prior	1985–92
Lady Eccles of Moulton	1986–95

Appendix 3: Chairman's Speech, Annual General Meeting
1 July 1992

I wonder how many of you here today were present at our first Annual General Meeting as a public company. It was on 26 June 1974 in The Connaught Rooms. Our share price on that day, if we adjust for Rights and Capitalisation issues, was around 6p, and the Company's market capitalisation was below £100 million, which compares to today's figure of over £8,000 million. That was the first time I addressed shareholders at an Annual General Meeting, and today, as you all know, is to be the last.

Little did I think at that first AGM that one day the Company would have the largest sales and the highest profits of any retailer in the country. But that indeed is what has happened.

It is perhaps appropriate this morning, therefore, to spend a moment reflecting on how our Company, which in 1969, the year I became Chairman, had only a ninth of the profit of the country's most profitable retailer, and less than half that of the most profitable supermarket company, has reached the position we have today.

The first point is that it is *not* because we sought to be the largest or the most profitable. Our objective was, as it always had been and is to this day, the very basic one of seeking to provide our customers with better quality, better prices and better service than any competitor.

Our success these past two decades is more than anything else due to sticking to that very clear, very simple, but very difficult objective. In doing so we were following the principles and the priorities established by the founders of our business in 1869 and held to by each generation since.

That tradition, one that might be described as the 'primacy of the customer', is part of our inheritance. Together with it goes another quality that successive generations of our Company have followed. That is the desire to constantly improve, what I have called 'the passion to innovate', the recognition that, however well we are doing today, we can always do better tomorrow. That goes with relishing competition, which is the best spur to have, in that commercial race called 'the pursuit of excellence' in which we are engaged.

Our trade has, of course, always been fast-changing and dynamic, although never more so than in the post-war period. Most food chain stores that flourished in the 1950s had failed by the end of the 60s and disappeared by the end of the 70s. Only those who moved the fastest, and adapted the most to meet customers' changing needs, succeeded. They became our strongest competitors to give us that essential spur to our competitive drive.

Since the 60s the standard of living in our country has increased by 80 per cent. Greater travel, better education, more leisure, greater mobility have transformed our customers' needs and lifestyles. This has been the background of the transformation in food retailing over these years. Our success has been because we recognised the changes needed and responded quicker and more effectively than others in our trade.

As the ancient Greek saying of 500 BC goes, 'Nothing is permanent but change.' The figures we quote in our Annual Report are a measure of some of the more important changes that have occurred in the Company during my Chairmanship. They reflect investment and growth on a massive scale. It has been that investment, through the development of new and much larger supermarkets, that has provided the means of improving the service to our customers, the means of improving operating efficiency, and the means of achieving higher quality, lower prices and a wider range than would have been conceivable if we had not invested as we have.

In 1969 our total sales area was a tenth of our supermarket sales area today, and 160 of our 240 shops were old counter shops. Very few of our stores had car parks, and those that did had multi-level ones. Town planners, in those days, were slow to recognise the changing needs of shoppers. They were slow to recognise that multi-level car parks were both an architectural disaster and a grossly inconvenient way of parking cars. They were slow to recognise that supermarkets needed to become both larger and easier to get to than was possible in the traditional High Street location. So in the early years the development of modern supermarkets was inhibited by the planners and what seemed to be their belief that only a prosperous minority would be able to shop by car.

Happily that attitude is now much changed, and our pace of modernisation and development has increased. In the 70s we opened an average of 12 stores a year. By the end of the 80s this had risen to around 20 a year. Over the same period the average size of stores increased threefold. This has meant we have sufficient space to give customers far greater choice and the convenience of being able to buy everyday household items along with their food shopping. The range of food and other goods we sell is four times as great as 20 years ago, and now we are able to have fish and delicatessen counters and in-store bakeries.

For me, as I think for all of us with responsibility for the policy of the Company, the true motivation in the great expansion since the 70s has been the determination to improve the quality of shopping, the quality of choice and the good value we offer to our customers. Our high level of investment raised operating standards, improved efficiency, lowered costs and made possible our high profit margin – although I should point out that our return on capital, whilst very good, is not significantly different to that experienced by the most successful food retailers in other countries.

Along with the ambitious development programme of new stores, we made considerable investment in new systems and new technology. We led our trade in the use of scanning at the checkouts and in new logistical systems to improve efficiency and lower costs of distribution. Our computer installations throughout the Company now have a power 2,000 times greater than they had only ten years ago.

Larger stores and the latest systems have resulted in higher productivity both in terms of sales per employee and sales per square foot. Today our productivity per employee is 19 per cent higher than ten years ago, and significantly higher than any other supermarket company. Our sales per square foot of selling space is double the national average, whilst the profit we earn per square foot is 67 per cent greater than any of our major competitors'.

The fact that today's customers greatly value the convenience of purchasing everyday items along with their food shopping has led to a huge expansion in sales of products other than food. Keenly priced petrol is particularly important, and all new shops will have petrol stations unless space or other restrictions make it impossible. Flowers, house-plants, newspapers and magazines are the latest departments that have enjoyed great success in recent years. The development of our non-food departments has been such that today over 30 per cent of sales are in products other than food. The overall share that we have of the nation's trade in food and all those product areas in which supermarkets trade is approximately 10.5

per cent. Looking at our market share purely in food, and including food eaten away from home which represents about one-third of all expenditure on food, our share is significantly lower than this.

Some of you will have seen press comments suggesting that the growth of the largest food retailers has reduced the level of healthy competition in our trade. I believe nothing could be further from the truth. The success and the growth of those retailers that offer the public the best value is a demonstration of competition working. The success and growth of smaller regional companies is a clear indication you do not have to be large to be successful. The success of the best of the limited-line discounters, as well as the success of the best of the hypermarkets – eg SavaCentre – is a demonstration that the public have a wider range of choice of *type* of food retailing than ever before.

The *amount* of choice is evident in the fact that for every Sainsbury supermarket there are over 250 other food shops, of which 14 belong to other major multiple food retailers. The combined share of trade enjoyed by the five largest food retailers in the UK is under 40 per cent, and this compares with France and Germany where it is estimated that the equivalent figures are about 30 per cent and 50 per cent respectively.

I am pleased to say that, contrary to some reports, UK food prices are generally lower than in other European countries. This in part is a tribute to our food industry as a whole, and in part due to the stronger place that retailers' brands have in the UK food trade, compared to other countries.

Our private label – the Sainsbury brand – is our greatest single trading success. For 40 years it has given our customers the best value in the market place and made possible our competitive price advantage.

As many of you will appreciate, 80 per cent of our sales and 90 per cent of our Group profit come from our UK supermarkets. However, we believe there is great potential for long-term growth of our subsidiary companies. Both SavaCentre and Homebase have been affected over the last two years by the recession in the non-food trade but, despite this, showed a good improvement in sales and profits last year. Shaw's suffered severely from the deep recession in the north-east of the United States, but I have every confidence that, this year, they will be back on track and will begin to benefit from the many changes we have initiated.

I am pleased to say that this year has started well. Inflation is lower than we had expected and sales volume slightly higher. The year's new stores opened to date are trading well, and we anticipate opening the 22 supermarkets listed in the Annual Report before the year end.

I have left to the last any reference to our Company's greatest strength, our outstandingly able, highly motivated and efficient staff. It is they who have brought the Company to the pre-eminent position it is in today. It is they whom I thank as their Chairman, and whom I suggest all shareholders should thank for their achievements, especially in the last year.

We have always given the highest priority to staff training, believing that if we are to achieve the highest standards in the trade it is necessary for staff training to be second to none. Last year we invested no less than £30 million in the training and development of our people.

I am proud of that figure as I am of our profit-sharing scheme. Since its inception we will have distributed to staff over £250 million in shares or cash. It is certainly the most generous profit-sharing scheme in the retail industry. An employee on average earnings, who has taken shares rather than cash since the scheme started in 1980, now has shares worth about £20,000. In total about one-third of all shareholders are JS staff.

Looking back over the last 23 years I should like to thank all who served the Company during those years and who contributed to the success we have achieved. I am thinking especially of our veterans, many of whom gave their working life to JS. They can claim the distinction of being part of the team who, in 20 years, have made this Company not only the most successful UK retailer, but also one of the most respected food retailers in the world.

I look forward to my retirement in November confident that the team under my cousin, David Sainsbury, with Tom Vyner and David Quarmby as Managing Directors, will take the Company from strength to strength. I know, too, that whatever the changes – and there will be many in the years ahead – they will uphold the traditions that have made JS the Company it is, the traditions that have guided each generation of the Company during the 123 years since my great-grandparents opened that small shop in Drury Lane with the name J Sainsbury over the door.

FAMILY TREE

John James = **Mary Ann** (*née Staples*)
1844–1928   1849–1927

John Benjamin
1871–1956
Director 1922
Chairman 1928

George
1872–1964

Frank
1877–1955

Arthur
1880–1962
Director 1922

Alfred
1884–1965
Director 1922

Paul
1890–1982

Alan
1902–98
Director 1933
Chairman 1956
President 1967

Robert
1906–2000
Director 1934
Chairman 1967
President 1969

James
1909–84
Director 1941

John D
1927–
Director 1958
Chairman and Chief
Executive 1969
President 1992

Simon
1930–
Director 1959
Deputy
Chairman 1969–79

Timothy
1932–
Non-executive
Director 1974–83
and 1995–99

David
1940–
Director 1966
Deputy Chairman 1988
Chairman 1992–98

INDEX